THE
HISTORY OF THE
BALTIC STATES

THE
HISTORY OF THE
BALTIC STATES

Kevin O'Connor

The Greenwood Histories of the Modern Nations
Frank W. Thackeray and John E. Findling, Series Editors

Greenwood Press
Westport, Connecticut • London

Library of Congress Cataloging-in-Publication Data

O'Connor, Kevin, 1967–
    The history of the Baltic States / Kevin O'Connor.
        p. cm. — (The Greenwood histories of the modern nations, ISSN 1096–2905)
    Includes bibliographical references and index.
    ISBN 0–313–32355–0 (alk. paper)
       1. Baltic States—History.   2. Baltic States—History—1991–   I. Title.   II. Series.
DK502.7.O2   2003
947.9—dc21   2003048527

British Library Cataloguing in Publication Data is available.

Library of Congress Catalog Card Number: 2003048527
ISBN: 0–313–32355–0
ISSN: 1096–2905

First published in 2003

Greenwood Press, 88 Post Road West, Westport, CT 06881
An imprint of Greenwood Publishing Group, Inc.
www.greenwood.com

Printed in the United States of America

The paper used in this book complies with the
Permanent Paper Standard issued by the National
Information Standards Organization (Z39.48–1984).

10 9 8 7 6 5 4 3 2 1

Contents

Series Foreword   vii
    Frank W. Thackeray and John E. Findling

Preface   xi

Abbreviations   xiii

Timeline of Historical Events   xvii

1   Unknown Europe   1

2   Early History   9

3   Russian Rule, 1721–1905   33

4   The Revolutionary Era, 1905–20   65

5   Independence, 1920–40   85

6   Soviet Rule, 1940–85   113

7   Reawakening, 1985–91   145

8   The Post-Soviet Baltic States   167

Notable People in the History of the Baltic States   201

Bibliographic Essay   205

Index   209

Series Foreword

The *Greenwood Histories of the Modern Nations* series is intended to provide students and interested laypeople with up-to-date, concise, and analytical histories of many of the nations of the contemporary world. Not since the 1960s has there been a systematic attempt to publish a series of national histories, and, as editors, we believe that this series will prove to be a valuable contribution to our understanding of other countries in our increasingly interdependent world.

Over thirty years ago, at the end of the 1960s, the Cold War was an accepted reality of global politics, the process of decolonization was still in progress, the idea of a unified Europe with a single currency was unheard of, the United States was mired in a war in Vietnam, and the economic boom of Asia was still years in the future. Richard Nixon was president of the United States, Mao Tse-tung (not yet Mao Zedong) ruled China, Leonid Brezhnev guided the Soviet Union, and Harold Wilson was prime minister of the United Kingdom. Authoritarian dictators still ruled most of Latin America, the Middle East was reeling in the wake of the Six-Day War, and Shah Reza Pahlavi was at the height of his power inIran. Clearly, the past 30 years have been witness to a great deal of historical change, and it is to this change that this series is primarily addressed.

With the help of a distinguished advisory board, we have selected nations whose political, economic, and social affairs mark them as among the most important in the waning years of the twentieth century, and for each nation we have found an author who is recognized as a specialist in the history of that nation. These authors have worked most cooperatively with us and with Greenwood Press to produce volumes that reflect current research on their nations and that are interesting and informative to their prospective readers.

The importance of a series such as this cannot be underestimated. As a superpower whose influence is felt all over the world, the United States can claim a "special" relationship with almost every other nation. Yet many Americans know very little about the histories of the nations with which the United States relates. How did they get to be the way they are? What kind of political systems have evolved there? What kind of influence do they have in their own region? What are the dominant political, religious, and cultural forces that move their leaders? These and many other questions are answered in the volumes of this series.

The authors who have contributed to this series have written comprehensive histories of their nations, dating back to prehistoric times in some cases. Each of them, however, has devoted a significant portion of the book to events of the last thirty years, because the modern era has contributed the most to contemporary issues that have an impact on U.S. policy. Authors have made an effort to be as up-to-date as possible so that readers can benefit from the most recent scholarship and a narrative that includes very recent events.

In addition to the historical narrative, each volume in this series contains an introductory overview of the country's geography, political institutions, economic structure, and cultural attributes. This is designed to give readers a picture of the nation as it exists in the contemporary world. Each volume also contains additional chapters that add interesting and useful detail to the historical narrative. One chapter is a thorough chronology of important historical events, making it easy for readers to follow the flow of a particular nation's history. Another chapter features biographical sketches of the nation's most important figures in order to humanize some of the individuals who have contributed to the historical development of their nation. Each volume also contains a comprehensive bibliography, so that those readers whose interest has been sparked may find out more about the nation and its history. Finally, there is a carefully prepared topic and person index.

Readers of these volumes will find them fascinating to read and useful in understanding the contemporary world and the nations that comprise it. As series editors, it is our hope that this series will contribute to a heightened sense of global understanding as we embark on a new century.

Frank W. Thackeray and John E. Findling
Indiana University Southeast

Preface

My interest in Baltic history dates to a master's thesis that explored the place of the new Baltic countries in the foreign policies of Weimar Germany and Soviet Russia after World War I. Unlike the many historians of the region who were born in or enjoy some sort of family connection to the Baltic region, I first visited the area in the summer of 2002, not long after completing a doctorate in Russian history. Therefore this book is written not by an expert on Baltic history, but by an historian of Russia who is interested in the concept of national identity in Russia (and in the former Soviet Union) and, in that context, in the relationship between Russia and the empire's western borderlands.

But this book is not about Russia. Its subjects are the three Baltic countries—Estonia, Latvia, and Lithuania—and the many peoples who have lived in the region for the past millennium. More specifically, however, the book depicts the struggle of three tiny nations in a remote corner of northeastern Europe to create identities for themselves and to secure and maintain their national independence in the nineteenth and twentieth centuries. I have attempted to consider these developments not through the lens of St. Petersburg or Moscow, nor from the vantage point of Tallinn, Vilnius, or Rīga, but rather from the perspective of a Western academic writing primarily for a general audience. Although I would like to think that my "outsider" status lends some credibility to my claim of treating the region's history in a balanced and evenhanded manner, on that score it is perhaps best to let the reader judge.

I wish to thank the many people who have helped in ways great and small in the preparation of this manuscript. I am grateful first of all to the many scholars whose erudition informs all aspects of the present volume. Partial funding for my visit to the Baltic countries was provided by Spalding University and Vidzeme Augustskolas in Valmiera, Latvia. My sincerest thanks to Richard Bærug and the faculty and staff at the Baltic International Summer School for providing a stimulating educational experience in Valmiera. I also owe great debts to Bozena Meckovskaja and the Lapicka family, as well as the many individuals I met while traveling through Estonia, Latvia, and Lithuania, for sharing their experiences and insights, all of which certainly enriched my perspectives on contemporary Baltic history. Many thanks also to cartographer Malcolm Swanston, who created the maps for this book. Greenwood Press editors Frank Thackeray and Kevin Ohe provided support and encouragement throughout the writing of this manuscript and saw to it that the resulting book was published without undue delay.

I would also like to express my appreciation to all the people who took the time to read various drafts of the manuscript, in whole or in part, including Emily Fritz, Brian McGee, and my father, Richard O'Connor, whose influence on my intellectual development I am only now beginning fully to appreciate. It is to my mother, Marianne, who has never failed to offer me her boundless encouragement and support, that I dedicate this book.

Finally, a note on names and spellings. For Estonian, Latvian, and Lithuanian words, I have retained all diacritical marks: thus Sąjūdis rather than Sajudis, and Rīga rather than Riga. Transliterations from Russian follow the U.S. Library of Congress style, with the exception of familiar names such as Yeltsin (rather than El'tsin) and Yakovlev (rather than Iakovlev). I have also retained the soft signs for words such as *oblast'* (region) and *glasnost'* (openness). The pluralization of nouns follows Russian rules: hence *kulaky* rather than "kulaks;" *gubernii* rather than "gubernias." Cities and towns are usually rendered by the contemporary local designation (Tartu), with alternate names following in parentheses (*Ger.* Dorpat). Dates of birth and death are provided for all major actors.

Abbreviations

b.	born in
B.C.E.	Before the Common Era
BALTBAT	Baltic Battalion
BALTDEFCOL	Baltic Defense College
BALTRON	Baltic Naval Squadron
C.E.	Common Era
CBSS	Council of Baltic Sea States
CC	Central Committee of the CPSU
CIS	Commonwealth of Independent States
CP	Communist Party
CPD	Congress of People's Deputies
CPSU	Communist Party of the Soviet Union
d.	died in
ECP	Estonian Communist Party (USSR)

ESSR	Estonian Soviet Socialist Republic
EU	European Union
GDP	Gross Domestic Product
Ger.	German (language)
KGB	Soviet state security force
LaCP	Latvian Communist Party (USSR)
Latv.	Latvian (language)
LDLP	Lithuanian Democratic Labor Party
LFL	Lithuanian Freedom League
LiCP	Lithuanian Communist Party (USSR)
Lith.	Lithuanian (language)
LKDP	Lithuanian Christian Democratic Party
LNIM	Latvian National Independence Movement
LPF	Latvian Popular Front
LSDP	Lithuanian Social Democratic Party
LVLS	Lithuanian Peasant Populist Union
NATO	North Atlantic Treaty Organization
NKVD	Soviet internal security force
NP	National Progress Party (Lithuania)
OMON	Soviet special forces
PFE	Popular Front of Estonia
PfP	Partnership for Peace
Pol.	Polish (language)
RKO	*Reichskommissariat Ostland*
RLA	Rīga Latvian Association
RSDWP	Russian Social Democratic Workers' Party
RSFSR	Russian Soviet Federal Socialist Republic

Rus.	Russian (language)
SSR	Soviet Socialist Republic
SR	Socialist Revolutionary
USA	United States of America
USSR	Union of Soviet Socialist Republics

Timeline of Historical Events

Ca. 3000–2000 B.C.E.	Finno-Ugric and proto-Baltic tribes settle on the Baltic shores.
8th–12th centuries	Baltic peoples trade and battle with Scandinavian Vikings and later with Slavic tribes.
1180	First attempt made to convert Baltic pagans led by Father Meinhard, a German priest.
1198	Pope Innocent III sanctions the first Baltic Crusade.
13th century	Latvia and southern Estonia are conquered by Germans. A Livonian state is formed.
1201	Rīga is founded by the Bishop of Livonia, Albert von Buxhoevden of Bremen.
1219	Northern Estonia is conquered by the Danes.
1253	Mindaugas is crowned the King of Lithuania.
14th century	Lithuanian territory is extended southward to the Black Sea.

1316–41	Grand Duke Gediminas rules Lithuania; encourages traders and merchants, including Jews, to settle in the region.
1343–46	Estonian peasant uprising forces Danes to surrender control of northern Estonia to Germans.
1386	The Lithuanian prince Jogaila marries into the Polish royal family, thus establishing a nominal union between Lithuania and Poland. Lithuania, Europe's last pagan kingdom, accepts Christianity.
1410	Lithuanian defeat of the Teutonic Knights prevents further German expansion eastward.
1520s	Lutheranism reaches the Baltic region.
1525	In Lübeck a Lutheran book of common prayers is published in Estonian, Livonian, and Latvian. All copies are subsequently destroyed.
1547	The first Lithuanian-language book is printed.
1558–83	Russian Tsar Ivan IV attempts to conquer Livonia, but is checked by Sweden and Poland. The Livonian Confederation is dissolved and most of Livonia is incorporated into Poland-Lithuania.
1561	Sweden acquires Tallinn and surrounding region.
1569	The Lithuanian and Polish crowns formally unite to form the Polish-Lithuanian Commonwealth.
1579	Vilnius University is established.
1584	Sweden annexes northern Estonia, creating the Duchy of Estland.
1629	Poland is forced to cede Livonia to Sweden.
1632	Swedes found Tartu University in the Duchy of Estland.
1699	Dissolution of Hanseatic League.
1710	In the Great Northern War (1700–15), Russian Tsar Peter I seizes Estland and Livland (southern Estonia and northern Latvia) from Sweden.

1772–95	Prussia, Austria, and Russia partition Poland. Lithuania and Courland (western Latvia) are annexed by Russia.
1816–19	Following the Russian defeat of Napoleon, serfdom is formally abolished in Estland and Livland. Initially the former serfs do not receive land with their freedom.
1824–79	Establishment of literary societies facilitates the formation of distinctive national identities among the Baltic peoples.
1840–60	Agrarian reforms are undertaken in Estland and Livland.
1845–48	Tens of thousands of Estonian and Latvian peasants are converted to Russian Orthodoxy.
1861	Lithuanian serfs are freed.
1863	A Polish insurrection, aided by Lithuanian peasants, is crushed by tsarist forces. Peasant unrest subsequently breaks out in Livland, Courland, and Estland.
1867–68	A famine is followed by the massive emigration of Lithuanians.
1880s–1890s	Russification policies are implemented in the Baltic territories.
1905	Revolution in the Russian Empire.
1914–18	World War I; Russia's Baltic territories are occupied by German forces.
1917	Russian Tsar Nicholas II abdicates throne in March as the tsarist regime collapses. Russia's new Provisional Government assents to the territorial unification of its Estonian province.
November 1917	Bolsheviks seize power in Russia.
February– March 1918	Russia and Germany agree to peace terms at Brest-Litovsk. Russia must surrender its western territories, including the Baltic provinces. Estonia and Lithuania proclaim independence.
November 1918	Latvia proclaims independence.

1918–20	Baltic states fight the Bolsheviks, White Russian armies, and German and Polish forces to defend their independence. Lithuania loses Vilnius region to newly independent Poland.
1920	Baltic states sign peace treaties with Soviet Russia.
1919–22	Baltic states carry out land reform and introduce democratic constitutions. They are also admitted to the League of Nations in 1921.
January 1923	Lithuania annexes the Klaipėda (*Ger.* Memel) region, formerly under international control.
December 1924	Communist coup attempt in Estonia fails.
September 1926	Lithuania signs nonaggression and neutrality pact with USSR.
1926–29	Antanas Smetona establishes dictatorship in Lithuania.
1934	Konstantin Päts and Kārlis Ulmanis establish dictatorships in Estonia and Latvia.
August–September 1939	Nazi-Soviet nonaggression pact; secret protocols award the Baltic states to the USSR.
June–August 1940	Baltic states are occupied by Soviet troops, then annexed to USSR.
June 1941	Massive deportations of Baltic peoples to Soviet Russia.
1941–44	Nazi occupation of Lithuania, Latvia and Estonia. Nearly the entire Jewish populations of these countries are murdered.
1944	Soviet forces reoccupy Baltic states. Westward flight of thousands of Balts continues through 1945.
1944–48	"Forest brothers" resist Soviet occupation. A few bands continue to resist into the mid-1950s.
1944–52	Massive deportation of Estonians, Latvians, and Lithuanians to other Soviet republics. This is accompanied by industrialization and the first waves of Russian and other Slavic immigrants.

1947	First collective farms established in the Baltic republics. Collectivization completed by 1952.
1949–51	Bloody purge of "bourgeois nationalists" from the Estonian Communist Party.
1956–64	Nikita Khrushchev's "thaw" loosens ideological restrictions throughout the USSR.
1970s	Nationalist and human rights movements grow in the Baltic republics.
1972	Rioting and demonstrations in Lithuania follow the self-immolation of a student.
1985	Mikhail Gorbachev is named CPSU general secretary. Launches reform program.
1987–88	Growth of environmentalist activity in the Baltic republics, which becomes the basis for resurgent nationalist movements.
April–June 1988	Popular Fronts are formed in Estonia and Latvia. Sąjūdis is formed in Lithuania.
November 1988–July 1989	Restrictive language laws enacted in the Baltic republics, followed by declarations of sovereignty within the USSR.
August 23, 1989	Baltic Way demonstration unites up to 2 million Balts in protest against the Nazi-Soviet pact of August 1939.
March 1990	Elections to Baltic parliaments. Vytautas Landsbergis is selected to head the Lithuanian government. Lithuania declares its secession from the USSR.
April–June 1990	Soviet embargo is imposed on Lithuania.
January 1991	Soviet paratroopers and KGB units attack the Vilnius television tower.
February–March 1991	Baltic peoples overwhelmingly vote in favor of independence in public referenda.
August 19–21, 1991	Hardline coup in Moscow attempts to depose Gorbachev and fails.

September 6, 1991	The USSR formally recognizes the independence of the Baltic states.
September 17, 1991	The United Nations admits Estonia, Latvia, and Lithuania.
November 1991	The Baltic Assembly is formed.
December 31, 1991	Commonwealth of Independent States (CIS) is created to replace the USSR. Baltic states opt not to join.
1992–93	Baltic economies hit bottom: high inflation and unemployment, declining production. New currencies are adopted in each country. New constitutions are adopted and elections are held. Peak of Russian emigration from Baltic states.
1994	Baltic economies begin to recover. The Baltic states join NATO's Partnership for Peace program.
August 1994	Russian troop withdrawal from the Baltics is completed.
September 28, 1994	A passenger ferry, the *Estonia*, sinks to the bottom of the Baltic Sea; 852 people die.
1995	The Baltic Battalion (BALTBAT) is established as part of Partnership for Peace program.
January 1995	A Free Trade agreement is concluded between the European Union and the Baltic states.
May 1995	Collapse of Baltija Bank sets off banking crisis in Latvia.
August 1998	Russian economic crisis temporarily interrupts economic recovery of Baltic states.
July 1999	Latvians elect first woman president of east central Europe, Vaira Vīķe-Freiberga.
November 2002	Baltic states are invited to join the NATO alliance.
December 2002	Baltic states are invited to join an enlarged European Union (EU). They are expected to become EU members in May 2004.

1

Unknown Europe

GEOGRAPHY, CLIMATE, AND POPULATION

The subjects of this book are three small and little-known countries in northeastern Europe: from north to south, they are Estonia, Latvia, and Lithuania. Because of their location along the northeastern part of the Baltic Sea—first called "Mare Balticum" by German chroniclers in the eleventh century—they are usually called the Baltic states, or simply "the Baltics." Estonia, the smallest of the three, in size is roughly comparable to Vermont and New Hampshire combined. Lithuania is only slightly bigger than Latvia, and each is about the same size as West Virginia. The location of the Baltic countries, across the sea from Scandinavia and between western Europe and Russia, has exerted a profound influence on their cultural and economic development, and continues to affect their sense of security.

The region's geography has few outstanding features apart from 2,750 miles of coast and over one thousand Estonian islands. In general, the Baltic region is low and flat, the highest points barely reaching 1,000 feet. While Lithuania has the most arable land and is the most reliant on agriculture, Estonia and Latvia are more heavily forested, with timber and wood products being their most important commodity exports.

Baltic climate is temperate. The weather in Estonia is maritime, but further south in Lithuania it verges on continental. Throughout the region winters are moderate and summers are cool, but whatever the season the Baltic region is often wet. While the sun sets early during the dark Baltic winters, at mid-summer Estonians enjoy 19 hours of sunlight a day.

In 1989 the Baltic countries, then republics of the Soviet Union, were together home to just under 8 million people, a figure comparable to the populations of present-day Austria or Chad. Unfavorable demographic trends during the 1990s, however, have contributed to an alarming decline in the population, which by the year 2002 had dropped below 7.5 million. While emigration from the Baltic countries, mostly Russians, has dwindled in recent years and the tendency toward declining life expectancy among males may be corrected, the low birth rates of Estonians and Latvians are unlikely to be reversed. Only Lithuania has experienced positive population growth in recent years.

PEOPLES OF THE BALTIC REGION

Isolated from the outside world for half a century, the Baltic countries are unfamiliar terrain to most Westerners, and are often confused with the equally unfamiliar Balkans. While this error is regrettable, there are, aside from the obvious fact that the words "Baltic" and "Balkan" sound somewhat alike to the Anglophone ear, understandable reasons why it is so common. Both the Balkans and the Baltic region lie at a European crossroad, and as such each has been both a transmitter of culture and a victim of the aspirations of larger and more powerful neighbors. Furthermore, the Baltic peoples of northeastern Europe, like the Balkan peoples of southeastern Europe, are ethnically and religiously diverse, and as a result all continue to struggle with the question of identity.

A significant difference in their historical experiences, however, distinguishes the peoples of these poorly understood regions: while Balkan peoples have frequently fought among themselves, native Balts generally have had peaceful relations with each other for nearly 600 years. Indeed, while the countries that once constituted Yugoslavia plunged into war following the collapse of communism, Estonians, Latvians, and Lithuanians have enjoyed a period of peace, if not exactly universal prosperity, since the end of Soviet rule. Having "returned to Europe" after a half-century of foreign domination, the Baltic peoples are intent on preserving the spirit of cooperation and solidarity that emerged during their struggle for independence over a decade ago.

A defining feature of the Baltic region is the flow of peoples—foreigners to the area—often preceded by bloody conquest. Having established themselves in the region by sword in the thirteenth century, the Baltic Germans, called *Baltische*, constituted the region's elite for over six centuries and profoundly influenced the culture of Latvia and Estonia. By 1940, however, the German presence had all but vanished, and the Soviet conquest that followed was accompanied by massive Russian immigration to the region. Jews were once prominent in Lithuania and to a lesser extent in Latvia, but nearly all were killed during the Second World War. Besides Russia and Germany, Sweden and Poland have also played important roles in the history of the region, but the small number of Swedes who lived in Estonia fled before the arrival of the Red Army in 1944; meanwhile, a substantial number of Poles regard Vilnius, for twenty years under Polish rule, as their home and continue to live there.

Of the Baltic countries, only Lithuania can make the claim of having enjoyed a period of national sovereignty before the twentieth century. Indeed, at the end of the Middle Ages Lithuania was Europe's largest state. By the sixteenth century, however, its history was tied closely to that of Poland, and by the end of the eighteenth century the Polish-Lithuanian state had disappeared from the map, with most of the Lithuanian areas being absorbed by the Russian Empire. Latvia and Estonia, on the other hand, are relative newcomers to the community of independent European states. Before creating new states at the end of World War I, Latvians and Estonians had spent five centuries under the rule of German barons, followed by nearly three hundred years of Russian domination. From 1918 to 1940, during a brief period of German and Russian weakness, all three Baltic countries were independent, and since 1991, when the Soviet Union suddenly imploded, they have enjoyed their independence once again.

Through it all, Estonians, Latvians, and Lithuanians have maintained a fierce attachment to their homelands and are proud guardians of their national cultures. Although they share, to some extent, a common historical experience, each of the Baltic peoples is unique. Lithuanians and Latvians are historically Baltic peoples, who speak old Indo-European languages. Whereas Lithuanians have been ethnically distinct since at least the thirteenth century, Latvians formed during the Middle Ages from the convergence of several Baltic tribes. Another Baltic people were the ancient Prussians, but following the Germanic conquest they were largely assimilated and disappeared as a distinct nationality.

Estonians, unlike the Latvians and Lithuanians, have Finno-Ugric origins. The Estonian language is closely related to Finnish and is more distantly related to Hungarian. The Estonians' linguistic cousins also include the Livonians (or Livs), who lived in northwestern Latvia but gradually assimilated into the neighboring Latvian tribes. Only a few, mostly elderly, Livonians remain, and like the Prussians they too will disappear.

Religious affiliation in the Baltic countries is almost as diverse as ethnicity. Estonians and western Latvians tend to be Lutheran, while many southeastern Latvians (the Latgale region) and nearly all Lithuanians are Catholic. The Russians of all three Baltic states are usually Orthodox. While Judaism has all but disappeared, with only a few thousand Jews remaining in the region, Islam has yet to establish any sort of presence in the Baltic states. Hare Krishnas and other unusual (to the Balts, at least) sects, completely unknown during Soviet times, can occasionally be found singing and dancing in larger cities such as Tallinn and Rīga.

CHANGE AND PROSPECTS

The spectacle of exotica such as dancing and singing Hare Krishnas testifies to the profound changes that have swept over the region since the early 1990s. Long gone are the bronze figures of Lenin and local communist leaders, all of which were toppled as the Soviet Union collapsed. Such tributes to Soviet power have been replaced by statues of Baltic national heroes—mostly writers, artists, and musicians of the nineteenth and early twentieth centuries—and monuments commemorating the Balts' struggle for freedom from foreign oppressors. The historic sections, or "old towns," of Vilnius (pop. 580,000), Rīga (pop. 796,000) and Tallinn (pop. 408,000) are presently undergoing a stunning transformation: cathedrals and other historic buildings are being restored while dozens of new and refurbished hotels, restaurants, bars, and clubs cater to the growing number of tourists arriving from Finland, Scandinavia, western Europe, and North America. The changes, however, are far deeper than a mere fresh coat of paint: since 1991 democracy has been restored to the region, and with that the people's freedom to choose.

From the bell tower of Tallinn's Council Hall, which provides the visitor with a panoramic view of this charming, brightly-colored Hanseatic town, one sees a healthy and prosperous "European" city—one that of course has benefited from the optimism of Scandinavian investors as well as the credit cards of thousands of vacationing Finns. The prosperity of Estonia's largest city, however, stands in stark contrast to the stagnation of southeast Estonia or the abject poverty of Latgale, an agricultural region in eastern Latvia, where an aging populace ekes out an existence on only dollars a day. Indeed, throughout the Baltic region thousands of young people are abandoning the bleak, unchanging countryside for the opportunities they hope to find in the cities. Behind them they leave those who are also less able to adapt to the changed circumstances, including the old and infirm— as well as tens of thousands of acres of deserted farmland. But even life in the cities, despite their tidy public spaces and well-stocked stores, has its drawbacks: gainful employment is far from guaranteed, and millions still live in decaying Soviet-era housing developments.

Despite these negative factors, in recent years the Balts have made tremendous progress in transforming their economies and setting up durable political systems. It has been argued that Estonians possess the best-developed sense of national identity among the Baltic peoples, and in embarking upon the massive project of transforming their society it is Estonia that acted most decisively and has advanced most rapidly. Estonians were the first to close their unprofitable factories and privatize the remainder; they set their gaze westward and cut most of their economic ties with Russia. Estonians like to think of themselves as Scandinavians, and do not hesitate to point out that their country's economy has undergone the most thorough transformation. Political stability has also been one of Estonia's great blessings over the past decade. Although dozens of parties contend for power (six of which are represented in the parliament or *Riigikogu*), and numerous prime ministers have come and gone, a sense of continuity has been provided by the Estonian presidency, the office of which was occupied by Lennart Meri from 1992 to 2001.

Lithuania, the boldest of the Baltic republics in its struggle with Moscow in 1990 and 1991, entered the post-Soviet era at a somewhat lower level of economic development than Latvia or Estonia. Although the country's leaders initially were reluctant to move decisively in the direction of free market reform, by the late 1990s the country was making noticeable progress. At the dawn of the twenty-first century Lithuania ranks higher than Latvia (but lower than Estonia) on the United Nations' Human Development Index. Although Lithuanians can be fiercely patriotic, nationalist tendencies are restrained by the fact that among the Baltic peoples they feel least threatened by the country's ethnic minorities. While Estonia is 65 percent Estonian and more than 30 percent "Russian-speaking" (this term includes ethnic Russians, Ukrainians and Belarussians living in the Baltics), Lithuania is the most ethnically homogenous of the Baltic countries, with approximately 80 percent of the population identifying itself as Lithuanian. Feeling more secure than the natives of Estonia or Latvia, the Lithuanians have taken active measures to integrate their Russian-speaking community and develop a positive relationship with Russia.

Latvia is the most diverse of the Baltic countries. A relatively prosperous Rīga gives the illusion of national affluence, but the standard of living in some Latvian regions is better compared to country life in Russia or

Ukraine. Latvia is indeed a divided country: only 56 percent of its people identify themselves as Latvians, while most of the rest are "Russian-speakers." Rīga, the country's capital city, is 70 percent Russian-speaking, yet, as in the other Baltic capitals, one finds no street signs in the Russian language. However, there is no shortage of Russian-language television, radio, or print media. This is often a source of consternation to many Latvians, who wonder when or if the Russians will ever fully integrate into Latvian society.

Despite the tensions between the dominant nationalities and their ethnic minorities, relations between the Estonians, Latvians, and Lithuanians are constructive. Nevertheless, one of the most surprising features of life in the Baltic region is how poorly the Balts know each other! For Latvians, the common stereotype of their Estonian neighbors is of slow-witted but harmless bumpkins. The Estonians, for their part, regard themselves as kin of the Finns to the north, with whom they share a certain cultural and linguistic connection. Moreover, since Estonia has managed to develop extensive economic ties with its northern and western neighbors, the Latvians and Lithuanians to the south often feel that the Estonians are abandoning them for Scandinavia.

Lithuanians are little more familiar to Latvians than Latvians are to Estonians. Whereas Lithuanians are oriented culturally toward Poland, Latvian and Estonian culture developed under German tutelage. Moreover, although the Latvian and Lithuanian languages share similar origins, they are mutually unintelligible. Under Soviet rule, their common language of communication was in fact Russian. Indeed, a common claim among the Balts (and other ex-Soviet peoples) is that in a room of ten people, if there is even only one Russian present, then the entire group will speak Russian. Although this may be an exaggeration, there is an underlying truth behind this claim: during Soviet times Balts and other non-Russians were expected to learn Russian, and few Russians living in the Baltic republics mastered the local language.

This situation is changing rapidly. While Russian recedes as a second language for today's Baltic students, English has taken its place. In the larger Estonian towns, knowledge of English is fairly common, and one has no difficulty finding natives who speak English in the larger Latvian or Lithuanian towns as well. Indeed, the Russian-speaking world of an older generation—one that was governed from Moscow—is disappearing, and a new world—one that requires knowledge of English for advancement—is taking its place.

Of course, this is not to suggest that in the course of globalization Estonians, Latvians, and Lithuanians will hurry to abandon their national languages and cultures for English and alien Western traditions. Far from it: the efforts to preserve and win the right to use their languages were too arduous to surrender them. It is now the Russians and other minorities of the Baltic countries who must learn to speak the official language and integrate into Baltic societies. Thus it is unsurprising that many Russian-speakers residing in the Baltics regard Baltic language and citizenship policies, especially in Latvia and Estonia, as discriminatory.

Times have certainly changed. At the height of Soviet power in the 1970s it was not unusual for academicians to consign the Balts to the fate of other assimilated and disappeared nations like the Livonians or ancient Prussians. The Balts' survival and recovery, which first drew the world's attention during the "Singing Revolution" of the late 1980s, are a testament to their strength and determination. Unlike many of the other former Soviet republics that experienced civil war, dictatorship, and poverty in the 1990s, the Baltic states are peaceful, democratic, and relatively prosperous. Given their turbulent history and well-traversed terrain, it is in some ways amazing that they exist at all.

How the Baltic countries came to be and how they survived the tumultuous twentieth century are the main subjects of this book. While making full disclosure of his admiration for the Balts' courage in their struggles against foreign oppression, the author intends to provide the readers of this book with a balanced, truthful, and hopefully appealing portrayal of the Baltic countries' remarkable journey from medieval times to the twenty-first century.

2

Early History

WHO ARE THE BALTS?

Before the tenth century B.C.E. the entire Baltic region, including Scandinavia, the lowlands of central Europe, and northern Russia, was covered by an enormous glacier. The gradual retreat and melting of the Scandinavian glacier was followed by the arrival of the first humans to the Baltic area, probably around 8000 B.C.E. To understand the prehistory of the region and its peoples from this time until around 1000 C.E., when written records concerning the region begin to appear, we must rely on archaeological evidence rather than historical documentation. From this scant evidence scholars have concluded that the inhabitants of this region were not in any sense a single identifiable people, but rather were broadly differentiated linguistically and ethnically.

Hunter-fisher tribes from the Finno-Ugric language group arrived from the Volga region of Russia between 3000 and 2500 B.C.E.: these were the linguistic ancestors of the contemporary Hungarians, Finns, Ingrians, Karelians, and Estonians. Finno-Ugric languages are unrelated to the Indo-European language group to which belong the Slavic, Germanic, Romance, and Baltic languages. Thus contemporary Estonians and their Finno-Ugric ancestors are not Balts in the linguistic sense, although today they are grouped together with the Latvians and Lithuanians as Baltic peoples in the geographic sense.

Unlike the Estonians, Balts, from whom emerged the Lithuanian, Latvian, and Prussian tribes, were Indo-European peoples. Estonians moved to the Baltic region from the Eurasian steppe somewhere north of the Black Sea around 2200 B.C.E., and for many centuries inhabited areas extending well beyond the Baltic littoral. On the basis of water names, scholars have concluded that Balts lived in today's Latvia, Lithuania, Belarus, the northwestern parts of Ukraine, and the western parts of Russia. Indeed, the area inhabited by the Baltic-speaking peoples in prehistoric times, before the arrival of Germans and Slavs, was perhaps six times as great as present-day Lithuania and Latvia, although it is hard to know whether they occupied the entire area at once or had migrated from one region to another. Pressure from migrating German and Slavic tribes during the first millennium C.E. pushed the Balts, Estonians, and Finns to the geographical locations in which they live today.

Like other early Europeans, the peoples living along the Baltic Sea did not yet exist as "nations." Proto-Estonians were divided into clans speaking different Finno-Ugric languages, which merged to form the basis of modern Estonian. A common proto-Baltic language probably existed between 1800 B.C.E. and 500 C.E., but evolved into West Baltic languages (Old Prussian and Jatving), which disappeared in the centuries after German conquest, and East Baltic tongues (Lithuanian and Latvian).

The Väina River formed the divide between the peoples who spoke Finno-Ugric and Baltic languages. Livonians (or Livs) were an exception in that they were a Finno-Ugric people concentrated in modern-day northern Latvia, but during the Middle Ages they were largely assimilated by proto-Latvian tribes.

The proto-Latvians included Couronians, Zemgalians, Latgalians, and Selonians, each of which had marked out territories for themselves by the end of the ninth century.[1] Taken together, these territories generally correspond to present-day Latvia. Lithuanians were concentrated further south, in the remote forests and swamps of the Nemunas River basin. West of the Lithuanians, in the territory of present-day Kaliningrad and northeastern Poland, lived the Prussians, but they were later either exterminated or assimilated by conquering Germans. The appearance and disappearance of numerous tribes through the ages reflect an important historical reality about this region of which modern Baltic peoples are keenly aware.

In the absence of a literary culture among the ancient Balts, our early sources are alien observers. The first reliable reference to the presence of

Balts in northeastern Europe is found in *The Germania* by the Roman historian Tacitus. Writing in the late first century C.E., Tacitus referred to these people as "Aesti," by which he likely meant the ancient Prussians.

Mediterranean civilization's familiarity with the Balts was not only a product of the latter's broad geographical distribution, but was also related to the rich deposits of amber found in the regions they inhabited along the Baltic coast. Amber is a hard yellowish fossil resin that was prized in ancient times for its magnetic qualities, for its alleged medicinal uses, and most of all for its ornamental uses. For the ancient Balts, amber was essentially money. Ancestors of Lithuanians and Latvians traded amber with the Romans, and the metal objects they received in return, including weapons and ornaments, turned the Balts into important transmitters of the metal culture to areas north and east of the Roman Empire. To the German tribes the Balts dealt furs, which were easily accessible in the northern forest zone occupied by the Finno-Ugric peoples. While the Balts acted as mediators in the north European fur trade, they also traded amber, bear skins, horses, cattle, wax, and slaves with their neighbors.

However, Balts, like their Slavic neighbors, were mostly farmers: they grew wheat, rye, and millet, while raising cattle and horses as well as goats, sheep, and chickens. They also grew flax and wove linen. Unlike their Slavic neighbors, who tended to create more communal rural dwellings, Balts lived on independent farms, much like early west Europeans.

Unlike both their eastern and western neighbors, however, Balts remained pagans into the thirteenth century and beyond, worshiping the spirits of the forests, mountains, fields, and water. Although there may have been some diversity of religious practice among the Baltic tribes, they shared in common a particular reverence for the earth—the giver of life and sustenance—as well as deities such as the sky god (*Latv.* Dievs, *Lith.* Dievas), the thunder god (*Latv.* Pērkons, *Lith.* Perkūnas) and the goddess of fate or happiness (Laima). The sky god and Laima were later assimilated by the Christian God and Mary. Other "gods" have been attributed to the Balts, but as Baltologist Endre Bojtár has pointed out, these are most likely the inventions of later mythologists who transformed Baltic idols and spirits into gods.[2]

A fateful feature of the Baltic tribes of the early Middle Ages was their lack of political unity or organization. Only Lithuanians managed to create a united kingdom. Estonians, lacking any centralized authority, lived as free peasants loosely organized into parishes and districts. Ancestors of the Latvians—the Latgalians, Zemgalians, Selonians, and Couronians—lived in a number of small, independent kingdoms. Lacking a monarch at the top of the hierarchy, as in feudal western Europe, Baltic peasants accepted the leadership of warlords who could equip themselves with horses and weapons, and supported the warrior aristocracy with taxes on their agricultural produce and their trade. Rulers were apparently little concerned with gaining territory or subjugating populations; they were content with a show of submission and payment of tribute from their vassals.

Whereas the Lithuanians first created their own state in the thirteenth century, Estonians and Latvians did not establish states until the twentieth. They were surrounded by more populous and better-organized neighbors, several of whom proceeded to build powerful states such as Sweden, Poland, and Muscovy (the core of the emerging Russian state). Scandinavian colonization of the eastern Baltic coast from the north occurred between 650 and 850 c.e. and lasted until the end of the Viking Age (800–1050) in the eleventh century. Slavic expansion into the eastern Baltic region from the southeast began before the fifth century and has persisted through recent times.

The Baltic area was significant to Slavs and Scandinavians alike due to its resources, its surging economic activity, and a geographical position that belied its growing importance in the transit trade between the West and the East. Indeed, the most important trade routes of the early Rus' flowed through the Baltic region, connecting northern Russia to the Black Sea and Constantinople via the Neva, Narva, Daugava (*Rus.* Dvina), and Dniepr rivers. Balts, however, did not control this trade, which fell instead to the more powerful Vikings and their Rurikid descendants who ruled the Russian princedoms.[3] In exchange for security, some Baltic chieftains even paid tribute to western Russian principalities such as Novgorod and Pskov, with the result that Orthodox Christianity made an early appearance in the region. By the twelfth century, the Baltic lands had also begun to attract the attention of German merchants—and the Catholic Church.

THE NORTHERN CRUSADES

To the west of the Baltic tribes were German warriors, transformed during the Middle Ages into European knights and possessing the missionary zeal of new converts to the faith. German attempts to bring Christianity to the pagans of the Baltic region, beginning with Pope Innocent III's (ca.1160–1216) authorization of a Holy War on the north in 1198, were symptomatic of Europe's crusading impulse during the High Middle Ages. The crusade against the remaining pagans of the northeast was undertaken with the same objectives as earlier crusades to the Near East: to defend Christian communities and save souls—and to create new sources of papal revenue to meet the Church's growing commitments and ambitions. Of particular concern to the German missionaries was the possibility that Russians might convert the Baltic pagans to Orthodoxy.

Like those who had marched to Jerusalem, the Northern crusaders were driven by their fidelity to the papacy and to the Roman Christian faith, as well as the knowledge that for their services they would obtain remission of their sins. The promise of heaven justified any misdeeds performed in the cause of spreading the faith. Whether or not they received their final reward, the crusaders in the northeast enjoyed success in battle, conquering most of the west Baltic heathen in the first decades of the thirteenth century.

In Livonia, a Latinized form of the name originally given by the Germans to the coastal settlements of the Livonians (or Livs), the process of conquest and conversion began in 1201 with the creation of the Brothers of the Sword (or Swordbrothers). This knightly order, whose members were clad in white cloaks adorned with a red cross and sword, was founded by Albert von Buxhoevden of Bremen (ca.1165–1229), the Bishop of Livonia and the founder of the city of Rīga, for the purpose of the subjugation and Christianization of the Baltic lands. Although the order was responsible only to the pope, Bishop Albert wished to maintain total power over it. The reality was that the Swordbrothers could hardly be controlled by either Albert or Rome. This fact, combined with the order's overenthusiastic (that is, violent) approach to conversion, became a major source of friction between them.

Not long after the crusaders' arrival in Rīga, the Livonians and Selonians, the weakest of the Baltic tribes, were soon either conquered or won over as allies. Albert shared the conquered territories with the Swordbrothers, who demanded one-third of all conquests. The native populations were then baptized and subjected to an occupying elite of priests and landlords. Next the Swordbrothers made an alliance with the Latgalians in the east in order to take the struggle north to the Estonian lands. Despite their alliance with Russian tribes, the Estonian lands were conquered by 1227 and placed under the direct control of Rome.

The subjugation of the Prussians was left to another band of crusaders known as the Order of Teutonic Knights, founded in Palestine in 1190. More numerous and better-led than the peoples of Livonia, the Prussians were better able to resist the Teutons, although they too were defeated by 1283, after nearly sixty years of fighting. The majority of Prussians converted to Christianity and were subjected to military and labor service, while their new rulers granted privileges to a favored elite.

After subduing the northern lands of the Baltic littoral, in 1236 the

Swordbrothers were defeated by the better-organized Lithuanians (allied with Zemgalians, who also remained unconquered for a period) in the south, and most of their leaders were killed. Consequently the Swordbrothers collapsed and became merely a northern branch of the Teutonic Order. The former Swordbrothers, now known as the Livonian Order, continued to rule a separate Livonian state, comprised of much of modern-day Latvia and southern Estonia. Counterbalancing the order was the Archbishop of Rīga, under whose authority several smaller states, including the Bishopric of Courland (the western part of modern Latvia), and the Bishoprics of Tartu and Saare-Lääne (both in modern Estonia), banded together.

Meanwhile, northern Estonia was held by the Danes until a peasant revolt known as the St. George's Day Uprising (1343–45), resulted in the region's sale to the Livonian Order in 1346.[4] Only the Balts living in the southwest of the conquered areas managed to remain free of foreign rule (and, for the time being, Christianity). In the mid-thirteenth century they united to form a Lithuanian state under King Mindaugas.

Thus from the thirteenth century onward most of the Baltic tribes were assimilated into a Christian world that was governed by the Holy Roman Emperor and the pope, and whose military arm in the region was the Livonian Order. Although the surviving leaders and the upper class were effectively Germanized, the languages and customs of the northern and eastern Balts were preserved by the enserfed peasants. For nearly six centuries these two groups, a foreign upper crust (*Baltische,* initially consisting of 200 or 300 knights, along with clergymen, merchants, and German noblemen who were invited to settle the colonies) and a subjugated native peasantry (*Undeutsche,* or non-German people), coexisted with each other in what was essentially a colonial relationship. While Prussia was incorporated into the German Holy Roman Empire, the peoples of the East Baltic remained almost entirely unfamiliar to the West during the Middle Ages.

THE POLISH-LITHUANIAN COMMONWEALTH

Unlike the politically less organized peoples in the northern and eastern parts of the Baltic littoral who fell under German rule, resistance to the invaders spurred the Lithuanians to unite under the leadership of a ruthless tribal king named Mindaugas (?–1263) around 1230. Mindaugas successfully fended off the Germans by concluding an alliance with them; under Teutonic pressure he formally accepted Latin Christianity and was awarded the Lithuanian throne in 1253. However, his policy of co-existence with the Teutonic Knights alienated his nobles, who after 10 years killed their king and reverted to paganism. Despite this setback for Christian expansion, the Lithuanian state, a territory of only about 80,000 square kilometers that was home to perhaps 300,000–400,000 subjects in Mindaugas's day, continued to grow as it absorbed the lands of other Baltic tribes and of nearby eastern Slavs.

Having rejected the Catholic West, for the next century Lithuania's rulers chose to pursue ties, partly through political marriages, with the Slavic and Orthodox East. By this time Kievan Russia, which had been reduced to the status of a Mongol tributary state during the thirteenth-century invasions, had lost its influence over the neighboring Slavic principalities, and many drifted into the Lithuanian orbit. In fact, by the middle decades of the fourteenth century the Lithuanian state of Grand Prince Gediminas (ruled 1316–41) was Muscovy's main rival for control over the Russian lands. At the same time, the growing military might of the Lithuanian state was a threat to the Knights of the Cross, another German military-missionary order that had invaded neighboring Prussia. Dismayed by the Lithuanians' reversion to paganism after Mindaugas's death in 1263, the Knights still hoped to convert Europe's last remaining pagans and raided Lithuanian territory at least once a year. Their immensely destructive wars against Lithuania lasted more than a century, during which time Lithuania's rulers continued to add territory in the east while strengthening their alliances with the neighboring Slavic principalities.

Despite his collaboration with the Orthodox East, Gediminas did not reject the political and material benefits of ties with the Catholic West, as he enjoyed excellent commercial relations with German merchants in the Baltic Sea area. Moreover, Gediminas encouraged western traders, artisans and landowners to settle in his realm—an important consequence of which was the emergence of a large Jewish community in Vilnius (*Pol.* Wilno, *Yiddish* Vilna), which became the Lithuanian capital in 1323. Still, urban development was much slower in Lithuania than in the Hanseatic towns of the Baltic coast (such as Rīga and Tallinn), and most townspeople were not foreigners but Lithuanians, supplemented by smaller numbers of German and Russian colonists, as well as Poles and Jews.

Although the nobles upon whom he relied for support were firmly opposed to Christianity, Gediminas provided protection for both the Catholic and Orthodox clergy residing in Lithuania, while continuing to allow all people to worship their own gods. Indeed, Gediminas even contemplated his own conversion in order to ward off future incursions by the Teutonic Knights, but he nevertheless remained a pagan until his death in 1341. It was not until 1386 that a Lithuanian monarch, Jogaila (1348–

Expansion of Lithuania to 1430. Courtesy of Cartographica.

1434), converted to Christianity. By this time the Grand Duchy of Lithuania, whose formerly pagan Lithuanian elite ruled over a mostly eastern Slavic and Orthodox population (perhaps eight million of the territory's 9 million inhabitants), was the largest kingdom in Europe. Stretching from the Baltic to the Black Sea, Lithuania occupied much territory, including modern Belarus and much of Ukraine, that in prehistoric times had once been possessed by East Baltic tribes but would later belong to the Russian Empire.

Thus from the fourteenth century onward, the Lithuanians faced a dilemma that has confronted the Baltic peoples ever since: whether to look to the Russian and Orthodox East or the Catholic West for cultural and political influences. Threatened by scheming relatives, allied with Muscovy's ruler Dmitri Donskoi, who intended to seize his throne, the Lithuanian Grand Prince Jogaila chose the West.

To save his throne, Jogaila (*Pol.* Jagiello), a grandson of Gediminas, was compelled to conclude a territorial pact with the Teutonic Knights (1380) and promised to Christianize the Lithuanians. He then accepted the offer of a marriage alliance and political union with Poland, a Catholic state that shared with Lithuania a common German enemy.[5] After marrying Jadwiga, the 10-year-old queen of Poland, in 1386 Jogaila was baptized and crowned Wladyslaw II, thus initiating a dynasty that lasted two centuries. The Christianization of the country soon followed, and with it was laid the foundation for the Catholic Church's superior position in Lithuania, as it received considerable land concessions in addition to legal protection.

Despite his earlier triumph, Jogaila's struggle with Lithuania's great nobles (and with the Germans) continued, and in 1392 he was forced to concede his title as Grand Prince of Lithuania to his cousin Vytautas (1350–1430), a rival in the succession struggles of the 1380s, while Jogaila himself remained King of Poland. Later, in 1410, Jogaila and Vytautas together headed a combined force of Lithuanians, Poles, and Czechs, and were able to defeat the Teutonic Knights in the Battle of Tannenberg (Grünwald), thus preventing the further eastward expansion of the Germans. Indeed, under Vytautas Magnus, generally considered the most important ruler of medieval Lithuania, the Grand Duchy reached the height of its territorial expansion and influence. To the east of Lithuania, however, lay an expansionist Muscovy, which liberated itself from Mongol domination during the fifteenth century and was bent on gathering the Russian lands—many of which were under Lithuanian rule.

Although the Polish and Lithuanian crowns were unified, for nearly two centuries the Lithuanian administration functioned separately under a legal code known as the "Lithuanian Statute." According to the terms of Jogaila's agreement with the Poles, the Lithuanian grand prince was required to "adjoin" Lithuania to Poland, thus ensuring that Lithuania would forever be the junior partner in the union. Some historians claim that this union retarded the development of the Lithuanian state and Lithuanian culture. Because Lithuania's social structure was not as firmly established as that of Poland—perhaps because of Lithuania's failure to adopt Christianity earlier—during the period of the Lithuanian-Polish union, the Lithuanian elites were essentially Polonized as they absorbed the language and culture being disseminated by the Polish church and nobility. Meanwhile, the overwhelming mass of Lithuanian subjects—the peasants—became enserfed, tied to the estates of the nobles.

In response to the growing power of Muscovy, whose expansionist impulses posed a potential threat to the dual state, in 1569 the Poles and Lithuanians signed the Treaty of Lublin, which abolished the state's confederate structure and replaced it with the Polish-Lithuanian Commonwealth (*Rzeczpospolita*). According to an edict of King Sigismund II Augustus (ruled 1548–71), the Polish kingdom and the Grand Duchy of Lithuania henceforth constituted a single indivisible state with a jointly elected leader. Following the Union of Lublin, for two centuries the *Rzeczpospolita* was one of the largest and most powerful states in Europe, with each side preserving its own territory, army, and treasury. Despite the preservation of its statehood within the Commonwealth, the reality was that Lithuania had an unequal position. The Polish aristocracy gained the upper hand over the Lithuanian aristocracy as it acquired lands and positions in Lithuania. Moreover, because of its elected monarchy, Lithuania was usually ruled by kings from other countries, including France, Sweden (the Vasa dynasty, 1571–1668), and Saxony (the Wettin dynasty, 1696–1763).

Another consequence of Lithuania's ties to Poland was their shared economic and political decline in the seventeenth and eighteenth centuries, with the result that Lithuanian peasants were by and large poorer than peasants in the Latvian and Estonian provinces. Moreover, in the predatory international climate of seventeenth- and eighteenth-century Europe, the weak and decentralized Polish-Lithuanian Commonwealth was unable to compete with its aggressive neighbors. Relations with Muscovy had been worsening since the fifteenth century, when Muscovite rulers, finally recovering from two centuries of Mongol rule, began laying claims to the Russian lands of the Grand Duchy of Lithuania. A particularly ferocious period was 1654 to 1667, when Swedish and Russian forces swept into Lithuanian territory. As a result of these battles, most of Ukraine was lost to Russia.

Because of constant warring, famine, and epidemics, Lithuanian areas became increasingly barbarous and depopulated, with the population of the Grand Duchy declining by nearly one-half between 1648 and 1697. The region was further damaged in the course of the Great Northern War (1700–15), fought by the armies of Tsar Peter the Great and the Swedish King Charles XII (discussed below).

Polish-Lithuanian fortunes fell further as the Commonwealth found itself in the path of the ambitious monarchs who ruled Austria, Prussia, and Russia. Together they conspired to divide the country in three successive partitions in 1772, 1793, and 1795. By the first partition, Russia's Empress Catherine the Great (ruled 1762–96) obtained much of the area that comprises modern Belarus along with Latgale (an ethnically Latvian area that was largely Catholic and politically Polonized); in the second, Russia incorporated the rest of Belarus, western Ukraine and much of Lithuania proper. In the final partition of 1795, Russia acquired the remainder of Ukraine and Lithuania (where the majority of ethnic Lithuanians lived), as well as the Duchy of Courland (*Ger.* Kurland). Thus did Lithuania and Poland disappear from European maps for more than a century.

Meanwhile, as noted earlier, during the long period of Polish domination, Lithuanian culture stagnated as Lithuanian elites became Polonized. However, in Lithuania Minor—that part of Lithuania that fell under German rule in East Prussia—Lithuanian culture tended to develop more dynamically than in the Grand Duchy. In 1547 the first Lithuanian-language book (by M. Mažvydas) and later the first complete Bible translation were both published in Königsberg (Kaliningrad of the present-day Russian Federation). Indeed, in the 1578–1831 period nearly twice as many books were published in Prussian Lithuania than in Lithuania itself.

LITHUANIAN JEWS

Until nearly the entire Jewish community in Lithuania was destroyed during World War II, Jews had a long and rich history in Lithuania, dating to Grand Prince Gediminas's invitation to merchants and craftsmen to settle in the area in the fourteenth century.[6] In the early fifteenth century, Gediminas's grandson, Vytautas, granted Jews privileges, including religious freedom, and protection of both person and property. As a result, during his reign the number of Jews in Lithuania grew to 6,000. Following the expulsion of Jews from Spain and the continued persecution of Jews in western Europe, by the sixteenth century Poland-Lithuania had become the new cultural center of Jewish life in Europe. At first concentrated in the Zamut region (including Vilnius and areas north and west of it), Lithuania's Jews, called "Litvaks," eventually established communities throughout the western part of the Grand Duchy.

During the period of the Commonwealth, Jews enjoyed considerable autonomy, even apportioning and collecting the Jewish poll tax, whose level was set by the *sejm,* an early assembly of notables. While the support of the Lithuanian nobility benefited a handful of wealthy Jews (who could even own estates and serfs), the vast majority of Lithuanian Jews endured difficult conditions, earning their living from petty trade and the occupation that was reserved for Jews by royal decree: money-lending. Although medieval Europe needed a banking system, the Catholic Church forbade Christians to lend at interest; hence Jews were to provide this service for the rest of society, and especially for Europe's royalty. While this meant that many Jews felt safe and protected within their defined area of residence, they nevertheless felt the brunt of an anti-Polish revolt of Cossack forces led by Bogdan Khmelnitskii in 1648, in which Jewish communities were singled out for destruction. Tens of thousands of Jews were murdered, maimed, or raped.

Despite the pogroms of the previous century, by 1765 there were at least 120,000 Jews living in ethnic Lithuania, and nearly 750,000 Jews in the Commonwealth. They formed about 20 to 30 percent of the population in the larger cities and more than 70 percent in some of the smaller towns. By this time, Vilnius was established as the most important Jewish center in Lithuania. However, under Russian rule, to which nearly all of Lithuania was subject by the end of the eighteenth century, Jews' legal and socioeconomic status deteriorated. The Russian Empire's western border, including Lithuania, was made part of the "Jewish Pale of Settlement." Jews living there were forbidden from settling in the Russian interior, and restrictions on Jewish life tightened throughout the first half of the nineteenth century.

GERMAN RULE

When the Russian Empire annexed Lithuania as a result of the eighteenth-century Polish partitions, Lithuanians could make the claim of having enjoyed a long period of independence and greatness as rulers of a large kingdom in the heart of Europe. Other Baltic provinces that came under Russian rule never had a national memory of such independence. Ruled by a succession of foreign regimes (including Sweden, Poland, and Rus-

Medieval Livonia c. 1500. Courtesy of Cartographica.

sia), the natives of Estonia, Livonia, and Courland were always subordinate to the Baltic German upper class that dominated the social and economic life of the region.

Within the boundaries of the Livonian Confederation, German knights who had been given land in the thirteenth century and afterwards became the new nobility, to which were added German noblemen who were invited to settle in the region. The knights continually clashed with the bishops over the matter of territorial control. The original formula for dividing new territories, which called for one-third to go to the Livonian Order and two-thirds to the Church (headed by the Archbishop of Rīga, who commanded his own army of vassals), gradually lapsed, with the result that far more territory came under the Order's control. The Church, however, controlled many of the institutions of Livonian life, such as parishes, congregations, clergy, and houses of worship. Only in 1330, after a long struggle, did Rīga acknowledge the suzerainty of the Order.

Merchants constituted the other elements of the ruling elite, and they too were usually German. Following the Livonian conquest, Hansa ("flock") merchants rushed into the Baltic region. German and Scandinavian merchants formed the Hanseatic League in the mid-twelfth century, and at its peak 200 later it was fostering trade links between more than 100 towns and outposts throughout the North Sea and Baltic Sea regions. These included Rīga, the area's first and largest commercial center, Tallinn (*Ger.* Reval), Tartu (*Ger.* Dorpat), Königsberg (Kaliningrad today), and Novgorod in Russia. As self-governing polities, the Hanseatic city-states operated independently of the surrounding principalities and kingdoms and for more than three centuries enjoyed peaceful relations with each other.

The Hanseatic League began as and remained an organization of German merchants; merchants who were not German faced severe restrictions in the Baltic. Thus Germans dominated not only the religious and political life of the Baltic, but also controlled the region's economy, which supplied western Europe with grain, wax, furs, flax, and timber. Imports included cloth, metal goods, weapons, salt, and various luxury items. By playing such a vital role in the West-East trade, the East Baltic region was incorporated into the economic life of Europe, dependent on western Europe's demands for its agricultural products and natural resources.

Although Baltic towns—Rīga in particular—were predominantly populated by German colonists, they became attractive destinations for indebted (and therefore fleeing) peasants, who were otherwise largely isolated from the institutions and structures introduced by their German overlords. Indeed, the flight of *Undeutsche* to the towns was a source of particular concern to Baltic landowners, since the peasants formed the foundation of an economic system that by the sixteenth century was largely based on serfdom.

Baltic peasants were expected to cultivate the land for the profit of the German landowners. However, Germans were not the only landowners in the wake of the conquest, for the leaders of the conquered Baltic tribes often became vassals of the German elites (and thus were gradually Germanized) and were given small portions of land in exchange for military service. Some Baltic peasants had small amounts of land, but the majority were landless, renting or owning small farms on the land of the larger manors in exchange for labor and rent (in the form of money or agricultural produce) requirements. However, by the fifteenth century the increasing tax burden on the small peasant farms resulted in their being swallowed up by the surrounding estates. For most peasants, accumulated debt and hereditary serfdom were the results; others moved to the cities to work as artisans and craftsmen.

The German landowners lived on manors that were separate from the native rural communities. The result was that native Balts lived a world apart from the German-speaking elite, speaking their own languages and paying their landowners rent, increasingly in the form of physical labor. This remained the case in Estonia and Livonia until the early nineteenth century, when serfdom was outlawed in most of the Baltic provinces. In Lithuania, this elite was mostly Polish (and also Russian after the eighteenth-century partitions), but the social, political, and economic nature of the relationship was similar.

RUSSIAN EXPANSION

In 1418 the Livonian Confederation was created from the five Baltic bishopric-principalities of the Holy Roman Empire. However, the lack of unity between the Church and the Order, and the declining power of the Hanseatic League weakened German rule in the Baltic. The Confederation finally collapsed in 1561 as Sweden, Poland, and Russia battled for control of the Baltic. Ultimately it was Russia that emerged as the strongest power in the region.

Finally liberated from Mongol rule late in the fifteenth century, Muscovy (from which the Russian Empire would emerge) was an aggressively expansionist state whose rulers were bent on absorbing neighboring Slavic princedoms while upholding the banner of Orthodox Christianity. By the mid-sixteenth century, Muscovy's power extended through all the Russian lands, having absorbed Novgorod, Tver', and other rival principalities during "the gathering of Russia" that proceeded under the rule of Ivan III (ruled 1462–1505) and his successors.

The Lithuanian princedom, which had expanded deep into East Slavic territory during the period of Mongol rule in Russia, was Moscow's rival for the gathering of the Russian lands, but Lithuanian princes were not equipped with the absolute authority enjoyed by Muscovy's grand prince. Instead, the grand princes of Lithuania, like their Polish counterparts, gradually turned into elected constitutional monarchs who heeded the counsel of a gentry elite (*szlachta*) to whom they granted unprecedented rights and privileges. Thus, as Lithuanian grand princes grew weaker, the power of the Muscovite autocracy reached a new peak under Ivan IV ("the Dread," popularly known in the English-speaking world as "Ivan the Terrible"), Russia's first true tsar. Instead of becoming a serious contender for power in Orthodox Russia, Lithuania remained a junior partner to Catholic Poland during a period when Poland-Lithuania and Russia were constantly fighting.

Almost all of Tsar Ivan IV's reign (1547–84) was spent at war. The main threat came from the steppe—the khanates of the south and east. Defeat of the khanate of Kazan' in 1552 was the first step in Russia's expansion beyond traditionally "Russian" lands. In the east, the road was now open to unknown Siberia; in the northwest, however, Ivan IV waged war against the Livonian Confederation. With its small hold on the coastline at the mouth of the Neva River, Russia had enjoyed only limited access to the Baltic, a condition Ivan IV sought to remedy by launching a war in 1558. Initial successes resulted in the disbandment of the Livonian Confederation in 1561 (much of its territory fell to Poland-Lithuania, Sweden, and Denmark), but the war dragged on for 25 years with few gains by the Russian state.

Amidst the chaos of war the Baltic peasants fended for themselves. A peasant uprising in the far north, one of the largest in Estonian history, began in the autumn of 1560 but was crushed the following year. While most peasants continued to farm, others abandoned agriculture to join mercenary armies or to loot (or both). Widespread famine was the result.

In the long run, Ivan IV's attempts to expand into the Baltic were catastrophic not only for Baltic peasants but for Russia itself. By 1569 it faced a united Poland and Lithuania, as well as a growing Sweden, each of which was concerned less with the fate of Livonia than with checking Muscovite expansion. Moreover, Russia's northern war diverted men and resources from the Tatar threat in the south and east. Shortly before his death in 1584, Ivan IV signed treaties with both Poland and Sweden renouncing all that Russia had gained in the first part of the war. A century later, Russia's rulers would again set their sights on the Baltic, but in the meantime the Baltic peoples continued their development largely under western political and cultural influence.

LUTHERANISM IN THE BALTIC

A defining moment in the history of western and central Europe was the Protestant Reformation, which ensured the permanent western orientation of Latvians and Estonians. Arriving in the Baltic area not long after the collapse of the Teutonic Order, this religious movement had a tremendous appeal in and impact on a region that, resentful of the Germans' attempts at forcible conversion to Catholicism, had never fully converted from paganism.

The Reformation in Europe officially began with Martin Luther's (1483–

1546) challenge to the papacy and the Roman Catholic Church. Luther, a German friar, argued against the Church's practice of selling indulgences (that is, the selling of one's pardon, and hence one's salvation) to parishioners, while he challenged its authority on numerous theological issues. The Catholic world quickly split into warring camps: those who remained loyal to the papacy were pitted against those who were either sincere followers of Luther or who otherwise did not wish to continue remitting taxes to Rome.

The ideas of the Reformation entered the Livonian Confederation by the 1520s, and Lutheranism soon became the prevailing religion in the urban areas of the region, while Lithuania remained Roman Catholic. (Prussia became a Lutheran state.) To Baltic peasants, the main message of the Reformation was that all men were equal before God—a serious challenge indeed to the hierarchical structure of feudal Europe—and unrest soon followed. Of course, Livonian peasants had little choice concerning which form of Christianity they would observe; that decision was left to the region's German-speaking nobility, many of whom initially fought against the reforms. Although by the 1530s the majority of the gentry had converted to Protestantism, Catholic bishops, the Livonian Order, and most cloisters remained active for several more decades.

The transition to Protestantism was facilitated by the Reformation's campaign to translate the Bible into indigenous languages, thus making Protestant Christianity more accessible to congregations in the Baltic region. The translation of the Bible into the vernacular is doubtless one of the great legacies of the Reformation in the Baltic region, as elsewhere in Protestant Europe. Still, for the peasantry, Christianity, whether in its Roman Catholic or Lutheran form, was not a matter of religious conviction but was something imposed from the outside; despite their outward obeisance to established religious authority, many peasants continued their pagan practices.

Despite Lutheranism's hold on the people of Livonia, the region once again fell into Roman Catholic hands. As the price for protection from Muscovy, in 1561 most of Livonia came under Polish-Lithuanian rule.[7] The Livonian Confederation was subsequently dissolved, and the former knights of the Order became the landed nobility of the province subsequently known as the Duchy of Courland and Zemgale, which owed its allegiance to Poland. Although much of Livonia was incorporated into the Catholic Poland of King Sigismund II Augustus, the area (called Inflanty during the period of Polish-Lithuanian rule) was not entirely Catholicized. Many of the region's inhabitants managed to retain their newly acquired Lutheran religious identity—as well as their old pagan traditions.

In the Lithuanian territories the Reformation's impact was less profound. Where Protestantism did manage to take root, it was often in its Calvinist variant, which by the mid-sixteenth century had become popular among the Lithuanian nobility.[8] Just as quickly as it arrived, however, Calvinism began to wane, and Catholicism began its recovery with the arrival in 1569 of Jesuit priests at the invitation of the Bishop of Vilnius.[9] Setting up mission stations and schools throughout Lithuania, the Jesuits' attempts at conversion were successful—and were aided by the fact that the Lithuanians who had earlier converted to Calvinism had not done so with any great conviction. Although the Catholic faith won out in Lithuania, the Protestant Reformation was responsible for the publication of the first books in the Lithuanian language, and hence for the beginning of a national Lithuanian literature.

RUSSIAN, POLISH, AND SWEDISH COMPETITION

For decades after the partition of Livonia, the Baltic region remained an object of contention between Sweden, Denmark, Poland-Lithuania, and Russia. A short period of relative peace, between 1583 and 1600, was followed by one of severe warfare. The seventeenth century was an era of heightened religious tension in Europe, culminating in the Thirty Years' War from 1618 to 1648. That the Baltic region would become a battleground between its Catholic and Protestant contestants was nearly inevitable. Although dynastic ties between Poland and Sweden muddle the picture somewhat, the state of relations between these two countries was that of protracted war, reaching a peak between 1600 and 1629.

The Swedes ended up the winners of the struggle, ultimately conquering most of the Baltic area (except for the southern regions of Latgale and the Duchy of Courland and Zemgale, each of which remained under Polish suzerainty) in 1629. With the Swedes controlling the most important cities on the east coast of the Baltic Sea—Tallinn, Rīga, and Narva—from this point onward Polish power in the Baltic was in retreat. For Sweden, the Baltic provinces were a source of grain and revenue; dominion over these territories also allowed the Swedes to control trade between Europe and Russia.

Of course, the main victims of the Livonian Wars and the Polish-Swedish struggles were the Baltic peoples themselves, suffering not only from the intense fighting that took place in the region, but also from disease (mainly the plague) and famine. Estonian historians estimate that during the Polish-Swedish war the Estonian population fell from more than 250,000 to as little as 100,000; some regions suffered the loss of as much as 75 percent of their population.[10] Some of the lost population was replaced by extensive immigration from Russia (including persecuted Old Believers—opponents of reform in the Russian Orthodox Church—who at the end of the seventeenth century began to settle on the northern and western coasts of Lake Peipsi), Finland, and other neighboring regions.

Estonians and Latvians of later eras romantically tend to view the era of Swedish rule as, if not exactly a golden age, at least a time of reform and relative liberalism sandwiched between the lengthier and more repressive periods of German and Russian rule. Although Germans, with their privileges intact, remained the main landowning class in what were now known as Livland (southern Estonia and northern Latvia) and the Duchy of Estland (northern Estonia), Swedes were placed in local administrative positions and in the *Landtage* (diets, or assemblies of notables), while some Swedish officials and generals received land. Meanwhile, Roman Catholicism and Russian Orthodoxy, favored respectively by Livonia's former Polish rulers and the Muscovites in Estonia, were in retreat as the Lutheran faith now enjoyed the protection of the Swedish monarchs.

King Charles XI (1672–97) is usually regarded as the most reform-minded of the Baltic region's Swedish rulers and even as a defender of the interests of the Baltic peasants. Like other monarchs of his day, he was bent on centralizing power in his realm, which meant tightening his control over the powerful Baltic nobility. A related goal was the improvement of tax collection in his Baltic territories, which he attempted through a massive policy of land expropriation beginning in 1681. As a result, nobles in Estland surrendered one-third of their land, while their counterparts in Livland gave up five-sixths. In each case many of the German nobles, upon whom the Swedish crown continued to rely for support, were allowed to retain their estates even where these were considered state property. Whether this policy did much to improve the conditions of the Livonian and Estonian peasantry, as is sometimes suggested, is debatable. Whatever the case, the German barons retained their loyalty to the Swedish crown and continued to exert a their influence on all aspects of life in the region.

While Livland and Estland developed under Swedish rule for most of the seventeenth century, the Duchy of Courland and Zemgale, whose peasants were mostly Latvian, was under loose Polish control. Unlike most other Polish territories, Courland and Zemgale had Lutheran populations, having followed the lead of the first Duke of Courland, Gotthard Kettler (1517–87). Since his day, Courland's nobles had enjoyed virtually unlimited control over their properties and the peasants who lived on them. Unlike the case in the Swedish-controlled territories of Livland and Estland, where many peasants received the protection of the crown (which nominally owned many of the estates), the rulers of Courland never considered undertaking any reforms to mitigate the worst aspects of serfdom.

Economically, the Baltic region, split between Polish and Swedish rulers, remained somewhat diverse, although serfdom remained its basis. Peasants labored on estates to produce agricultural goods, and then carted these goods to markets in commercial centers along the waterways. Rīga was the largest of these commercial centers in the Baltic region, and by the mid-seventeenth century had become the biggest city in the Swedish realm, with a population in the 1680s of perhaps ten thousand—at least 50 percent of whom were Latvians.[11] Grains, wood products, and naval supplies were brought to Rīga from throughout the Baltic littoral, and Rīga's merchants supplied the region with finished products from abroad. With the dissolution of the Hanseatic League in 1699, Baltic commerce was more open than it had been in centuries, with Swedish, Danish, and English ships competing to carry Baltic products.

It was also during the period of Swedish rule that Estonian and Latvian began their development as literary languages. This owes much to the efforts of Lutheran clergymen who responded to the need to reach their parishioners in their own vernacular. A few books in Latvian and Estonian, mostly of a religious nature, had appeared as early as the first quarter of the sixteenth century. About 40 books, mostly theological tracts, were published in Estonian in the seventeenth century, while perhaps as many as 60 new titles were printed in Latvian during this period, especially in the latter half of the century.[12]

Among the most important pioneers of Latvian-language publishing was Georg Mancelius (1593–1654), a Lutheran clergyman and professor of theology at the University of Dorpat (now the University of Tartu). Although born in Livland to German-speaking parents, he recognized the importance of being able to communicate his sermons to the Latvian peasants and learned their language. Mancelius published not only his hymn collections, but also a work called *Lettus* (1638), which contained a Latvian-German dictionary, which remained in use for more than a century. Also noteworthy was Ernst Glück's (1651–1705) translations of the New and Old Testaments. While such writers made great contributions to the development of literary Latvian, for the overwhelming majority of Latvian and Estonian peasants, until the late nineteenth century it was the oral tradition of folk songs, stories, and other spoken expression that remained the main means of transmitting local culture from one generation to the next.

Until that time and with few exceptions, education was limited to the children of the Baltic German elite, as well as Swedes and Finns. The first Estonian university was established in Tartu (*Ger.* Dorpat) in 1632; it supplied the region with future pastors, doctors, schoolteachers, and state officials. Elementary education began in the 1680s with the founding of parish schools of Estonia, thus affording a few Estonian peasants—girls as well as boys—access to learning. Around the same time, the first parish schools in Livland were opened in Vidzeme. In nearly all these cases, however, the language of instruction was German—a condition that did not change substantially until the nineteenth century under Russian rule.

THE GREAT NORTHERN WAR

The end of Swedish rule in Livland and Estland was a direct consequence of Muscovy's reemergence as a contender for power in the region. As noted earlier, Muscovy's first attempts to expand its power into the Baltic region, during the Livonian Wars, were disastrous, leaving the country severely weakened and vulnerable to the predatory actions of its northern and western neighbors. Following the instability of the Time of Troubles (1598–1613), during which Muscovy nearly suffered the fate of becoming a Polish province, the country gradually recovered and established a new ruling dynasty which was to last until 1917—the Romanov dynasty.

In 1672 this dynasty produced Peter Alekseevich Romanov (ruled 1689–1725), who as a boy delighted in war games and dreamed of building a great navy. Crowned Peter I in 1689, but known to history as Peter the Great, the new tsar set his gaze toward the Baltic Sea, which at this time remained a Swedish lake. Meanwhile, Peter's lifelong adversary Charles XII (ruled 1697–1718) ascended the Swedish throne at age fifteen and quickly made a reputation for himself as a military commander of genius. Soon these soldier-kings were locked in a war for mastery over the Baltic provinces, known as the Great Northern War (1700–21).

Once again, the Baltic area was the scene of great devastation, with Peter's scorched-earth policy, famine, and plague being responsible for the catastrophic loss of human life: as much as 40 percent of the population in Latvian lands were killed, and perhaps 60 or 70 percent in Estonia.[13] A peace treaty was not signed until 1721: under its provisions Russia acquired Livland, Estland, and other territories in the region, along with perhaps 300,000 new Latvian and Estonian subjects. With its Baltic conquests, Russia had formally become an empire, and its new acquisitions were now counted among its provinces.

Despite the devastation of the Great Northern War, the Baltic German ruling class emerged stronger than ever, thanks to the extremely favorable terms of surrender offered by the Russian tsar. Peter I returned to the landowners the land expropriated by the Swedish crown in the last decades of the seventeenth century, while confirming the rights of the Lutheran Church and German as the language of administration and the courts. Corporate bodies known as *Ritterschaften*, formed in the sixteenth century by the Baltic German nobility, retained their privileges, and Germans controlled the provincial *Landtage* of Estland and Livland.

With its privileges confirmed by subsequent Russian tsars and tsarinas, during most of the eighteenth century the nobility was able to strengthen its political hold in the Baltic provinces, while German merchants controlled the economic life of the cities. Maintaining the privileges of the Baltic landed elite, however, also meant restoring and upholding the serf status of much of the Baltic peasantry during the first century of Russian rule in the region, a subject to which we shall return in the next chapter.

NOTES

1. The names of the proto-Latvian tribes may also be rendered Kurlanders, Zemgals, Latgals, Sels, etc.

2. See Endre Bojtár, *Foreword to the Past: A Cultural History of the Baltic People* (Budapest: Central European Press, 1999), 307–317.

3. The Viking Rurik was the founder of the earliest Russian state, centered in Kiev, in the ninth century. His descendants ruled numerous Russian principalities east of the Baltic areas.

4. The St. George's Day Uprising is usually portrayed by Estonian historians as a fight for freedom.

5. Jogaila rejected an arrangement proposed by his mother for him to marry the daughter of the Muscovite Prince Dmitri Donskoi. One can only speculate what a dynastic union with Orthodox Russia would have meant for the future of Lithuania.

6. Some historians have hypothesized that Jews reached Lithuania around the time the Kievan state embraced Orthodox Christianity in the late tenth century. According to this theory, Jews who had been living in the Rus' principalities were subsequently expelled; many moved to towns that then belonged to Lithuania. See Masha Greenbaum, *The Jews of Lithuania: A History of a Remarkable Community 1316–1945* (Jerusalem: Gefen Books, 1995), 2–3.

7. Although most of Livonia fell into Polish-Lithuanian hands, parts of Courland and the island of Ösel (Saaremaa today) were ceded to Denmark, while northern Estonia came under the control of Sweden, a Lutheran country.

8. Calvinism was based on the theology developed by John Calvin (1509–64), a French religious reformer.

9. Jesuits were members of the Society of Jesus, an order of Roman Catholic priests and monks dedicated to foreign missions and education.

10. Rein Taagepera, *Estonia: Return to Independence* (Boulder, Colo: Westview Press, 1993), 24; Toivo U. Raun, *Estonia and the Estonians* (Stanford, Cal.: Hoover Institution Press, 1987), 28.

11. Andrejs Plakans, *The Latvians: A Short History* (Stanford, Cal.: Hoover Institution Press, 1995), 52–53.

12. Raun (1987), 32; Plakans (1995), 55–59.

13. The Great Northern War occurred in the wake of a famine in Estonia in 1695–97 that took an estimated 70,000 lives—20 percent of the Estonian population. By the end of the war the Estonian population had dropped from about 350,000 to 100,000. Taagepera (1993), 26.

3

Russian Rule, 1721–1905

The previous chapter described how, as a consequence of the Great Northern War, Russia obtained from Sweden the Baltic provinces of Livland (northern Latvia and southern Estonia) and Estland (northern Estonia). These arrangements, later affirmed by the Treaty of Nystad (1721), provided Russia with a Baltic coastline and thus significantly improved Russia's strategic position in northeastern Europe. The rest of the area comprising the contemporary Baltic countries remained under Polish control until the last decades of the eighteenth century, when Poland was partitioned in three stages. Austria and Prussia received some Polish territories, but the bulk was swallowed by Russia, including Ukrainian, Belarussian, and Lithuanian areas in the east, as well as Courland and Latgale (which together form the southern part of contemporary Latvia).

Because Livland and Estland came under Russian control considerably earlier and were governed by a ruling class of Baltic Germans, here they are treated separately from the Lithuanian territories, which were annexed in 1795 and whose landowning class was Russo-Polish. In general, Russian state policy distinguished between the Baltic provinces (including Courland, acquired in 1775) and the Polish-Lithuanian provinces, confirming the privileges of the loyal Baltic German elite in the former, while looking upon the elites of the Polish provinces with great suspicion, es-

The Baltic Provinces of
the Russian Empire c. 1850

FINLAND
Gulf of Finland

Reval (Tallinn)

Narva

St. Petersburg

Baltic
Sea

Estland

Hiiumaa

Lake
Peipsi

Saaremaa

Pskov

Gulf of
Riga

Livland

Pskov

Courland

Riga

Vitebsk

Mitawa
(Jelgava)

R   U   S   S   I   A   N

Dvinsk (Dunaberg)

Memel

Kovno

E   M   P   I   R   E

Tilsit

Kovno (Kaunas)

Vilna

East
Prussia

Vilna (Vilnius)

Suwalki

Suwalki

Grodno

Grodno

N

0   100 km

0   100 miles

The Baltic Provinces of the Russian Empire c. 1850. Courtesy of Cartographica.

pecially after the Polish uprising of 1830. In each case, however, the Russian government attempted to integrate these borderland territories into the administrative and legal framework of the Russian Empire by encouraging the use of the Russian language and, more cautiously, conversion to Orthodoxy.

This "Russification" policy accelerated significantly during the last decades of the nineteenth century, partly as an official response to the growth of national movements on the empire's periphery, including the Baltic provinces. In an era of rising nationalism throughout Europe, however, the "awakenings" of the Latvian, Estonian, and Lithuanian peoples were of less concern to the Russian state than the continued loyalty of the Baltic German elites. It is to the Baltic Germans we shall turn first.

BALTIC GERMANS AND THE RUSSIAN STATE

Baltic Germans constituted the ruling class in the areas that today comprise modern Estonia and Latvia from the thirteenth century until the beginning of the twentieth. As previously noted, Germans came to the Baltic region as traders (the Hansa merchants) and crusaders (Teutonic Knights), subduing the native Estonians, Latvians, Livonians, Prussians, and other tribes as they established themselves as the ruling authorities. The order they brought with them was much like the one that existed in western Europe at the time—a feudal system with a small landowning elite ruling over the dues-paying peasant masses. Unlike western Europe, however, the division between elite and peasantry in the Baltic lands had an ethnic basis: German nobles owned most of the land, German priests constituted the religious authorities, and German merchants dominated urban commerce. The indigenous populations, speaking their own languages and maintaining their own separate cultures, supported the German-speaking elite with their labors. This division became especially pronounced in the sixteenth and seventeenth centuries, as the native peasantry became enserfed.

Although the medieval German crusaders were Roman Catholic, Germans were also responsible for bringing the ideas of Martin Luther to Livonia and Estonia and converting much of the native peasantry to Protestantism. Thus in the matter of religion, Baltic Germans and the Latvian and Estonian peasantry shared something in common. In almost every other respect, however, the relationship was colonial. This was reflected in the Baltic Germans' generally condescending attitude toward the natives and their reputedly harsh treatment of Latvian and Estonian peasants. These non-Germans (*Undeutsche*) were barred from entering the urban professions and faced other restrictions.

Because the Baltic German aristocracy were a trusted and even admired elite, Russian tsars allowed them an unusual degree of autonomy. These provinces were the empire's most westernized, and as such the local governments and courts of the region were to serve as models for the rest of Russia, which Peter I sought to reform along European lines. The Petrine reforms of the eighteenth century strove to create a more rational and efficient Russian state, for which Germans had the necessary technical and political expertise. Not only were Baltic Germans allowed to administer local government in the Baltic provinces, they also served in St. Petersburg as diplomats and administrators, filling the ranks of the country's swelling bureaucracy—and often replacing the German-speaking foreigners upon whom the state had earlier relied.

Above all, Baltic Germans were well represented in the officer corps of the Russian army, as Peter I valued their education, experience, and familiarity with Western technology and warfare. As in state service, they replaced the foreigners (including men of Scots, French, German, Polish, and Swedish origin) upon whom the Russian armed forces had relied since the seventeenth century. Of the entire officer corps of the Russian army in the 1730s, perhaps as many as one-quarter were Baltic Germans.

The service of Germans was also necessary for the Russian state to achieve its diplomatic and economic goals in Europe. Russian ambassadors to Britain were almost always Baltic Germans, and since German was the *lingua franca* of the Baltic region and central Europe, nobles from Estland and Livland (as they were called under Russian-German rule) played a vital role in furthering Russia's foreign policy objectives in Europe. Their service was also necessary for the maintenance and development of Russia's Baltic commercial and financial connections with western Europe. In short, the Baltic Germans were valuable intermediaries between Russia and the German-speaking parts of Europe, especially in the first half of the eighteenth century.

In exchange for the loyalty of the Baltic German nobility, every Russian tsar from Peter I to Aleksandr II (ruled 1855–81) confirmed their privileged status in the Russian Empire; only Aleksandr III (1881–94) and his son Nicholas II (1894–1917) refused to continue the tradition. Despite the loyalty of the *Baltische*, a number of Russian rulers were greatly concerned with the anomalous position of the Baltic provinces and of the western borderlands in general. The tsarinas Anna (1730–40) and Elizabeth (1740–62) much admired the Baltic Germans and allowed them considerable autonomy in running Baltic affairs, but the accession of the German-born

Empress Catherine II in 1762 heralded some changes in the status of the Baltic Germans and the provinces they governed.

As a product of the eighteenth century Enlightenment, Catherine II (the Great) strove to achieve a higher degree of uniformity, rationality, and centralization in the empire's law and government, while retaining the absolutist basis of her rule. As one of the Enlightenment's main philosophical concerns was the rights and dignity of individuals, Catherine's attention was drawn to the plight of the empire's peasants, which underlined the relative backwardness of her adopted land. A one-month visit in 1764 to the provinces of Estland and Livland allowed Catherine to familiarize herself with local conditions, especially those of the peasants, whose lot she wished to improve as a model for the rest of the empire. Although little progress was made in this sphere, the official discussions that followed Catherine's visit helped pave the way for the emancipation of Estonian and Latvian serfs fifty years later.

Turning her attention to the organization and functioning of local government in the empire, Catherine enacted reforms that reorganized the empire into *gubernii* (provinces) and *uezdy* (districts). With some modifications by her son Paul I (1796–1801), after the final Polish partition in 1795, the region that today embraces the modern Baltic countries of Estonia, Latvia, and Lithuania were administered as the provinces of Estland, Livland, Courland (ruled together under a single governor-general from 1801–76, and afterwards governed separately), Kaunas, and Vilnius (the latter two *gubernii* comprise modern Lithuania).[1]

While in the Ukrainian and Belarussian lands Catherine and her successors implemented Russification measures designed to integrate the newly annexed regions into the legal and political framework of the empire, in Estland and Livland Russian rulers proceeded more cautiously— mostly out of admiration for the institutions of the local nobility, but also because of their concern that the Baltic Germans might form an organized resistance to St. Petersburg. Still, Catherine's efforts to bring uniformity to the empire entailed some loss of privilege for the Baltic German nobles. However, these were quickly restored during the brief reign of Catherine's son Paul I, who required in return that Baltic landowners provide recruits for the Russian army. With the support of admiring Russian rulers after Catherine II, the Baltic German nobility maintained their autonomy until the accession of Tsar Aleksandr III, a supporter of Russification who abolished the nobility's special rights.

Apart from their political and economic dominance, Baltic Germans made significant contributions to the social and cultural life of the region from the medieval era through the period of Swedish rule and under the two centuries of Russian domination. As noted earlier, among the most prominent Baltic German institutions was the University of Dorpat, founded by the Swedish King Gustavus Adolphus in 1632. Although closed during the Great Northern War, it was reopened during the reign of Tsar Aleksandr I (1801–25), and remained one of the leading universities in the Russian Empire while attracting leading academicians from Germany.

Secondary schools existed in Baltic towns since the thirteenth and fourteenth centuries, and expanded considerably under Russian rule during the nineteenth century. The Baltic educational system was almost purely German: the language of instruction was German, and German teachers provided instruction to the children of affluent Germans in the towns and to a small number of Estonians and Latvians. Although the central authorities, lacking their own resources, encouraged Baltic Germans to take a leading role in providing a basic education to provincial youth, by the mid-nineteenth century some Russian officials began to recognize the dangers inherent in an educational system that threatened to lure Latvian and Estonians toward German rather than Russian culture.

While Germans dominated the economic, political, and social life of the Baltic provinces, their numbers were small. Germans always constituted less than 10 percent of the population of the Baltic provinces, and by the end of the nineteenth century were probably less than 6 percent of the overall Baltic population. In the mid-nineteenth century, for example, the German-speaking population amounted to about 125,000 out of a total population of 1.6 million for Livland, Estland, and Courland. While predominant in Baltic cities until the mid-nineteenth century, in the Baltic countryside Germans lived on isolated manors in a sea of Estonian and Latvian peasants. Indeed, many landlords were of the absentee variety, spending most of their time in the towns.

It is this arrangement that, perhaps more than any other, helps to explain the loyalty of Baltic Germans to the Russian state. St. Petersburg provided the German minority with the political support necessary for maintaining their rule in the Baltic provinces. Although Baltic Germans had nurtured a distinctive ethnic identity as Germans (in contrast to the simply "non-German" peasants—the *Undeutsche*), they were divided across three provinces and were physically and politically separated from their spiritual homeland. Thus they were not a unified group and entertained no "national" aspirations. While Baltic Germans guarded their historic rights and privileges (including the privilege of not having to learn Russian—although the German nobles could communicate with their Russian counterparts in French), they were loyal servants of the tsar. Likewise, most Russian rulers regarded the Baltic Germans as honest and particularly useful subjects. This began to change after 1871, when the German lands of central Europe were unified, and in the following decades the new Germany developed into one of the great world powers. Following this development in the heart of Europe, Russian authorities sought to undermine the authority of the Baltic German elite, whom they suspected of drawing Estonian and Latvian peasants into the German cultural orbit.

ESTONIAN AND LATVIAN PEASANTS

Estonians were the predominant ethnic group of Estland and northern Livland. In the early eighteenth century, after the famine of 1695–97 and the disasters of the Great Northern War, there were perhaps only 100,000 persons living in Estonian lands; however, by 1782 the population of Estland and northern Livland had reached close to 500,000, and by 1858 perhaps as much as 750,000, with more than 60 percent of Estonians concentrated in northern Livland.[2]

Ethnic Latvians lived in southern Livland, Courland (annexed in 1795), and Latgale (annexed in 1772, and later incorporated into the Vitebsk *guberniia*, or province). In the early eighteenth century the number of people living in Latvian-speaking areas was perhaps 465,000, rising to 873,000 at the end of the century.[3] The western areas were the least ethnically mixed, containing only Latvian-speaking peasants and German landowners. The southeastern parts of Courland were considerably more heterogeneous: here the population consisted of Latvians, Germans, Poles, Jews, Belarussians, Lithuanians, and Russians.

In contrast to the relatively simple case of the Estonians, who emerged as an identifiable ethnolinguistic group before the German invasion of the thirteenth century, the question of when Latvians became "Latvians" is complex. As noted in Chapter Two, the ancestors of modern Latvians were Latgalians, Couronians, Zemgalians, Livonians, and Selonians. It is possible that under the impact of the German invasion in the thirteenth century, the old political elites and thus tribal identities gradually withered, and the Latgalians, being the largest of the older groups (and thus the source of the name "Latvia"), came to dominate the others. It is also possible that the presence of uninvited, aggressive foreigners encouraged the subordinated peoples to unify, thus facilitating their emergence as "Latvians." Whatever the case, by around 1500 the old group identities had been submerged into a broader, although not necessarily very deep, Latvian identity. Like the Estonians to the north, these Latvians were peasants and remained subordinated to a German elite, who generally saw the

Latvians, Estonians, and remaining subpopulations simply as *Undeutsche;* this remained the case throughout the years of Swedish rule and Russian rule.

Following the disasters of the Great Northern War and annexation by Russia, conditions for Latvian and Estonian peasants stabilized and their status as serfs underwent little change for more than a century. However, whatever rights they had gained under Swedish rule they now lost for under Russian rule the peasants again belonged to the manor. Baltic land-lords, who remained overwhelmingly German, were often absent from their estates, preferring life in the towns to the isolation of their manors.

Although numerous—by the mid-nineteenth century there were more than 1,000 manors in the Estonian areas alone—Baltic manors were not as large as those in other parts of the Russian Empire. Unlike the Lithuanian manors, which were comprised of thousands—sometimes tens of thousands—of peasants, estates of more than 200 or 300 peasant households were relatively rare in Livland and Estland. Each noble landholding was divided into two areas for cultivation: the noble's estate, which consisted of a single consolidated unit, and the "peasant" land, which was held in scattered strips for periodic redivision by Latvian and Estonian peasants. Peasants worked "peasant" land in exchange for dues payable to the land-owners; this sometimes involved money payments but usually meant providing labor (*corvée*) for the estate land. Until the mid-seventeenth century, manors made most of their profits from the grain trade; afterwards, and especially from the second quarter of the eighteenth century onwards, there were increasing efforts to distill spirits for export to Russia.

In the eyes of the peasants and critics of serfdom, it was an exploitive system that landowners used to extract an increasing amount of labor from the peasants, who could not leave. Indeed, under the control of the Baltic barons serfdom was intensified for the purpose of expanding grain production for export to the West. It is likely that the resulting rise in the amount of obligatory peasant labor on the estates was responsible for the peasant unrest of the final decades of the eighteenth century in these provinces.

EMANCIPATION AND ITS CONSEQUENCES

Emancipation for most of the Baltic serfs preceded that for serfs in other parts of the Russian empire by nearly half a century and had a dramatic effect on the development of Estonian and Latvian social and cultural life, while to some extent helping to transform the region's economy. Emancipation was not a product of the efforts of Estonian and Latvian peasants, although there were indeed occasional peasant disturbances arising from poor economic conditions; nor was it an initiative undertaken by the Baltic German nobility, who felt that there was little need for change. Exceptions did exist, however, such as the clergyman Johann George Eisen von Schwarzenberg (1717–79), who argued that it was necessary to abolish serfdom and replace the feudal manor economy with a system that favored money rent. However, it was far more common for German landowners to criticize such reform efforts than to attempt to implement them.

Rather than being a German initiative, the process of emancipation arose out of the Russian government's concern for the condition of the peasantry—and its potential for producing tax revenues for St. Petersburg—during the rule of Catherine the Great. Visiting the province in 1764, Catherine was appalled by Baltic landlords' "despotic and cruel" treatment of their serfs and urged the landlords to reform, lest change be imposed upon them by the imperial government. The empress directed the Livland *Landtag* to assure peasant rights to movable property and provide other protective measures, but little came of it. However, Catherine's grandson Aleksandr I, an enthusiastic reformer during the early years of his reign (1801–25), acted more resolutely to improve the peasantry's condition not only in the Baltic provinces, but throughout the empire. The more advanced and efficient Baltic regions were to serve as test cases, and the Baltic German nobility were expected to take the initiative in working out the details.

Ultimately the tsar concluded that the *Landtag* was incapable of coming up with acceptable reforms, and the matter was taken up by the imperial government, which drafted a new peasant law for Livland and imposed it on the barons. Although serfdom was not abolished, the Livland Peasant Law of 1804 gave the peasantry hereditary land tenure. This, of course, the barons viewed as an encroachment on their exclusive right to own land. The law also provided for the creation of peasant judicial institutions and placed limitations on the landlords' rights over the lives of peasants on their estates. Despite its significance as an early attempt to reform serfdom on the western fringe of the Russian Empire, the Livland Peasant Law was never fully implemented by the time full emancipation came to the Baltic provinces more than a decade later.

Emancipation came to Estland, where the condition of the peasantry was the worst among the Baltic provinces, in 1816, to Courland in 1817, and to Livland in 1819. (Latgalian peasants were emancipated only in 1861.) The emancipation laws, the terms of which were worked out by committees representing the local nobility, were implemented incrementally in order to minimize disorder during the transition period, which took about 14 years. Baltic peasants were granted personal freedom and their own courts; however, they were denied land, which was retained by the lords. Politically, the peasants remained under the control of the German nobility, who retained judicial and police powers, including the right to administer corporal punishment.

While the landowners retained their traditional control over the peasants, emancipation meant that they gave up their traditional obligation to look out for their well-being. Some historians view the post-emancipation decades until around 1860 as a period of protracted agricultural crisis. During this time landless Estonian and Latvian peasants paid rent (in either labor or, less commonly, money) to the noble landowners, who, striving to maintain their high standard of living (which they believed was necessary for upward social mobility) as world prices for agricultural products fluctuated, fell deeper into debt. Many landowners continued to rely on the distilling of alcohol as the surest means of increasing their income—more than 80 percent of Livland's estates were involved in distilling—but even the market for alcohol was unreliable. For peasants, the worst period was the winter of 1845–46, when bad harvests resulted in famine. Thousands of peasants begged to be allowed to move to the Russian interior.

Although considerable restraints remained on the peasantry's freedom of movement until the 1860s, emancipation meant that greater numbers of Baltic peasants now had the freedom to join other occupations. However, most remained agricultural laborers, working on the manors of the German landlords. This situation changed somewhat by the 1860s, following the introduction of legislation designed to boost local self-government and facilitate peasants' access to land, combined with pressure on the German nobility to abolish labor rent and make more land available to peasants. Money rents began replacing labor rent in much of the region, and rural properties increasingly came under peasant ownership. By 1877 peasants owned more than 40 percent of agricultural land in Livland; in Estland, where the peasantry was poorer, the process was considerably slower. In neither case was the peasant problem solved, as many Estonian and Latvian peasants continued to suffer from landlessness (caused in part by a swelling population) and debt. Thousands drifted to the interior of Russia to find land and work in factories.

Another effect of emancipation was the introduction of surnames. Until then, Latvian and Estonian peasants were usually known only by their Christian names and the names of their manors and fathers. Since the new surnames names were usually given by the German landowners, many emancipated peasants received German or German-sounding names, which stuck until the early twentieth century when surnames were nativized.

Of course emancipation inaugurated many changes in Baltic rural life, but the introduction of the potato in the nineteenth century, although quieter, was nearly as momentous. Peasants in Courland had begun growing potatoes in the seventeenth century, but attempts to force other Baltic peasants to grow the crop failed. Only in the beginning of the nineteenth century was a breakthrough achieved, and soon the potato became the most important field crop in many areas. Because of its profitability, flax also gained popularity in Lithuania, Latgale, and southern Estonia. In all the Baltic provinces the raising of dairy cattle and pigs was common.

RELIGIOUS LIFE

The lives of Latvian and Estonian peasants, like those of their German landlords, were closely tied to the Lutheran Church, which in addition to regulating the spiritual lives of the Baltic population provided much of what little education existed before emancipation. Pietism, a movement originating in Germany that stressed Bible study and personal religious experience, also made inroads in the Baltic region from the 1720s to the 1740s, especially in Estonia, but since it remained basically within theological circles it was never really a threat to the predominance of the Lutheran faith. However, Moravianism, a branch of pietism that was brought to the region by traveling German craftsmen, brought pietist ideas closer to the ordinary peasants. With its emphasis on humility, morality, and equality, Moravianism played an important role in increasing the peasantry's self-consciousness. Since the Baltic nobility and clergy were unable to keep the movement under control, from 1743 to 1764 it was prohibited by the Russian state. Nevertheless, a new wave of Moravianism, with its renewed emphasis on civil rights, spread through the Estonian lands in the early nineteenth century. By 1839 membership in the Moravian Brethren in the Baltic exceeded 66,000; however, by the 1860s the Lutheran Church had managed nearly to eradicate the movement.

Although the Russian state upheld the position that Lutheranism enjoyed, the laws of the empire nevertheless favored Russian Orthodoxy. The offspring of mixed marriages in the Baltic provinces were expected to be baptized and raised as Orthodox Christians, and Lutheran pastors were prohibited from proselytizing among the tsar's Orthodox subjects. The state's influence over the region's religious life was somewhat strengthened after 1832, when church organizations in Estland and Livland were placed under the direct supervision of the General Consistory for the

Evangelical-Lutheran Church, an organ in St. Petersburg. Lutheran churches nevertheless remained under the influence of the region's German nobilities.

Although an Orthodox bishopric was established in Rīga in 1836, until the late nineteenth century the Russian government made little attempt to encourage the Baltic population to convert to Russian Orthodoxy; its concern there was mainly with meeting the needs of the small existing Orthodox community in the Baltic provinces. Despite the Russian government's general reluctance to proselytize in the Baltic provinces, the situation appeared to change in 1841 when thousands of peasants suddenly requested to be accepted into the Orthodox Church. Suffering from crop failures in the late 1830s and famine in 1840s, many peasants mistakenly believed that the tsar would grant them lands in the warmer Russian south if they expressed the desire to adopt the sovereign's faith. Out of respect for the ancient rights and privileges of the Baltic provinces, Tsar Nicholas I (ruled 1825–55) was reluctant to accept further petitions; nevertheless, he concluded that the Baltic peasants' conversion to Orthodoxy was acceptable as long as it was based on religious conviction rather than anticipated material rewards, which the Russian government never promised in the first place.

Between 1845 and 1848 at least 75,000 Estonians and Latvians in Livland converted, despite the government's repeated affirmations that no material benefits would be awarded as a result. This lesson was learned by the end of the decade, and Estonian and Latvian peasants quickly lost their zeal to convert to Orthodoxy. Although the problem remained that it was illegal for Orthodox Christians to convert to another faith, this difficulty was partially and gradually resolved by a secret edict, issued in 1865, which lifted the requirement that children of mixed marriages be raised as Orthodox. As for adults wishing to reconvert, they could only hope that tsarist authorities would look the other way as thousands embraced Lutheranism once again in the 1870s. Because of this competition, along with the rise of secular trends, the Baltic Lutheran Church would have to take greater care in meeting the needs, spiritual and material, of its members. However, until the twentieth century, this church continued to be dominated by the Baltic German elite, and Germans remained the great majority of its clergymen.

ORIGINS OF THE NATIONAL AWAKENINGS

The first century of Russian rule saw plodding but nevertheless significant progress in the development of Latvian and Estonian as literary languages. In the first years, few books were published in Latvian; however, from 1722 to 1835 an average of nearly ten new titles were published in Latvian each decade.[4] Estonian-language publishing was less developed, with an annual average of 3.2 books and brochures being published in Estonian during the second half of the eighteenth century, but rising to more than thirteen per annum in the 1830s.[5] Religious books continued to predominate, but an interest in secular themes became apparent by the end of the eighteenth century in both Latvian and Estonian literature. Until the nineteenth century, most books published in the local vernacular were written by Baltic Germans who had acquired Latvian or Estonian as second languages.

Although Baltic Germans had traditionally maintained a condescending attitude toward the peasants who worked on their manors, by the late eighteenth century this mind-set gradually gave way to curiosity about the peasant culture of the Latvians and Estonians. This development was part of a general European trend in the development of national identities. For late Enlightenment intellectuals, observations of peasant attitudes, expressions, and traditions yielded clues to understanding humanity as a whole. At the same time the study of peasants also facilitated the construction, however artificial, of separate and distinct national characters for the peoples of Europe.

In German lands, intellectuals emphasized the *Volk* (people), with its oral traditions of legends, fables, and songs, as the key to understanding the essence of Germanness. Around this time, Germans in the Baltic also began to "discover" the local peasantry, identifying them too as *Volk* possessing their own characteristics and traditions. This scientific approach to the Baltic peasantry was taken most famously by Johann Gottfried Herder (1744–1803), who lived in the Baltic area for some time and taught in Rīga in the late 1760s. Herder was interested in the language and folklore of both the Latvian and Estonian peasantry, and included several Estonian folksongs in his *Stimmen der Völker in Liedern* (*The Peoples' Voices in Song*), published in 1787. It was also during this period that Gotthard Stender (1714–96) began to publish his fairy tales for Latvian peasants.

Scholarly publications dealing with the Estonian and Latvian languages followed in the first decades of the nineteenth century. In 1824, 14 Lutheran clergymen from Livland and Courland founded the Society of Friends of Latvians; one of its purposes was the study of Latvian language and folklore. This was followed in 1838 by the founding of the Estonian Learned Society, whose members were likewise interested in the study of Estonian folklore.

Meanwhile, Baltic Germans played important roles in the publication of newspapers in the vernacular. A weekly Latvian newspaper, *Latviešu avīzes* (*The Latvian Newspaper*), began to appear in the 1820s, after the emancipation of peasants in Livland. Although the newspaper was published by Baltic Germans, Latvians wrote the articles. Around the same time, *Marahwa Näddala-Leht* (*Countryfolk Weekly*) appeared in Estonian. Indeed, until the 1860s Germans had maintained a near-monopoly on the Latvian- and Estonian-language presses, and most German intellectuals believed that Baltic peasants would eventually be assimilated into German culture. This was the danger that aroused the concern of authorities in St. Petersburg.

One important consequence of Latvian- and Estonian-language publishing was the rise in literacy among Baltic peasants. Perhaps as many as one-third of all peasants in Courland could read in the first decades of the nineteenth century, and the majority of Latvian youth in Livland were literate by this time.[6] Estonian peasants were further behind, although those living in northern Livland enjoyed more rapid progress than Estonians in Estland. Nevertheless, by mid-century the literacy rate for all Estonians over the age of 10 approached 90 percent.[7] Thus in the decades after emancipation in the nineteenth century, with the appearance of the Latvian and Estonian intelligentsia, a significant reading public, and the development of Latvian and Estonian as literary languages, the preconditions existed for the "national awakenings" of the Baltic peoples.

In most areas of national development, the Lithuanians were behind the Estonians and Latvians. Lithuanians were territorially divided, residing on each side of a border that separated the Russian Empire from Prussia. But even more damaging to the development of a sense of Lithuanian national consciousness was the fact that over the course of the four-hundred-year Polish-Lithuanian union the Lithuanian elites had largely assimilated into Polish culture. Although a separate Lithuanian literary language existed, beginning with the publication of religious literature by Lutheran clergymen in the sixteenth century, until the emancipation of the Russian peasantry in 1861 and the Polish and Lithuanian insurrection two years later, the Lithuanian national idea remained submerged in the Polish national idea.

THE LATVIAN AWAKENING

The national "awakening" of the Baltic peoples should be viewed in the larger context of rising national consciousness throughout Europe in the nineteenth century. In France, the birthplace of modern nationalism, the phenomenon was stimulated by the 1789 Revolution, during the course of which French intellectuals and political leaders came to see the French as a people possessing a special destiny. In the wake of Napoleon's attempt to liberate Europe from its monarchs and aristocrats, intellectuals in other parts of Europe began to explore and define their own national communities. In general these "imagined communities"—Europe's new nations—developed on the basis of their members' sense of common ancestry as well as a shared language, set of customs, mythology, religion, and territory.[8]

In western Europe, the national awakenings of the nineteenth century stimulated the development of nation-states, so that by the 1860s the various Italian states had united to form modern Italy while most of the lands where German was spoken united under Prussian leadership to form modern Germany. In central and eastern Europe, the process of forming nation-states was more problematic, as the inhabitants of these comparatively underdeveloped regions were subjects of the Austrian, Ottoman, and Russian empires. For mid-nineteenth century Latvians, Estonians, and Lithuanians, there could be no question of reconstituting their provinces as separate and independent nation-states like Germany, Holland, or Greece: their status as subjects of the tsar appeared to be permanent and, in the age of great empires, perfectly natural. National consciousness among the Latvian and Estonian peoples was spurred not by a desire for independence, but by the perceived unfairness of their continued subservience to an alien German nobility.

In Latvia, as elsewhere in the Baltic provinces, the complaints were both cultural and economic. As late as the mid-nineteenth century, Baltic Germans still dominated the Latvian-language press. The development of a Latvian intellectual class in the decades after emancipation, however, made it possible for Latvians to take control over their own language. As a result, by the end of the 1860s native Latvian-speakers were the authors of more than half of all Latvian-language texts, most of which were stories and poems. However, more political matters were often on the minds of the publishers of the weekly newspaper *Pēterburgas avīzes* (*Saint Petersburg Newspaper*), which began its run in 1862. Latvian writers used this organ to ridicule the Baltic Germans' pretensions to cultural and political superiority, but after three years the newspaper was accused of sedition and closed.

As in many other embryonic nations, Latvian national consciousness was shaped by perceived injustices, focusing in particular on the uneven landholding system and the Germans' treatment of Latvians as a peasant underclass. Unlike the national movements in the Habsburg lands of central Europe, the goal of Latvian nationalists was not independence or even autonomy, but recognition of the dignity of the Latvian nation and its equality with other peoples. Latvians wanted to be recognized as more than just a peasant people; they wished to assume a cultural and economic presence that reflected their greater numbers in the provinces in which they resided.

One significant problem that this "nation" faced was its territorial disunity: Latvian-speaking peoples lived in the *gubernii* of Livland, Courland, and Vitebsk (which included Latgale, and was administered as a Russian province), and tended to think in local terms. Another was that upwardly mobile Latvians tended to assimilate into one of the dominant cultures—German or Russian. For the Latvian intellectuals, the key to overcoming these difficulties then was to foster the idea that all Latvians were one people (*tauta* in Latvian) sharing a collective identity, a shared historical experience, and a common destiny. This was to be achieved by educating the Latvian peasantry and developing the Latvian language from a peasant tongue to a language of culture on a par with other literary languages.

For Latvian activists such as Krišjānis Valdemārs (1825–91), an economist and an editor for *Pēterburgas avīzes,* this also meant drawing closer to the politically powerful Russian government, to which many Latvian intellectual leaders remained faithful, while increasing their distance from the culturally and economically dominant Baltic Germans, who were the main objects of their grievances. Although they were often resented, Germans were not always perceived as malevolent. Latvian nationalists recognized that there were many liberal-minded Baltic Germans who were sympathetic to the awakening of the Baltic peoples. Nevertheless, anti-German feeling was typical of most Latvian nationalists, and most Latvians understood that their place as subjects of the Russian Empire was permanent.

During the second half of the nineteenth century, Latvians formed numerous organizations, whose goals and character, they assured tsarist authorities, were nonpolitical. The largest and wealthiest of these was the Rīga Latvian Association (RLA), founded in 1868 ostensibly as a relief organization to aid victims of famine. In reality the RLA was actively involved in cultural development, and even had its own newspaper, *Baltijas vēstnesis,* an advocate for Latvian causes and ideas. Latvians also created numerous agricultural and self-help associations. Indeed, by 1887 there were well over two hundred Latvian organizations of various kinds. Although women, whose lives were still centered on the home, generally were little involved in the most important activities associated with the national awakening, there were nevertheless some opportunities for women to engage in public affairs. In 1818, for example, the Rīga Association of

Women was established for the purpose of providing aid to the needy. Fifty years later the Rīga Latvian Charity Association was formed, and women played a prominent role in its leadership and activities.

The awakening continued through the period of Russification (discussed below), as Latvian scholars looked to the countryside to define the essence of "Latvianness." Valdemārs's protégé Fricis Brīvzemnieks (1846–1907), a school inspector who accepted a certain degree of Russification as a necessary measure to counter the German cultural influence, collected Latvian folklore in the 1870s and 1880s in the belief that a widespread familiarity with it would increase the Latvian people's sense of national belonging. Jānis Cimze (1814–81), a composer and music teacher, laid the groundwork for this activity by organizing the systematic collection of Latvian folk music. His work was continued by Andrejs Jurjāns (1856–1922), who became the most important name in Latvian music folk study in the early twentieth century, and Krišjānis Barons (1835–1923), who along with publishing numerous folk tales is reputed to have collected around 35,000 thousand *dainas*—the traditional four-line Latvian folk songs—in about 200,000 variations.

It was also during this period that Andrejs Pumpurs (1841–1902) published *Lāčplēsis* (*The Bear-Slayer*), which soon became recognized as a Latvian classic. This epic poem was loosely drawn from a pagan Latvian legend about a hero who overcomes the monsters (which Pumpurs reworked as Teutonic Knights) who guard scrolls containing ancient Latvian wisdom. The poem's publication in 1888 helped shape a nation's consciousness concerning the historic (and contemporary, to its readers at that time) struggle between Latvians and Germans, and influenced later writers and politicians who continued the national struggle against foreign oppressors.

While the Latvians of southern Livland and Courland experienced a national awakening from mid-century onward, until the 1890s Latgalians, who were mostly Catholic and living in the Russian *guberniia* Vitebsk, were largely isolated from these intellectual and popular currents. Latgale had been governed as a Russian rather than a Baltic province, and Latgalians' history had diverged from that of their western brothers. For them serf emancipation came more than four decades later (1861), socioeconomic development lagged behind, and the Latgalian elites tended to be Polish and Russian rather than Baltic German. Because of this isolation, and because of the ethnic heterogeneity of the province in which they lived, national identity among the Latgalians was not as well developed as in the Latvian regions of Livland and Courland. Until the twentieth century, their cultural ties to the western Latvians were minimal; only during the revolutionary tumult of 1905 was Latgale brought into the fold of the nascent Latvian "nation."

THE ESTONIAN AWAKENING

The national awakening of Estonians occurred during roughly the same period as that of their Latvian neighbors, each coinciding with the relatively liberal reign of Tsar Aleksandr II (1855–81). Like the Latvians, Estonian intellectuals who guided the creation of Estonian nationhood had to steer a course between the economically and culturally dominant Baltic Germans on one side, and the Russian political authorities on the other.

The two leading first-generation Estonian intellectuals were the physicians Robert Faehlmann (1808–50) and Friedrich Reinhold Kreutzwald (1803–82), each of whom was both a product of the German educational system (that is, they were Germanized Estonian intellectuals) and a significant contributor to the early development of Estonian national consciousness. Kreutzwald, who was the compiler of the Estonian national epic *Kalevipoeg* (*Son of Kalev*), had an especially profound impact on the Estonian national awakening. *Kalevipoeg*, published in 1857–61, promised that its mythological hero, the ancient ruler of Estonia, would one day return to usher in an era of happiness. The story reflected Kreutzwald's beliefs that Estonians could overcome their socioeconomic conditions and that through education they could achieve and preserve Estonian nationhood. Faehlmann, on the other hand, believed that Estonians were unlikely to develop as an independent nationality, insisting that they were more likely to be assimilated into German culture.[9] He argued that this fate was superior to the alternative of Russification, which would be more difficult for Estonians and moreover would end their progress.

Under the politically repressive rule of Nicholas I, such intellectuals exerted little influence on the development of national life in the provinces where Estonians lived; indeed, *Kalevipoeg* found a wide audience only decades later. This situation began to change for Estonians in the 1860s, as the Russian government of Aleksandr II, fearing that in an age of nationalism the Baltic Germans might seek to Germanize the Latvian and Estonian peasantry, began to pay more attention to developments in the Baltic region. Here there was a coincidence of interests with the Estonians, who sought aid from the tsarist government against the power of the Baltic German establishment. Between 1864 and 1869 delegations of Estonian peasants appeared in St. Petersburg, petitioning for the extension of Russian reforms to the Baltic, evidently as a means of mitigating what they perceived as the deleterious effects of German economic, administrative, and cultural dominance.

Some historians have pointed out that Estonian peasants shared a disposition similar to that of the Russian peasants, who looked for the "good tsar" to rescue them from the "wicked nobility."[10] For Estonian (and Latvian) peasants, this indeed made some sense, as the impetus for reform in the Baltic region in earlier periods had come from St. Petersburg. It appears, then, that the petitioning Estonian peasants of the 1860s sought a degree of administrative Russification, involving the introduction of Russian judicial reforms and institutions for local government (*zemstva*). They added that they would also welcome the substitution of Russian for German as the major foreign language in Estonian schools. Naturally, this would not only have the effect of reducing German cultural influence on Estonian students but also offer them opportunities for career advancement in the empire.

Intellectuals such as Carl Robert Jakobson (1841–82) and Johann Köler (1826–99) shared the Russophile perspective (in contrast to Faehlmann's German orientation) of these peasant petitioners. As leaders of Estonian society they even headed a delegation that in 1881 presented a memorandum to the new Tsar Aleksandr III requesting the introduction of land, legal, and educational reforms that favored Russification. In the view of Jakobson, a schoolteacher and writer, only the benevolence of the Russian tsar could break the Germans' hold on the Estonians. Likewise, Köler, a professor at the St. Petersburg Academy of Fine Arts, saw the tsarist government as a positive force for the development of Estonian national life.

Other Estonian intellectuals who emerged in the 1860s and 1870s questioned this gravitation toward political power and were more inclined to accept the leadership of the German community, as Robert Faehlmann had done in earlier decades. Johannes Jannsen (1819–90), a schoolteacher, journalist, and editor of the Estonian newspapers *Perno Postimees* (*The Pärnu Courier*, 1857–64) and *Eesti Postimees* (*The Estonian Courier*, 1864–80), believed that the Estonians should continue to work within the existing system, as Estonians were not yet sufficiently developed as a nation to take any important initiatives on their own.[11] Likewise, Jakob Hurt (1839–1907), a theologist, collector of folk songs, and perhaps the greatest ideologist of Estonia's national awakening, urged a conciliatory relationship between Estonians and Germans in which the former accepted the political leadership of the latter. Yet Hurt also believed in the basic goodwill of the Russian government, and saw little prospect of cultural Russification in the region. Estonians, he insisted, should focus on their spiritual and cultural mission, leaving political and military greatness to the larger nationalities.

Still others such as Lydia Koidula (1843–86), Jannsen's daughter, rejected both the Germanophile and Russophile perspectives, fearing that allying with one or the other could result only in the Estonians' denationalization. Estonians, she suggested, should look to Finland as a model for national development, and remove themselves from the growing Russian-German confrontation. All Estonian intellectuals, however, whether Russophile, Germanophile, or distrustful of both the dominant nationalities, believed that as much education as possible should be in Estonian and that Estonian should have at least equal rights with Russian as the language of administration.

The most profound manifestation of the Estonian national awakening was the tradition of the national song festival. The first festival, at which about 1,000 musicians and singers were joined by 20,000 other participants from different regions of Estonia, was held in Tartu on June 18–20, 1869. As in Latvia, which held its first song festival four years later, the event symbolized the reawakening and unity of the new nation. The tradition of song festivals continued into the twentieth century, and played an important role in the Balts' struggle for independence from Soviet rule in 1987–91.

Of course, the Estonian national awakening of the late nineteenth century could not have occurred without a significant increase in educational opportunities for Estonians, especially in Estland, which had long lagged behind northern Livland. Moreover, with the growth of publishing houses and a periodical press, educated Estonians also had more Estonian-language materials to read during the last decades of the nineteenth century.

Despite this progress, the organization of Estonian civic life lagged behind that of the better-developed Latvians, in part because urbanization and modernization came to the region somewhat later. As late as 1881, more than 90 percent of Estonians lived in the countryside, leaving Baltic Germans to direct much of Estonian cultural and social life in the cities. Although Estonians did organize their own local societies and clubs as well as song festivals, German cultural influence remained strong. Even Estonian intellectuals tended to communicate with each other in German until the turn of the century. The development of Estonian civil society really flourished only in the two decades preceding the 1917 revolution, during which time the Estonian cities emerged as among the most modernized and urbanized in the empire, and Estonians themselves became more urban and wealthy. However, until this development took place, the

Estonians remained essentially a colonial people under the tutelage of a foreign elite.

RUSSIFICATION

Despite the undeniably chauvinistic elements of Russification, the policy is better viewed as an instrument through which St. Petersburg attempted to further the centralization and modernization of the Russian state. However, rather than blunting the growing national consciousness of the Estonian, Latvian, and Lithuanian peoples, the Russification policies of the last decades of the nineteenth century only intensified their national awakenings.

The Baltic provinces had been subject to a relatively mild form of Russification, mostly administrative, ever since the reign of Catherine II, and further reforms were extended to the region during the reign of Aleksandr II in the 1860s and 1870s. A more sweeping wave of Russification was implemented under Aleksandr III, a supporter of Great Russian nationalism in an age of rising national feeling throughout Europe. Although the Baltic provinces were certainly objects of this policy, its impact there was not as great as in Poland (including the Lithuanian provinces), whose population St. Petersburg viewed as particularly seditious, especially after the uprisings of 1830–31 and 1863–64.

A new Baltic policy aimed at integrating the provinces into the political, legal, and economic framework of the Russian empire began in 1865, at the height of the Great Reforms. Most significant was the 1867 decree that required official documents in the Baltic *gubernii* to be in Russian. A major effect of Russification in the Baltic was the undermining of some of the authority of the great German landowners, who were now compelled to cooperate on the matter of land reform and abstain from the use of corporal punishment on the peasants. Thus many ordinary Estonians and Latvians welcomed the introduction of Russian administrative measures in the Baltic provinces.

Indeed, to some extent Russification came to the Latvian and Estonian lands by invitation. As noted earlier, in the 1860s Estonian peasants petitioned the tsar for the extension of Russian reforms to the Baltic region, mostly in order to curb the influence of the Germans. Likewise, in 1882 the Rīga Latvian Association encouraged the peasants to present their grievances to Russian officials in Rīga. Thousands of petitions from Latvian peasants arrived in the provincial capital. Some requested reform of the judicial system and local government along Russian lines; they also asked for an administrative reorganization of the three Baltic provinces

(Estland, Livland, and Courland) into two that would recognize the predominance of the two main populations, Estonians and Latvians. Petitioners also requested the right to use Latvian and Estonian as the language of instruction in rural schools.

With the assassination of Tsar Aleksandr II in 1881 and his replacement by the reactionary Aleksandr III, the influence of Slavophile intellectuals on officials in St. Petersburg increased.[12] Meanwhile, the appointment of new governors for the Baltic provinces in 1885—who were considerably less pro-German than their predecessors had been—appeared to herald a more complete assimilation of Estland and Livland into the Russian Empire. Unlike earlier attempts to Russify the region, which had focused mostly on administrative centralization and modernization, now the ambitions of the tsarist government, increasingly concerned about the Germanization of Latvians and Estonians, included winning over these peoples to Russian Orthodoxy and the Russian nationality.

The intensified Russification program of the 1880s focused on Russian culture and in particular on local use of the Russian language in administration and in the schools. In 1885 all primary schools in Estland, Livland, and Courland came under the control of the Ministry of Education in St. Petersburg, thereby weakening the power of the German nobility and Lutheran Church. Two years later Russian was made the language of instruction except in the lower classes of primary schools. The University of Dorpat, a German institution, had made competency in Russian a requirement since the 1840s, but in the early 1890s Russian was made the language of instruction and the institution was given a Russian name, Iur'ev University. This was quickly followed by an influx of Russian-speaking students, which in turn induced many Baltic Germans to pursue university studies in Germany.

Russian was also made the language of communication between Baltic government offices and higher authorities in St. Petersburg, and by 1889 linguistic Russification was extended to Baltic municipal governments, in which a small number of Estonians and Latvians were at last granted the right to participate. The *Ritterschaften* and provincial *Landtage*, along with peasant communal organizations, however, remained exempt from linguistic Russification. That the Baltic provincial administrations were never touched by these reforms suggests that Russification was neither systematic nor thorough.

Russification policies also affected the judicial systems of the Baltic provinces. Russia's judicial reform of 1864 had transformed the country's legal system into one of the most liberal in Europe; in comparison, the judicial systems of the Baltic provinces now seemed antiquated. With the introduction of the Russian judicial system in 1889, Baltic courts were subordinated to the St. Petersburg Court Chamber. Russian was made the language of the Baltic courts—no doubt the resulting communication problems made the administration of justice a difficult task—but the jury system was not introduced since there were still too few Russian-speakers available for jury service. The government pondered the introduction of *zemstvo* institutions (local self-government) into the Baltic provinces, ostensibly to undermine German authority, but never followed through on the matter.

Increased official support for Russian Orthodoxy in the western borderlands, especially in Ukrainian and Polish areas, also played a role in the Russification policies of the 1880s and 1890s. With the introduction of new religious regulations, the Russian state attempted to create conditions in the Baltic region more conducive to the future spread of Orthodoxy while simultaneously weakening the Lutheran Church. After 1885 no Protestant church could be built without permission from the Holy Synod in St. Petersburg, and Lutheran partners in mixed marriages were expected to convert to Orthodoxy. In a reversal of an earlier edict, their children were to be raised as Orthodox Christians. Lutheran pastors who defied the religious laws of the Russian Empire—by, for example, baptizing children of mixed marriages as Lutherans—were subject to punishment. As a result nearly every Lutheran clergyman in Livland was involved in criminal proceedings. Because of these measures, or perhaps despite them, the Orthodox Church managed to attract thousands of new converts from Lutheranism during this period. Yet at no time under tsarist rule did Orthodox believers comprise more than 10 percent of the total population of these provinces.

Despite the new cultural thrust of Russification, it is doubtful that the tsarist government had any serious plans to turn Latvians or Estonians into Russians. The government did, however, hope to diminish the threat that Germanization appeared to pose to Russia's hold on this vulnerable region, especially given the fact of Germany's political unification in 1871. In recent years scholars have been careful to point out that the Russification policy in the Baltic (as elsewhere) had been overrated, that it was implemented only halfheartedly, and that the Russian state had lost its resolve to Russify by the mid-1890s.[13] Only in education did the Russian government continue to pursue a Russification policy after 1895, although a decade later concessions were made to local languages in Baltic elementary schools.

It seems clear that the Russian government was more concerned with the cultural pull exerted by a dynamic Germany on the empire's westernmost provinces than it was with the national awakenings of the Latvian and Estonian peoples. However, officials in St. Petersburg were disappointed that rather than being attracted to Russian culture, the Baltic peoples were more concerned with their own national cultures. Whatever the government's real intentions, the development of the Baltic nations was already too far advanced by the 1880s for any kind of cultural assimilation to take place, and by the mid-1890s the state's enthusiasm for Russification in the Baltic provinces had waned.

Paradoxically, the effect of cultural Russification on the Baltic peoples was to intensify their sense of "Estonian," "Latvian," or "Lithuanian" identity. Although upwardly mobile Latvians had long understood the necessity of learning German and, after the advent of Russification in the 1880s and 1890s, Russian, their sense of belonging to the Latvian nation was undiminished. Having been awakened, the Baltic peoples began to resist assimilation into the cultures of their German and Russian rulers. For this generation, upward mobility no longer required the loss of one's native nationality, as by the turn of the century the Baltic Germans' power over the economic and cultural life of the region had substantially diminished. Now Estonian and Latvian intellectuals increasingly spoke to each other in their own languages. Despite the tsarist government's attempts to impose Russian culture on the Baltic peoples, the local intelligentsia emerged more self-confident than ever.

POLISH LITHUANIA

Developments in Lithuania, most of which was acquired by Russia during the Polish partitions of 1772, 1793, and 1795 (the remainder was under Prussian control), took shape somewhat differently than in the Latvian and Estonian provinces. Divided into several *gubernii*, the Lithuanians were never subjected to the sort of experiments that were attempted in Estland and Livland in the early nineteenth century. In contrast to the privileges the Russian government granted to the Baltic Germans and the autonomy their provinces enjoyed within the empire, the elites of the incorporated Polish areas were not granted autonomy or comparable rights and privileges. Like the Baltic Germans, however, the Lithuanian elites were far removed from the cultural life of the peasants who worked their land. Indeed, most of the educated class could not even speak the Lithuanian language, used almost exclusively by Lithuanian peasants. As had been the case for more than two hundred years, the Lithuanian upper classes lived in the cultural world of the Poles, the center of which was the University of Vilnius, reestablished in 1803.

The aristocratic class in the Polish-Lithuanian lands, which numbered in the hundreds of thousands, was considerably larger than the 150,000 or so confirmed Russian nobles in Russia proper, despite the fact that the overall population of Russia was obviously many times larger than that of Poland-Lithuania. Unlike their Russian counterparts, however, many of the Lithuanian nobles were in fact poor and landless. In the empire they found that their opportunities were rather limited: Lithuanian noblemen could serve in the tsar's army, which in turn was a prerequisite to obtaining a position in the civil service; however, Russian officials were appointed to the more important posts in Lithuania.

Meanwhile, the Lithuanian nobles who had estates—and Lithuanian estates tended to be vastly larger than estates in the Latvian and Estonian lands—endured the exodus of thousands of Lithuanian peasants following the partition and Russian occupation. Mostly this was a consequence of St. Petersburg's requirement that the gentry provide the Russian army with peasant recruits. The neighboring Grand Duchy of Warsaw (constituting the Polish lands not under Russian control), a nominally independent state created in 1807 by the French Emperor Napoleon Bonaparte (ruled 1804–15), attracted yet more fleeing Lithuanians.

Not satisfied with his conquest of much of the rest of Europe, in the spring of 1812 Napoleon, who for the preceding five years had enjoyed a peaceful arrangement with Tsar Aleksandr I, attempted to conquer Russia as well, using the Duchy of Warsaw as a launching pad. Although in Lithuania the occupying French troops spoke of liberty, they in fact treated the region as conquered territory, seizing food supplies and attempting to levy recruits for Napoleon's Grand Army. Failing to achieve their military objectives before the onset of the Russian winter, Napoleon's army retreated and rapidly disintegrated. Thousands of soldiers swept across Lithuanian territory, bringing with them arson, famine, and epidemics. Vilnius was the graveyard of about 40,000 of these soldiers. The extent of the human losses resulting from the war with Napoleon and Russian reoccupation was revealed by a census taken in 1817, which showed that Lithuania had lost one-third of its population since 1811.

After France's defeat Russia became the master of the continent, and the Polish-Lithuanian territories were reincorporated into the empire. Although the slogans of the French soldiers—"liberty, fraternity, equality"—had gained currency among many Lithuanians and Poles during the wars, the Russian government was not in a revolutionary mood. Nevertheless, as a concession to his Polish subjects, Tsar Aleksandr I set up the Kingdom of Poland, with himself as sovereign, in 1815. Provided with Europe's most liberal constitution and a parliament, the Polish kingdom was to act as a model for future Russian reforms. The kingdom (often referred to as Congress Poland) was not, however, a restoration of Poland-Lithuania, for it included only a small portion of its land and population, centered around Warsaw. While the resurrection of a Polish state provided some Poles and Lithuanians with hope for the future, most were never reconciled to union with Russia or any limits on Poland's sovereignty.

In late November 1830 Poles instigated an ill-fated uprising against the Russians, and by March of the following year the unrest had spread to Lithuania. Following defeat at the hands of imperial forces, the Polish constitution was abolished, the University of Vilnius was closed, and the entire region was brought into closer association with Russia proper. In Lithuania, most estates belonging to the Catholic Church and the nobility were confiscated and were subsequently transferred to Russian landlords. Meanwhile, as Tsar Nicholas I worked to centralize the institutions of the Russian Empire, his government implemented a Polish policy aimed at repressing Polish political and cultural life. The result was another Polish insurrection in 1863, which aimed at restoring the Polish-Lithuanian state within the borders of 1772. This failure invited further Russian repression and Russification measures. Despite Russian attempts to introduce land reform aimed at winning the loyalty of Polish (and Lithuanian) peasants, Poles of all classes were welded together to face a common enemy.

In general, Russification in Poland-Lithuania was much harsher than in the northern Baltic provinces. After the 1863 rebellion, Catholic monasteries and churches, viewed by tsarist officials as hotbeds of treasonous activity, were temporarily shut down throughout the Polish and Lithuanian provinces, and Russian became the official language of all *guberniia* and *uezd* offices. Henceforth court proceedings were conducted in Russian (although one could testify in Polish), and by the 1880s the Russian language was made obligatory in Polish and Lithuanian elementary schools.

Freed from serfdom in 1861—and disappointed at the result—Lithuanians also participated in the 1863 uprising. Although they made no claims to independent Lithuanian statehood, like the Poles they were brutally repressed. As part of St. Petersburg's effort to solve the "Polish question," the tsarist government attempted to split Lithuanians from the Poles, recognizing Lithuanians as a separate culture in the hopes that they would be assimilated into the Russian nationality. Lithuanian-language schools were shut down, and in an attempt to convert the Lithuanians to the use of the Cyrillic alphabet it was forbidden to print Lithuanian language books in Latin letters. (However, it was still permissible to print Polish-language books in Latin letters.) These prohibitions remained in effect until 1904. Nevertheless, Lithuanian-language printing continued in

Prussian Lithuania (also called Lithuania Minor, a mostly Lutheran area), from where they were smuggled into Russian Lithuania. This linguistic connection between the Lithuanians of Russia and Prussia ultimately became a rallying point for the national idea, and the book smugglers are now celebrated as national heroes.

The Lithuanian clergy played a vital role in resurrecting the Lithuanian national idea. During the period of post-insurrectionary repression the Lithuanian peasantry had become a source of recruits for the Catholic priesthood, effectively cementing the bonds between the Church and ordinary Lithuanian worshipers and creating the basis of the Lithuanian intelligentsia. Such was the background of Motiejus Valančius (1801–75), a writer and since 1849 the Bishop of Samogitia, who emerged from the Lithuanian peasantry to become one of the most significant figures in the national awakening. Focusing his efforts on the peasants, whom he regarded as the key to Lithuania's future, he urged Lithuanians to embrace the virtues of temperance. His success on this score was disastrous for state revenues, which were dependent on taxes on alcoholic beverages, and did little to earn him favor with the authorities in St. Petersburg, whose Russification policies he actively resisted. The bishop also promoted historical research and writing by his clergy and had their works—written in Lithuanian—illegally smuggled into Russian Lithuania from East Prussia.[14]

Perhaps the most important figure in the Lithuanian national renaissance was the physician Dr. Jonas Basanávičius (1851–1927), considered by many Lithuanians to be the patriarch of the nation. Although Basanávičius studied to become a priest, he graduated from Moscow University with a medical degree. In 1883 Basanávičius, living in Prague at the time, began publishing a newspaper called *Aušra* (*The Dawn*). For three years the newspaper, which was printed in Prussia and smuggled into Russian Lithuania, acted as the intellectual center of the Lithuanian national movement, collecting and publishing information on the history of Lithuania and the Lithuanian people with the goal of evoking Lithuanian national consciousness. For Basanávičius and many other Lithuanian intellectuals, however, the main danger to the Lithuanian people was the spread of Polish language and culture; Lithuania's place in the Russian Empire was beyond question.

Indeed, by this time the Lithuanian educated class was forced into choosing whether to identify with the Poles or the Lithuanian "people"—the peasants. Some nobles, especially after 1863, followed the lead of an increasingly assertive intelligentsia and made efforts to harmonize their interests with those of the peasants. Only in the last decades of the nineteenth century, with the emergence of a new democratic intelligentsia (mostly of peasant origin), did the idea of restoring an independent Lithuanian state—free from Russian rule and separate from Poland—begin to mature.

Despite the changes taking place inside Lithuania, because of tight internal controls and a large emigrant population, much of the impetus behind the Lithuanian awakening came from outside Lithuania. After the famine of 1867–68 tens of thousands of Lithuanians emigrated to other parts of the Russian Empire—including Siberia, Latvia, and Ukraine—as well as to Great Britain and Canada. The greatest number went to the United States, where they were concentrated in East Coast cities such as New York, Baltimore, and Boston, as well as inland industrial cities such as Chicago and the coal-mining areas of Pennsylvania. Mostly, Lithuanian immigrants were attracted to the industrial centers; few took up agricultural work. By 1900 more than 10,000 Lithuanians were arriving in American cities each year—a number that increased to more than 20,000 per annum by 1907.[15]

Paradoxically, Lithuanian communities in America enjoyed considerably greater freedom to be Lithuanian; as a result, in the last decades of the nineteenth century Lithuanian cultural life was more robust outside Lithuania than in the homeland. The first Lithuanian-language newspaper in America, *Gazieta Lietuviska* (*The Lithuanian Newspaper*) appeared four years before Dr. Basanávičius's *Aušra*. Other cultural activities by Lithuanian-Americans, particularly in the areas of theater and music, also enjoyed considerable success.

While Lithuanian cultural and social life flourished in American cities, in Lithuania itself national development stagnated until the early 1900s. It was only in 1901 that Lithuanians were at last granted their own church, St. Michael's Church in Vilnius, which in turn immediately became a center of Lithuanian nationalist activity. Around the same time, Lithuanians in Vilnius were able to found a publishing house and start a new newspaper, *Vilniaus Žinios* (*Vilnius News*). They also founded the Lithuanian Scientific Society and organized Lithuanian art shows.

By the time revolution broke out in Russia in 1905, the decrees against the use of the Lithuanian language had been revoked, and the Lithuanian press and literature were vigorous. Economically, however, the Lithuanians remained far behind other peoples in the western parts of the empire. According to the Russian census of 1897, 93 percent of all Lithuanians in Lithuanian-majority areas were peasants; just a handful claimed to be merchants, and only a very small percentage of town-dwellers in Lithuanian areas were ethnic Lithuanians. The others were mostly Jews, Poles, and Russians. Lithuanians, who had once been the most culturally and politically advanced of the Baltic peoples, had stagnated under Russian rule.

For Lithuania's Jews the picture was somewhat more promising, at least in the demographic sense. Between 1847 and 1897, the Jewish population of the Lithuanian provinces nearly tripled to a total of 755,000. They constituted 43.4 percent of the population in Kaunas (*Yiddish* Kovna) province (where ethnic Lithuanians were only 11.2 percent), while forming a majority in many small towns.[16] This was partly due to the measures taken by Tsar Aleksandr II, the liberator of the serfs, who removed some of the restrictions on Jews. Now allowed access to higher education, Jews were able to settle outside the Pale of Settlement, enter the professions, take civil service positions, and assume an active role in civic life. However, the government's consistent goals of getting Jews to assimilate and eventually accept Christianity were far from realized by the time Aleksandr III ascended the throne in 1881. A political reactionary and a fervent supporter of Russification, Tsar Aleksandr III was responsible for the enactment of various anti-Jewish measures known as the May Laws, which, among other things, placed new restrictions on the business practices of Jews in Russia and called for the creation of a virtual Pale within the Pale of Settlement.

Increasingly subject to spontaneous violent pogroms, many Jews began to leave during the last decades of the nineteenth century: some fled to neighboring Prussia (in many cases, on their way to western Europe or America); others went to southern Russia. Those who remained behind often made their living as craftsmen—most often as tailors and shoemakers—industrial workers, and traders. Moreover, by the end of the nineteenth century, Jewish traders had become an essential link in the distribution of agricultural products. However, few Jews made their living from farming; in Kaunas province, for example, just 1 percent of Jews were agricultural laborers.

Like ethnic Lithuanians, who were experiencing a cultural renaissance in the last decades of the nineteenth century, Jews enjoyed a Jewish enlightenment movement, demonstrated by an increased interest in the Hebrew language, which hitherto had been almost exclusively the language of religious study. Some Lithuanian Jews also began to show interest in the Zionist movement, which aimed to establish a Jewish national home in Palestine. Many Jews enthusiastically contributed to and collected funds for this cause, and a few began emigrating to the Holy Land. Others who were more interested in improving the working conditions and economic situation of the Jewish proletariat gravitated toward the socialist camp. In

1897 Jewish socialists in Lithuania founded the Bund, an organization that demanded both improved conditions for workers, and civil rights and cultural autonomy for Jews. Its influence peaked around the time of the revolution of 1905.

NOTES

1. As a result of the Napoleonic wars, new Lithuanian territory (hitherto under the control of Prussia) was added to the Russian Empire. Following the Congress of Vienna in 1815 this area became established as the *guberniia* of Suvałki.

2. Raun (1987), 49–50.

3. Plakans (1995), 87–88.

4. Ibid., 67.

5. Toivo U. Raun, "Estonian Attitudes Toward Russification before the Mid-1880s," in Edward C. Thaden, ed., *Russification in the Baltic Provinces and Finland, 1855–1914* (Princeton, N.J.: Princeton University Press, 1981), 293.

6. Plakans (1995), 68.

7. Raun (1987), 55.

8. The phrase "imagined communities" was coined by Benedict Anderson in his landmark book of the same title. See *Imagined Communities*, rev. ed. (London: Verso, 1991).

9. Faehlmann held a post at the University of Dorpat and in 1838 became a founder of The Learned Estonian Society, an organization dedicated to the study of Estonian folklore.

10. Raun (1981), 292.

11. Jannsen is reputed to have received money from the Baltic German establishment, thus compromising his reputation as a leader of Estonia's national awakening.

12. Slavophilism was a school of thought that emphasized putatively Russian values and traditions, such as Orthodox spirituality and Russian moral superiority, as the key to Russia's future. Beginning in the 1840s the Slavophiles were often contrasted with Westernizers, who sought to improve the country by adopting some of the ideas and institutions of western Europe.

13. Hans Rogger, *Russia in the Age of Modernisation and Revolution, 1881–1917* (New York: Longman Publishing Group, 1983); Astrid S. Tuminez, *Russian Nationalism Since 1856* (Lanham, Md.: Rowman & Littlefield Publishers, Inc., 2000), 39–42.

14. An even earlier pioneer of the Lithuanian national awakening was the writer Simonas Daukantas (1793–1864), who composed the first histories in the Lithuanian language in the 1820s and 1830s and died shortly after the 1863 insurrection.

15. All together, the migration from Lithuania to the United States involved about 50,000 people during 1869–98, and another 250,000 from 1899 to 1914. Dov Levin, *The Litvaks: A Short History of the Jews in Lithuania* (Jerusalem: Vad Yashem, 2000), 29.

16. Ibid., 77, 80.

4

The Revolutionary Era, 1905–20

URBANIZATION AND INDUSTRIALIZATION

By the turn of the century, the Baltic area was among the most industrialized and urbanized regions of the Russian Empire.[1] As the beneficiaries of rising living standards and an improved demographic situation, Latvian and Estonian families had never enjoyed greater prosperity than they did during the decades that preceded World War I. Literate, confident, and increasingly integrated into the institutions of their German and Russian rulers, Balts had every reason to look forward to future prosperity as subjects of the tsar in the multinational Russian Empire.

According to the 1897 census, the population of the Latvian territories was 1.9 million, of which about two-thirds were of Latvian nationality. Latvians were overwhelmingly a rural people, but this was changing rapidly: whereas in 1897 only about 28 percent of Latvia's population lived in urban centers, by 1913 this number exceeded 40 percent. Rīga, with a population of 282,000 (growing to 517,000 in 1913), was the area's most important metropolis and the sixth-largest city in the Russian Empire. It was also becoming a more heavily Latvianized city, as the proportion of Latvians residing in Rīga rose from 23.6 percent in 1867 to nearly 45 percent by 1897. Although Rīga was also home to significant numbers of

Russians, Poles, and Jews, it was the German influence that was always strongest there. However, with the arrival each year of thousands of Latvian peasants, the Germans' share of the city's population declined rapidly in the last decades of the nineteenth century. By 1897 Germans constituted only 16 percent of Rīga's residents, down from 43 percent in 1867.

The Estonian regions experienced similar demographic trends. Between 1881 and 1897 the population of Estland and northern Livland increased from 881,455 to 986,000, of whom more than 90 percent were ethnic Estonians. The relatively unimpressive growth rate of the Estonian regions is partially explained by rising Estonian emigration to other parts of the empire, including the Volga River region and the Caucasus; this was offset by the migration of Russians from the interior to the growing Estonian cities. By 1897 the urban share of the Estonian population rose to 19 percent, with the two largest Estonian cities being Tallinn (64,572) and Tartu (42,308), followed by Narva (an early industrial center) and Pärnu. As in Rīga, the proportion of Germans in Estonian cities began to decline during this period: in 1897 only 16 percent of the population in cities in Estland and northern Livland was German, while Estonians made up 68 percent of the urban inhabitants, and Russians, 11 percent.[2] Given the rising number of Estonians and Latvians in Baltic cities, the growing economic power of the native inhabitants, and the long history of the region's colonial status, it is not difficult to understand why many Balts came to regard Germans and Russians as alien presences in their cities.

In Lithuanian territories, still divided between Russia and Germany, the situation was quite different. Although the total population of Lithuania had reached 2.7 million by the turn of the century, Lithuanian cities saw little growth. Vilnius could claim around 200,000 inhabitants at the turn of the century, but it was barely touched by heavy industry. Moreover, the few cities that there were in the region did not even enjoy a Lithuanian character: in 1897, Lithuanians comprised only 2.1 percent of the population in Vilnius and 6.6 percent of the population of Kaunas. Lithuanians remained overwhelmingly a rural and agricultural people, while the cities in the three Lithuanian *gubernii* (Vilnius, Kaunas, and Suvałki) contained many Poles and Russians, and a large number of Jews. Indeed, Vilnius, whose population in 1897 was 40 percent Jewish (and 31 percent Polish), was regarded as the "Lithuanian Jerusalem"—the center of Jewish cultural life in northeastern Europe.

Partly because serfdom was not abolished in the Lithuanian provinces until 1861—and consequently few Lithuanian peasants were literate or mobile—industrialization arrived in the region late, and remained below Estonian and Latvian levels throughout the period of Russian rule. Thus, although Lithuanian towns enjoyed great ethnic and cultural diversity, unlike the cities of the north Baltic they grew little under tsarist rule.

While the Lithuanian provinces retained their overwhelmingly rural character, economic development in the Estonian and Latvian areas underlined the importance of these provinces to the Russian empire. Among the most important growth areas were cloth manufacturing and alcohol distillation, along with food-processing and the tobacco, leather, metal, timber, and paper industries. By the end of the nineteenth century the major Baltic cities were linked to the interior of Russia by railroad, and handled 30 percent of Russia's foreign trade. Indeed, from St. Petersburg's perspective, the port cities of Courland, Livland, and Estland were integral to Russia's economic success—and their place in the empire was regarded as permanent.

However, parallel with the economic progress evident in the Baltic region was the increasing weight that Latvians and Estonians carried in the socioeconomic and cultural life of their provinces. By 1900 the Latvian and Estonian countryside was socially differentiated, with new classes of landowners consolidating control over small, medium, and even some large landholdings—mostly at the expense of the heavily indebted Baltic Germans. In the cities, Latvians and Estonians had developed a bourgeoisie and a working class. What they lacked, however, was political influence, which still remained a monopoly of the Baltic Germans and the Russian government.

NEW POLITICAL MOVEMENTS

In 1896 Vilnius gave birth to the first political party in the Baltic region, the Lithuanian Social Democratic Party (LSDP). Given the almost total absence of an urban proletariat in Lithuania, the party's existence was perhaps anomalous. In principle the LSDP stood for solidarity with the empire's Polish and Russian working class; most of all, however, it was nationalist—a feature that would be characteristic of nearly all of Lithuania's future political parties. The earliest evidence of the party's commitment to Lithuanian statehood was its 1904 program, which contained the demand for an "autonomous, democratic republic, composed of Lithuanian Poland and other countries on the basis of a loose federation."[3]

If creating a truly independent Lithuanian state remained at this stage impractical—and to most nearly unthinkable—more perplexing still would have been the problem of defining a Lithuanian state in national terms, given the large numbers of Jews and Poles residing there. Other Lithuanian parties, such as the Lithuanian Democratic Party (formed in 1902) and the League of Lithuanian Christian Democrats (1905), faced the question as well, but none went further than demanding autonomy for an ethnographic Lithuania within a democratic Russia.

In Rīga, where industrialization had produced a large working class, social democracy exerted even greater appeal than in Lithuania. Since 1891 Marxist ideas had appeared in print in Latvia on the pages of the newspaper *Dienas Lapa* (*Daily Paper*), whose staff took a leading role in the formation of illegal workers' groups in the larger Latvian cities. In 1897, two years after a series of strikes in Rīga and Libau, the newspaper's staff, along with some left-wing student groups, were arrested and jailed; some were temporarily expelled from the Baltic provinces. Consequently, large numbers of Latvian intellectuals and activists became disillusioned with a government upon which they had earlier relied for protection against the Baltic German landlords. Now the Latvian intelligentsia's resentment was directed against not only the dominance of the Baltic Germans, but also at an exploitative political and economic system at the head of which stood the Russian tsar. In their view, just as workers were an exploited class, Latvians were an exploited nation. By 1904, the Latvian Social Democrats, founded as an expatriate group in Zurich the previous year, were prepared to publish their demands:

> We demand that each nationality which is a member of the Russian Empire should have the right to determine its own fate; that each nationality should have the right to maintain its own culture and to develop its spiritual strengths; and that the language of each nationality should have the right to be used in schools, local administrative institutions, and local courts.[4]

Although not all Social Democrats agreed with this position, the manifesto, like the Lithuanian Social Democratic Program, suggests that by the time the 1905 Revolution broke out, the nationality question in the Baltic provinces had assumed a position of prominence not only as a cultural issue but as a *political* issue as well. Latvia's Social Democratic Union, formed in 1903, went even further, advocating the unification of the Latvian peoples (including Latgale, then administered as part of Russia's Vitebsk *guberniiā*) and their complete separation from Russia.

Estonian intellectuals of the 1890s, such as Jaan Tõnisson (1868–1941?), tended to be more optimistic about their relations with the tsarist regime. Editor of the first Estonian daily, *Postimees* (*The Courier*), since 1896 and later one of the founders of the Estonian Republic, Tõnisson advocated loyalty to the tsarist regime (although he opposed Russification) and collaboration between Estonians and Germans (although he resented their privileges) in order to advance their common goal of Baltic development. Much criticism in the Estonian press was directed at the Russified educational system, as Estonian nationalists demanded that the language of instruction be Estonian in all elementary schools and secondary schools.

By the early 1900s, however, calls for more radical economic and social change, emanating from intellectuals who represented the Estonian working classes, began to be heard in the newspapers *Uudised* (*The News*) and *Teataja* (*The Herald*). The latter was founded and edited by future Estonian president Konstantin Päts (1874–1956). Some workers and radical intellectuals in Estonia's bigger towns sympathized with the Russian Social Democratic Workers' Party (RSDWP). Tallinn, for example, became an important Menshevik center, although Bolsheviks also enjoyed a presence there.[5]

THE 1905 REVOLUTION AND ITS CONSEQUENCES

The revolution of 1905 was a consequence of the social and economic transformation that took place in the Russian Empire in the decades following the abolition of serfdom and the Great Reforms of Tsar Aleksandr II. With the growth of capitalism and industrialization, new social classes emerged, including the bourgeoisie and the proletariat, each seeking its place in an inflexible political system. For many of the new professionals, liberalism under a constitutional monarchy was the answer. In 1905 these moderates organized the Constitutional Democratic Party (Kadets). The emergence of a labor movement in the industrializing regions of the empire, however, offered more radical possibilities.

An underground Marxist political party, the Russian Social Democratic Workers' Party, appeared in 1898, and three years later began to compete with the Socialist Revolutionaries (SRs)—who advocated peasant socialism based on Russian traditions—for the support of Russian radicals. In the early years of the twentieth century, Russia suffered from strikes, student protests, and peasant disturbances. While SRs conducted a terror campaign against government officials, the country stumbled into a losing war with Japan in 1904, thereby nearly unhinging the tsarist regime. The revolt began the following January, when the St. Petersburg police fired on a workers' demonstration and killed 130 people. The massacre, which came to be known as "Bloody Sunday," placed a sea of blood between

Tsar Nicholas II and his people and galvanized popular support for the revolutionary movement. In the summer, a new wave of strikes and peasant uprisings spread throughout the empire.

The revolution of 1905 revealed the depth of discontent in the Baltic provinces. In January sympathy strikes broke out in Tallinn, Narva, Pärnu, Rīga, and other large cities. The countryside was soon engulfed in violence, mostly directed at the Baltic Germans. By the time the violence subsided, 184 manor houses had been burned down and 82 Baltic Germans killed. Taking the side of the Baltic barons, the Russian army suppressed, often with great brutality, the rebellions of the countryside and towns. The worst occurred in Tallinn, where on October 16 tsarist forces fired into a peaceful crowd, killing 94 people and wounding 200 more. Soon afterwards martial law was declared in Livland, Courland, and Estland. Under pressure from the revolutionary movement, the tsar signed the October Manifesto, which promised civil liberties—including the right to organize political parties—and a representative assembly.

Although these concessions satisfied few, activists in the Baltic provinces took advantage of the new opportunities, as representative bodies convened to discuss the fate of the Estonian, Latvian, and Lithuanian peoples. In late November an All-Estonian Congress met in Tartu. This body reflected the division in the Estonian national movement between reformers and radical revolutionaries; some radicals went so far as to demand the expropriation of large estates. One issue, however, united both moderates and radicals, and that was autonomy for Estonia—although even on this matter there was much disagreement on the details. Latvians likewise organized meetings to discuss the fate of the Latvian nation. Whatever the disposition of Latvian intellectuals prior to the events of 1905, the subsequent punishment of thousands of Latvians (including more than 2,700 executions) destroyed much of whatever support there had previously been for the tsarist regime.

In the Lithuanian *gubernii*, where the proletariat was considerably smaller and less radical than in the Baltic provinces, the 1905 revolution was more peaceful—although here too nearly 3,000 Lithuanians were arrested in its wake, while many others fled. Since the Lithuanians' concerns were more national than social, unrest in the countryside was directed less at Russo-Polish landlords than at the Russian state. In November 1905 the Vilnius Diet, chaired by Dr. Jonas Basanávičius and attended by 2,000 representatives, met to debate the future of Lithuania. Its demands were the most radical yet of any nationality within the Russian Empire: the Lithuanian delegates wanted nothing less than national autonomy within ethnic Lithuanian boundaries, along with a democratically elected parliament. The diet also called for the use of the Lithuanian language in schools and in local government.

Attempting to recover from the shock of revolution, the Russian government found that it had little choice but to make concessions, including the granting of permission to use the Estonian, Latvian, and Lithuanian languages in the schools. However, the regime coupled its compromises with repression of the Baltic nationalists. Many revolutionaries were imprisoned, sent to Siberian exile, or expelled from their homelands. Not only were the Baltic peoples denied the sort of political autonomy they sought, the tsarist regime sought once again to collaborate with the Baltic German elite. However, Baltic Germans were in a quandary: administrative Russification had eroded much of their power in the decades before 1905, yet an alliance with Latvians and Estonians against St. Petersburg was unthinkable for both sides. Although most Baltic Germans cast their lot with St. Petersburg, hoping that with the tsar's support their traditional position in Baltic society would be reinforced, others rejected the tsarist government and emigrated to Germany. Caught between the hammer and the anvil, for many Baltic Germans there could be no reconciliation with either the tsar or the Baltic nationalists.

After the 1905 revolution the tone of politics in the Baltic provinces became more restrained. The periodical press expanded rapidly, and with the abolition of preliminary censorship in 1906 it enjoyed considerable freedom of expression, including the liberty to discuss Russification issues. However, censorship was not completely abolished, and radical newspapers such as the Estonian-language *Teataja* and *Uudised* were shut down.

Balts could also voice their concerns in the State Duma. With the creation of this imperial parliament the Balts were represented in St. Petersburg for the first time. Despite their low numbers (especially in the third and fourth Dumas, following a change in the electoral law that effectively worked against the non-Russian nationalities), representatives from the Baltic provinces were generally moderate, seeking reform rather than revolution. Estonian and Latvian deputies talked mainly about agrarian reform, with the result that branches of the state-sponsored Peasant Land Bank were established in the Baltic *gubernii*.

Although the revolution of 1905 did not result in the Estonians, Latvians, and Lithuanians being granted the sort of autonomy envisioned by some, the subsequent decade of parliamentary politics provided them with both the leadership skills and the experience necessary to cope with the challenges that would be presented by the Great War.

WORLD WAR I AND GERMAN OCCUPATION

On August 1, 1914, Germany's Kaiser Wilhelm II declared war on the Russian Empire of his cousin, Tsar Nicholas II. The war lasted for more than four years, and at its conclusion the map of Europe was fundamentally revised: gone were the great multinational empires of eastern, central and southern Europe, replaced by a number of smaller, weaker successor states. Following two revolutions and a civil war between 1917 and 1921, tsarist Russia, minus its western borderlands, was reinvented as a one-party state, later to be called the Soviet Union.

Although as a result of these circumstances Latvia, Estonia, and Lithuania achieved their independence, in August 1914 national self-determination seemed a remote prospect to even the most ambitious Baltic nationalists. Contemporary observers could only conclude that a German victory would mean incorporation of the Baltic provinces into the Reich; a Russian triumph, on the other hand, would likely reinforce the existing relationship between St. Petersburg and the provinces and therefore would bring few benefits to the empire's subject nationalities.

Latvians and Estonians initially gave their full support to the tsar and fought in his army. For Baltic Germans, however, the choice between kaiser and tsar was agonizing. For the war's first six months they could only try to convince the suspicious authorities in St. Petersburg of their unswerving loyalty; but with the failure of the Russian army and Germany's occupation of much of Lithuania and Courland (southwestern Latvia) by autumn 1915, many Baltic Germans became collaborators.

The main effect of Germany's occupation of these regions was the massive dislocation of local populations: 570,000 Latvians—about one-third of the population—and much of the industry of Courland were evacuated to neighboring territories. All together, during four years of war more than 2.6 million refugees from Polish, Lithuanian, and Latvian territories left to find safety in Russia proper; this included perhaps 75–80 percent of Lithuania's Jewish population.

The material and economic damage was equally great. In autumn 1915 Lithuanians observed the retreating Russian troops emptying Lithuanian factories and burning their bridges. Although Estonia and northeastern Latvia managed to avoid German occupation until September 1917, when Rīga and the larger Estonian islands (Saaremaa, Muhu, Hiiumaa) were seized, the peoples residing in unoccupied territories suffered nonetheless—principally from shortages, unemployment, and the runaway inflation that resulted from Russia's attempt to finance the war effort by printing more money.

Military administration in the occupied territories, called the *Land Oberost*, was headed by Field Marshall Paul von Hindenburg, chief of the German High Command, and his second-in-command, General Erich Ludendorff. Although German military leaders had long been convinced that it was necessary to weaken Russia permanently by setting up a ring of barrier states on her western border, at the outset of the war Germany's goals in the Baltic were not entirely clear.[6] One possibility was the annexation of Lithuania and Courland; another alternative, endorsed by some Baltic émigrés, was German colonization of the entire Baltic region. In any case, in a speech to the Reichstag in April 1916, Chancellor Bethmann-Hollweg made it clear that Germany would not be returning the Polish, Lithuanian, or Latvian territories to the Russian Empire.

Whatever the ultimate fate of the *Land Oberost*, for the moment the territory was an indivisible administrative unit run exclusively by Reich Germans. At the very least the Baltic territories were to provide the occupying army with food and raw materials; moreover, they were to send agricultural and industrial products to the Reich. Besides having to submit to requisitions, the nearly 3 million inhabitants (compared to 5 million before the war) of the *Land Oberost* faced restrictions on their freedom of movement and in communications. Moreover, a German policy of divide and conquer, aiming to pit the national groups against one another (such as Lithuanians against Poles, Poles and Lithuanians against Jews), was coupled with the goal of bringing German *Kultur* to Lithuania and Courland—a particular concern of Ludendorff's. Lithuanians, constituting the largest national group in the occupied region, were repressed the most, and a number of their leaders were arrested and jailed.

BALTIC NATIONAL MOVEMENTS IN 1917

With the war going badly for Russia and hunger threatening its cities, demonstrations against the government broke out in early 1917. The largest protests occurred in Petrograd (as the German-sounding St. Petersburg was renamed in 1914), where 150,000 workers went on strike. As the intensity of the protests in Petrograd escalated, Tsar Nicholas II ordered that the disturbances be suppressed. His unsuccessful last-ditch attempt to save his throne by dissolving the Duma underlined the tsar's waning authority, leaving him little choice but to abdicate. On February 23 (March 8, new style), 1917, the last Romanov ruler surrendered the Russian throne.

As the revolution took its course, spontaneously organized workers' and soldiers' councils, called soviets (first formed during the 1905 revolution), quickly acquired immense authority, especially in Petrograd. Meanwhile, a provisional government was formed on the basis of the old State Duma. However, this bourgeois-democratic body, which continued to pursue Russia's losing war against Germany, was countered by the Petrograd Soviet, a socialist-dominated institution that embodied the popular forces which had overthrown the old government. This political arrangement was known as "dual power"—a situation that appropriately symbolized the country's political paralysis and ambiguous future. For the empire's non-Russian nationalities, the fall of the tsarist government represented an opportunity to pursue their dreams of political autonomy, as the new Provisional Government would have little choice but to recognize the growing authority of Baltic nationalist leaders and establish partnerships with them.

While some sort of autonomy became a realistic goal for the peoples of Russia's western borderlands, the situation was far from ideal. Aside from the obvious inconvenience of German occupation, a main problem for the Lithuanians was the threat posed by a reconstituted Poland. Whatever their plans for Lithuania, the German authorities occupying the region had to take into account the wishes of the more numerous Poles—and for the Poles, Lithuanian independence, whether in the form of the restoration of the Grand Duchy of Lithuania or a smaller ethnic Lithuania, was undesirable and even threatening to their own plans to reconstitute a Polish state. Yet at the same time, any German concessions to the Poles—such as the restoration of an independent Polish Kingdom, announced by the German government on November 5, 1916—would seriously threaten the Lithuanians' hopes of freeing themselves from Poland's cultural domination. It was in this context that Lithuanian leaders worked to win formal recognition from the occupying Germans. Nevertheless, some Lithuanians, suspicious of German intentions and fed up with the deportations, compulsory work, requisitions, and personal maltreatment to which their co-nationals were subjected, placed their hopes in a Russian victory to achieve their national goals.

The prospect of a Russian victory all but disappeared with the February Revolution against the tsar. However, the revolution created the conditions for the spontaneous growth of national movements espousing the principle of self-determination. In May 1917, just months after the tsar's abdication but well before the Bolshevik seizure of power in Russia, 320 elected representatives of Lithuania's political parties met in Petrograd to discuss the future of Lithuania. The congress was split: while Lithuanian parties on the political left called for an autonomous Lithuania in a Russian federation, the majority on the right and center was able to squeeze through a resolution calling for complete independence. Still, the Russian

Provisional Government would not provide specific assurances of national autonomy for the Lithuanians, as had been promised the Poles at the beginning of the war.

While the government in Petrograd was reluctant to address the nationality problem, the Germans understood how the slogan of "self-determination" could be applied to advance their own goal of attaching the Baltic territories to the Reich—or at least detaching them from Russia. With German permission, in September 1917 Lithuanians in Vilnius organized a twenty-member Lithuanian National Council (*Taryba*), mainly representing the Lithuanian bourgeoisie, which unanimously voted for the establishment of "an independent state of Lithuania." In return, the *Taryba*, chaired by future Lithuanian president Antanas Smetona (1874–1944), vaguely agreed that the future Lithuanian state would enter into close military, economic, and political relations with the Reich. The effect of this arrangement was to bring closer to fruition the German High Command's goal of turning the entire Baltic region into a German dependency.

While Lithuanian politicians ultimately tried to gain advantages from German occupation, the situation in the Latvian and Estonian territories was less promising, as they (with the exception of German-occupied Courland) remained in Russia's hands, with little prospect of independence. Indeed, Latvians had initially responded to the German invasion by forming Latvian army units to defend Russian positions in the Baltic. However, by 1917 the circumstances had changed and Latvians were presented with new opportunities to advance their autonomist goals. Following the February Revolution, soviets immediately appeared in Rīga and other unoccupied Latvian cities, where they appealed to workers and soldiers with their promises of radical social and political change. Meanwhile, Kārlis Ulmanis (1877–1942) and Miķelis Valters (1874–1968) formed a new political party, the Agrarian Union, to appeal to the interests of Latvian farmers.

With open political activity at last possible, in late March Latvians in southern Livland formed a Provisional Provincial Council to replace the old aristocratic *Landtag*, but this body—like Latvian politics in general—was beleaguered by antagonism between socialist and bourgeois forces. While no such provincial assembly was created in German-occupied Courland, competing visions of an independent Latvia—one that would include southern Livland, Courland, and Latgale—were nevertheless debated throughout the Latvian provinces. Some Latvian activists called for the right of national self-determination for the Latvian people within their ethnic borders; others went even further and called for Latvia's complete independence from Russia. However, the Provisional Government in Petrograd refused to recognize an autonomous or united Latvia. An even bigger obstacle to Latvian autonomy was internal disunity among the Latvians, as many peasants and workers—increasingly drawn toward Bolshevism—were more concerned with the class struggle than the national one.

Like Latvians, Estonians had also entered the war as loyal subjects of the tsar, but eventually began to understand that Russia's weakness provided an opportunity for them to achieve their own national ambitions. With the fall of the imperial government in February 1917, Estonians, like most Finns, Latvians, and Lithuanians, saw little reason to continue defending the old order, and in fact were the first to take advantage of the new conditions. Immediately after the February Revolution in Petrograd, Jaan Tõnisson called for Estonian autonomy and pressured the Provisional Government to agree to the reorganization of self-government in the north Baltic region. With the establishment of an Estonian representative assembly (*Maapäev*) at the end of March, the old Baltic German- and Russian-controlled institutions of local government were abolished. Perhaps most importantly, with the administrative unification of northern Livland and Estonia, Petrograd agreed to recognize the existence of "Estonia"—a concession granted to neither the Latvians nor the Lithuanians.

Estonian political parties quickly emerged to fill the seats in the *Maapäev*, for which elections were held in May and June. Rather than urging outright separation from Russia, most deputies agreed that Estonia should become part of a democratic Russian federation. However, during the summer of 1917 real power lay not with the *Maapäev*, but with the socialist-dominated soviets, in which Russian sailors, soldiers, and workers were predominant. Bolsheviks fared well in local elections in August and, as a rising force in Estonian politics, challenged the authority of the *Maapäev* to speak for all Estonia. But with the Germans advancing and capturing Rīga in mid-August, it looked as if Estonia too would become an extension of the Reich.

THE OCTOBER REVOLUTION

By the time the Bolsheviks seized power in Petrograd in October 1917, the Lithuanians, Latvians, and Estonians had already taken decisive steps in the direction of national independence. The national cause in each of these countries had been consolidated, although in each case the socialist (and, in general, internationalist) left was more amenable than the bourgeois right and center to federation with a democratic Russia. But just as democracy in Russia ended with the Bolshevik seizure of power, so ended any prospect of a federal arrangement between Russia and the nascent Baltic countries.

With the authority of the Provisional Government waning, on October 25 (November 7, new style), 1917, Vladimir Lenin's (1870–1924) Bolsheviks, the radical wing of the Russian Social Democratic Workers' Party, seized the moment to execute a successful coup d'etat in Petrograd. Like Petrograd, cities in both Latvia and Estonia had seen the growth of a significant Bolshevik presence since the fall of the tsarist government the previous February. By the summer of 1917, Bolsheviks were a rising force in the soviets of Estonia and had achieved majorities in some Latvian soviets. (Indeed, Latvian Bolsheviks played a significant role in the revolution in Russia itself.) Consequently, in the wake of Lenin's coup, power was immediately proclaimed by the soviets—on whose behalf the Bolsheviks claimed to speak—in these countries.

This power, however, proved to be of only short duration. In order to strengthen their hold over the Russian heartland, the Bolsheviks desperately needed to end the losing war with Germany. Under the terms of the Treaty of Brest-Litovsk, signed by Bolshevik and German representatives on March 3, 1918, the Bolsheviks ended the war and in so doing agreed to surrender vast stretches of border territory, including Courland and Lithuania. The fate of these territories was to be determined "in agreement with their populations." Later, in August, the Bolsheviks renounced Russian sovereignty over Livland and Estland.

As German authorities and Bolsheviks made deals that decided the fate of the peoples of central and eastern Europe, the resolutions of the impromptu assemblies of Latvians, Lithuanians, and Estonians attracted little notice. Nevertheless, the Baltic peoples were using the window of opportunity provided by the confusion in Russia to shape their own futures. In mid-November 1917, a Latvian National Assembly met in the unoccupied city of Valka (on the border of Estonia) and declared that "Latvia"—including Southern Livland, Courland, and Latgale—was an autonomous unit within Russia. Two months later, on January 15, 1918, the National Assembly went a step further and declared the existence of an independent Latvian republic.

Meanwhile, on December 11, 1917, the *Taryba*, effectively a German-Lithuanian puppet government, proclaimed "the restoration of the independent state of Lithuania with its capital city of Vilnius."[7] Having received the necessary assurances from the *Taryba* (where Jonas Basanávičius had replaced Antanas Smetona as president) of its future close collaboration with Germany, on March 25, 1918, Kaiser Wilhelm decided to recognize the independent (but in reality German-occupied) Lithuanian state.

As for the Estonians, although they were the first of the Baltic peoples to make demands of the Russian Provisional Government for self-government, they were the last to declare their outright independence. With the Bolsheviks retreating from Estonia, on February 24, 1918, an Estonian Committee of Elders, acting on behalf of the dispersed *Maapäev*, declared the country's independence and simultaneously created a new provisional government. But detachment from Russia was still a far cry from independence, for on the next day German troops moved into Tallinn, where they stayed until mid-1918.

As World War I entered its final stages in 1918, the nascent Baltic states of Latvia, Lithuania, and Estonia had declared to the world the fact of their existence, but their futures still remained uncertain.

WARS OF INDEPENDENCE

In the spring of 1918, with a string of German victories in the east, a successful campaign in the west, and the prestige of the German High Command at an all-time high, the declarations of independence of the Latvians, Estonians, and Lithuanians bore little relationship to reality on the ground. The Treaty of Brest-Litovsk, extorted from a severely weakened Russian state, succeeded in detaching Lithuania and western Latvia from Russia, but by this time nearly the entire Baltic region was under German occupation. While Berlin acknowledged the existence of an independent Lithuanian state, it expected this state to be bound in perpetuity to the Reich.

Although reformers in the German Reichstag pressed for national self-determination for the Baltic peoples, the German High Command continued to manipulate the situation in the region in the hope of, at minimum, permanently depriving Russia of her western borderlands, and maximally, attaching the Baltic countries to the Reich. The most effective way to do this was to rely on the traditional lords of the region, the Baltic Germans, to express the popular will of Latvians and Estonians. The prototype for this plan was created in German-occupied Courland, where a representative assembly, the *Landesrat*, composed of Baltic Germans and seeking the closest ties to Germany, on March 8, 1918, offered the crown of the Duchy of Courland to Kaiser Wilhelm II. According to the reasoning of the German annexationists, with Germans "policing" the entire Baltic region, why shouldn't the experiment be repeated in Livland and Estonia?[8] While ostensibly observing the principle of self-determination, the Reich would then see the entire *Baltikum* fall into its hands.

There is little doubt that the Baltic German elite rejoiced at the prospect of the entire region becoming Germanized; the nobles of Livland and Estland were even prepared to offer land to German colonists from the Reich. However, Germany's recent good fortune in war was not to last much longer; and Latvian and Estonian resistance, combined with objections from the Reichstag, effectively ruined the Kaiser's plan.

To some extent, the fate of the Baltics lay in the hands of the Allied powers—Britain, France, Italy, and the United States. But during this period the Allies' main concern in the region, apart from reopening the eastern front and winning the war against Germany, was to maintain the territorial integrity of the Russian state, whose Bolshevik leaders, they believed, would quickly pass from the scene. Reluctant to acknowledge the full independence of the Baltic states, the Allies nonetheless encouraged them to resist the Germans.

The collapse of the German war effort came not in the east, however, but in the west. Despite Germany's quick successes in a spring offensive, the Allies, reinvigorated by a fresh infusion of American forces, were able to turn the Germans back. By autumn 1918, with Allied forces threatening to invade the fatherland, General Ludendorff sought an armistice. In quick succession a revolution in Berlin in November deposed the Kaiser, a new German government was installed, an armistice was signed, and Soviet Russia annulled the Treaty of Brest-Litovsk. As a result, once again the Baltic region fell into chaos.

Following the German collapse, in Estonia a provisional government was revived, headed by Konstantin Päts. This government, however, had to contend for power with the socialist-dominated Tallinn Soviet. This state of disarray provided the Bolsheviks, who were counting on a German evacuation and possibly a German revolution, with an opportunity to spread the revolution westwards. Supported by Estonian Bolsheviks who had earlier escaped to Soviet Russia, the Russian invasion of Estonia began on November 22, 1918, thus igniting the Estonian War of Independence. At first, the Estonian defense was a failure: within a week, the Red Army conquered Narva and proclaimed the Estonian Workers' Commune, headed by Jaan Anvelt (1884–1937), as an autonomous part of Soviet Russia. As other Estonian towns quickly fell during the westward advance, the Bolsheviks instituted a Red Terror that claimed more than 500 lives.

Meanwhile, in December Latvian Bolsheviks returned to those Latvian areas not occupied by the Germans and set up a provisional Soviet government headed by their longtime leader, Pēteris Stučka.[9] The Latvian Bolsheviks were soon met by the Red Army, which captured Rīga in early January. As in Estonia, a wave of terror immediately followed, with the Bolsheviks imprisoning and executing many of their enemies. The Kārlis Ulmanis-led Latvian Provisional Government that had been established in November was forced to flee to German-occupied Courland, where for the time being it enjoyed German protection.

What followed next was a curious postscript to World War I, in which Germans, defeated on the western front, were effectively given a green light to continue their struggle in the east. With the Red Army moving westward in an effort to "liberate" Estonia and Latvia from the retreating Germans, the Allies decided to invoke Article XII of the Armistice Agreement, which required that Germany withdraw its armed forces from the east *only* when the Allies thought it desirable. Although the new Weimar government, installed after the Kaiser's flight in November, hoped to build friendly relations with the Baltic countries, it nevertheless concluded that Germany would receive better peace terms from the Allies if it participated in the Baltic counteroffensive against the Bolsheviks.

Little more than two months after Russia's proclamations of Soviet republics in Estonia, Latvia, and Lithuania in December 1918, the German Free Corps (*Freikorps*), led by General Rüdiger von der Goltz (1865–1946), entered Latvia; Estonia and Lithuania were left to organize their own defenses. To add to the confusion, thousands of Latvian soldiers loyal to the provisional government of Kārlis Ulmanis joined an alliance of Baltic Germans (who wished to maintain their privileged position in the country) and *Freikorps* (lured by false promises of land) to fight their common enemy, the Latvian Bolsheviks. These combined forces were able to liberate Latvia from the weak Bolsheviks, but in the process the Baltic Germans overthrew the Ulmanis regime and in April 1919, with von der Goltz's cooperation, set up a puppet government headed by Andrievs Niedra (1871–1942).[10]

Having saved the Baltic states from Bolshevism, in the late spring of 1919 von der Goltz continued the German advance beyond Rīga to the east. The Allies, however, now insisted that the Germans evacuate Rīga and leave the region as quickly as possible. Underscoring the Allies' intention to replace the German anti-Bolshevik forces with native troops, Allied aid soon began flowing in to the Latvian and Estonian governments, thus perhaps unintentionally stimulating Baltic nationalist ambitions. As the German-backed Niedra government slipped into irrelevance, in July Ulmanis reclaimed the legitimacy of his provisional government. With his plans to create a Baltic bridge connecting the Reich to a restored

"White Russia" defeated, General von der Goltz was finally recalled in October 1919. However, *Freikorps* stragglers continued the anti-Bolshevik crusade for months afterwards.

Whatever one makes of this odd campaign in the Baltic, it helped clear the Latvian republic of the Soviet invaders (and White Russians) and helped mold a Latvian national army.[11] However, the actions of the Baltic German *Landeswehr* and the protracted military activity in Latvia did little to improve relations between the Baltic Germans and their Latvian masters in the new republic. Under the government of Kārlis Ulmanis, the Baltic Germans realized that they would have little choice but to accept the end of their dominance.

Estonians managed to liberate themselves from the Soviets without any "help" from the *Freikorps*—in fact the Estonians fought and defeated von der Goltz's forces on the Latvian border in June 1919. They did benefit, however, from the assistance of Finnish, White Russian (who pledged to fight for a "Russia one and indivisible," having no intention of recognizing the right of any nationality of the old Russian Empire to self-determination), Latvian, and Baltic German forces, in addition to aid from the Allied powers. By spring 1919 Estonia was cleared of Soviet troops and the provisional government was secure enough to elect a Constituent Assembly, which in turn voted unanimously to affirm Estonia's independence. Relations with Russia, however, remained questionable as the fractured giant continued its civil war. Nevertheless, by early 1920 the Bolshevik government in Moscow (the new capital of Soviet Russia), concerned that the Estonians and others would join a united anti-Bolshevik front that would permit the victory of White forces, were ready to make peace with Estonia.[12]

According to the terms of the Tartu Peace Treaty signed on February 2, 1920, Soviet Russia recognized Estonian independence de jure and forever renounced rights to Estonian territory. Likewise, Latvia's Ulmanis government, restored to power after the routing of von der Goltz's forces the previous summer, signed an armistice with Soviet Russia. A peace treaty followed on August 11, 1920, in which Russia recognized Latvia's independence. Curiously, although more than 220,000 Latvian refugees returned from Russia between 1919 and 1927, at least 150,000 Latvians, many of whom were convinced socialists, decided to remain in the Soviet Union.[13]

Lithuania also endured a Soviet regime—the Lithuanian-Belarussian Republic, proclaimed in December 1918 following the premature withdrawal of German forces—but the Bolsheviks managed to occupy only about two-thirds of the country. Since Bolshevism had not produced a native organization in Lithuania as it had in Latvia or Estonia, the Lithuanians' war against the Red Army was truly a national rather than a civil war. Volunteer regiments were formed to fight for the country's independence, and by late August 1919 the Lithuanians were able to drive the tired and poorly supplied Red Army from their territory.

Vilnius changed hands numerous times during Lithuania's wars of independence. The city was occupied by the Germans until late 1918, then by the Bolshevik Lithuanian government, and since April 1919 by Polish forces who claimed it and the surrounding region for Poland. Meanwhile, plundering White Russian forces (composed, in fact, mostly of German soldiers) commanded by Pavel Bermondt-Avalov appeared in northern Lithuania in the summer of 1919 with the aim of reintegrating Lithuania into a monarchist Russia. Thus at various points in 1919 the Lithuanians faced the Bolsheviks in the east, the Poles in the west, and White Russian (and German) forces on the northern front.

On September 11 Soviet Russia proposed negotiations, as it had with Latvia and Estonia at the same time. The peace treaty was signed the following July, with Russia renouncing all claims to Lithuanian territory while recognizing Lithuania's rights to Vilnius. Having driven out the Red Army, the Lithuanians, aided by the Latvians, succeeded in turning back Bermondt's army by December. Now the main threat was Poland, which launched an offensive against the Soviets in April 1920 in the hopes of regaining the territory that had once belonged to the old Polish-Lithuanian Commonwealth. Although the Poles ultimately failed to create a greater Poland, they managed to retain Vilnius and some other territory that the Lithuanians claimed was historically theirs. Kaunas became the provisional capital of the new Lithuanian state, but the Vilnius issue remained a sore spot in Lithuanian-Polish relations for years afterward.

No longer part of Russia, and freed from the dominance of the Baltic German elite, the peoples of Estonia, Latvia, and Lithuania embarked upon the creation of independent states with high hopes. But for the Baltic countries, it has never been possible to pursue the interests of nation and state completely independently of the will of their larger neighbors and other great powers. Indeed, in the final analysis, it was the collapse of two great powers, Germany and Russia, which made possible the establishment of three tiny states along the Baltic Sea.

Although the Allied powers were willing to provide some material help (which had to be repaid) in their struggle against the Bolsheviks, the Baltic countries were able to secure Allied recognition only in 1921 and 1922—after the outcome of the Russian civil war had been decided. Having abandoned the cause of the White Russians, the Allies now endorsed the idea of a *cordon sanitaire*—a belt of states that would confine Bolshevism to the east and keep Russia and Germany apart. In the postwar period, the requirements of the great powers would again play decisive roles in determining the fate of the Baltic peoples.

NOTES

1. The statistics used in this section were drawn from several sources. See, for example, Plakans (1995), 88, 108; Raun (1987), 71–73; Andreas Kappeler, *The Russian Empire* (Harlow, UK: Pearson Education Limited, 2001), 397–407.

2. Overall, the demographic situation was bleak for the Baltic Germans. From 1881 to 1897 the total number of Baltic Germans in Estland, Livland, and Courland dropped from 180,423 to 152,936, owing partly to Russification and partly to some German emigration.

3. Alfonsas Eidintas, Vytautas Žalys, and Alfred Erich Senn, *Lithuania in European Politics: The Years of the First Republic, 1918–1940* (New York: St. Martin's Press, 1998), 17.

4. Thaden (1981), 260.

5. Mensheviks and Bolsheviks were wings of the Russian Social Democratic Workers' Party, formed in 1898. Both claimed to be Marxist in orientation, but Mensheviks (or Minoritarians) were closer to European social democratic traditions than the Bolsheviks (Majoritarians), who endorsed the use of violence as a means of seizing power. Both wings of the party were illegal in Russia prior to 1917.

6. In his classic and controversial *Graff nach der Weltmacht* (1961), Fritz Fischer argued that Germany's expansionist ambitions sparked World War I and were consistent with her territorial goals in 1939. The English-language version is titled *Germany's Aims in the First World War* (New York: W.W. Norton, 1967).

7. Lithuanians generally regard this resolution as a sort of first draft of the country's declaration of independence, pending more favorable conditions. Another declaration of independence, made by the *Taryba* on February 16, 1918, noted that the new Lithuanian state "is separating that state from any state ties that have existed with other nations." Thus Lithuanians usually regard the latter resolution as the country's "official" declaration of independence. When Germany chose to recognize the Lithuanian state in March 1918, it did so on the basis of the *Taryba*'s resolution of December 1917 (which affirmed the Lithuanian state's ties with Germany), not the one of February 1918.

8. Since Lithuania lacked a German elite, there were no Baltic German assemblies to use to achieve the Reich's foreign policy goals in the region, as there were in Estonia and Latvia. Nevertheless, in the summer of 1918, the *Taryba* toyed with the idea of placing Duke Herzog Wilhelm von Ur-

ach, to be known as Mindaugas II, on the Lithuanian throne; but after the German collapse it no longer needed this ploy and reverted to a republican form of government with a three-man presidency led by Antanas Smetona.

9. Latvian Rifle Guards played an important role in the October Revolution in Petrograd and in the subsequent civil war.

10. An excellent treatment of this unusual campaign is Robert G. L. Waite's *Vanguard of Nazism: The Free Corps Movement in Postwar Germany, 1918–1923* (Cambridge, Mass.: Harvard University Press, 1952).

11. One incentive for men to join the army and fight the Bolsheviks and Germans was the Latvian provisional government's promise of land to veterans of the war of independence as part of a general land reform. For Latvians, private farm ownership was more appealing than the Bolsheviks' preference for state farms. This, along with the Red Terror, partly explains the Soviet government's rapid loss of popular support in Latvia.

12. Naturally, the leaders of the Baltic states were wary of taking part in any effort to overthrow the Bolshevik government, as "White" rule might have meant the end of their existence as independent countries.

13. Plakans (1995), 120.

5

Independence, 1920–40

Of the numerous "successor states" carved out of the collapsed empires of central, eastern, and southern Europe, Estonia, Latvia, and Lithuania were among the least well-known to outsiders. Indeed, prior to World War I, it was common for Westerners—like tsarist officials in St. Petersburg—to view the eastern Baltic region as an integral part of Russia itself; beyond the empire's western borders little was known of the unique languages and traditions of the Estonian, Latvian, and Lithuanian peoples. The collapse of the Russian state in 1917, however, offered the Baltic peoples a unique opportunity to pursue their own separate destinies, apart from and independent of the empire.

Despite endorsing the principle of national self-determination during the war, the Allies did not plan on the addition of three new sovereign states to the map of northeastern Europe. While the Baltic countries were disappointed not to receive from the Western powers immediate and unqualified support for their independence, they did receive some Western aid for their defense against Bolshevism. But Bolshevism's roots in the region were weak and the Red Army was too busy fighting a three-front civil war against various anticommunist forces to be a decisive factor in the Baltic. To save the revolution in Russia, Lenin concluded, it was necessary to amputate. His government, now located in Moscow, recognized the independence of the three republics in a series of peace treaties signed on February 2 (Estonia), July 12 (Lithuania), and August 1 (Latvia), 1920. Yet it was only in 1921–22, after hopes for a democratic Russia—within which, the Allies hoped, the Baltic peoples would enjoy national autonomy—had been dashed, that the new states were accepted as members of the League of Nations and given de jure recognition by the Allies.

The Western powers left the new states in an ambiguous position. Concerned about the possible spread of Bolshevism beyond Russia, Allied leaders conceived of the Baltic republics, along with other successor states of central and eastern Europe, as part of a cordon sanitaire—a belt of buffer states to separate the German and Russian pariahs and to keep Bolshevism confined to the east. Otherwise the new countries were left to settle their own problems, including those with their neighbors.

These problems were indeed formidable. Estonia, Latvia, and Lithuania each faced the daunting task of building a viable and durable state while overcoming the extraordinary material and human losses that they endured during World War I and the wars of independence. They had to construct new political systems, rebuild their economies, and settle their borders among themselves and with their larger Polish, German, and Russian neighbors. Moreover, with the new states having been created on the basis of national self-determination for the Estonian, Latvian, and Lithuanian majorities, each country's national minorities—especially the Russians and Germans who had once controlled the political and economic life of the region—would have to accommodate themselves to the new circumstances. In all of these respects there are obvious parallels between the 1920s and 1990s, when the Baltic states attained their independence once again.

Although their experiments in parliamentary democracy ultimately failed, as each country succumbed to authoritarian forms of government by the 1930s, the Baltic peoples managed to create viable nation-states. Even a half-century of Soviet rule, beginning during World War II, would not be able to erase the historical memory of two decades of independence.

RECONSTRUCTION AND REFORM

The fighting that took place between 1914 and 1920 took a tremendous toll on the populations and economies of each of the Baltic countries. In 1911, the population of the territory that would later comprise the Republic of Estonia was approximately 1,086,000; by 1920 it had fallen to 1,059,000.[1] During the fighting, thousands of Estonians, many of whom were communists, left for Russia, where they joined the tens of thousands of Estonians who had already been living there for several decades.

Estonia's suffering, though certainly significant, was far exceeded by the staggering toll taken on Latvia and its people. From a prewar population of about 2.5 million, by 1920 the population of the Latvian areas had plummeted to 1.58 million. Much of the decline is attributable to the large number of refugees—perhaps 750,000—who fled to Russia or elsewhere. Curiously, only about 236,000 ultimately chose to return. The physical destruction wrought by war—one-tenth of Latvia's buildings were destroyed—and the prolonged sieges of Rīga were accompanied by mass flight from the cities, as the urban population fell from 40 percent to less than 24 percent between 1914 and 1920.[2]

Lithuania endured almost continual occupation by foreign armies between 1914 and 1920 and like Latvia suffered from enormous material destruction and loss of life. In 1923 the population of the Lithuanian Republic, excluding the Klaipėda (*Ger.* Memel) and Vilnius territories, was about 2,035,000, down from 2,676,000 in 1897. Of those who remained, about 84 percent were ethnic Lithuanians; the rest were mostly Jews, Poles, and Russians.[3] Likewise, Estonians (88 percent) and Latvians (about 75 percent) were clearly predominant in their respective states.

Serious economic disruptions were common to all three Baltic states as a result of the war, and were compounded by the Allied blockade of Russia in 1919 as well as debts to Britain, France, the United States, and (in the Estonian case) Finland for their assistance during the wars of independence. In Latvia, where the fighting was heaviest, the economic situation was especially stark: most of the major industrial and transportation equipment had been moved to the Russian interior during the war, and much of the agricultural land was devastated and lay fallow. The situation was aggravated by the fact that Baltic agriculture and industry had been heavily dependent on Russia, which was now suffering its own economic catastrophe and was effectively cut off from the Baltic states. As a result, the Baltic economies had to be reoriented toward the West, whose enterprises, to be sure, saw the Baltic region as a natural bridge to potential Russian markets.

With many rural regions in ruins, one of the most pressing concerns for the Baltic leaders at the end of the wars of independence was the matter of land reform, which aimed to transfer control of the land from relatively rich landlords to the destitute native peasantry. In 1918, 58 percent of all agricultural land in Estonia was in the hands of large estate owners, and 90 percent of these large landed estates were held by Baltic Germans. Likewise, in Latvia, 57 percent of all agricultural land was owned by Baltic

Germans.[4] In Lithuania, the land was traditionally held largely by Poles, but after the rebellions of 1830 and 1863 much of it was transferred to Russians, whom the tsar saw as more loyal than the treasonous Poles. With much of the land in the hands of non-native elites, in 1918 a large proportion of Lithuanian (perhaps 20 percent), Latvian (40 to 50 percent), and especially Estonian peasants (more than 60 percent) remained landless. Independence from Russia now offered the republics' new leaders the unprecedented opportunity to rectify this imbalance—and to break the political and economic hold that the nobility had enjoyed in the region for centuries. Moreover, in the wake of the Baltic peoples' triumph over Bolshevism, land redistribution made good political sense, as it would blunt the appeal of communism to thousands of Baltic peasants.

In each of these countries, the subject of the debate was not whether land reform would take place, but rather how much land would be redistributed and what form compensation would take. The first experiment in Baltic land reform occurred in Estonia and was the most sweeping. In the summer of 1919, Baltic Germans proposed that the state take one-third of the land on their estates, but Estonia's Constitutional Assembly rejected this along with other moderate proposals in favor of a far more radical solution. Under the terms of the agricultural law adopted in October 1919, 96.6 percent of the holdings classified as large estates—lands that together comprised more than 50 percent of the entire republic—were expropriated without compensation.[5] The lands were then redistributed to small farmers, with priority going to veterans of the wars of independence. As a result of Estonia's land reform, the total number of Estonian farms more than doubled during the 1920s and Estonian land hunger was essentially satisfied; however, it took some time before the new small landholdings became profitable.

As in Estonia, in Latvia the compromise solutions proposed by large estate owners were rejected. Convinced of the need for drastic reform, in September 1920 Latvian leaders introduced agrarian legislation under which all privately owned properties comprising more than 110 hectares would be nationalized and placed in a land fund for redistribution to landless peasants and veterans of the wars of independence. The parliament (*Saeima*) voted by a narrow margin that there would be no compensation to the estate owners. However, the Latvians decided that estate owners whose properties were expropriated would be allowed to keep up to 50 hectares. Although rural debt remained a problem in Latvia, the number of farmsteads doubled between 1922 and 1935 and agricultural productivity steadily improved.

In Lithuania, a country that was considerably more rural than either

Latvia or Estonia (according to the 1923 census, 84 percent of Lithuanians lived in towns of fewer than 2,000 inhabitants), the main land reform law called for landlords to be left with no more than 80 hectares. The rest was to be redistributed to veterans and peasants; the estate owners who surrendered their property (some had supported the Poles in the war) would be compensated over a period of 36 years. In reality little of this was ever actually paid.[6]

What transpired in the Baltic area in the early 1920s was surely the largest and most sweeping land reform ever undertaken by democratic governments. However, one should not overlook the general trajectory of the region's landholding patterns during the decades preceding independence, as peasant landownership was continually growing at the expense of the traditional owners. In a way the leaders of the Baltic states were continuing the Russian rural reforms enacted by Peter Stolypin 20 years earlier. Like Stolypin, Baltic leaders wanted to create as many individual landholders as possible, in the hopes that this would lay a solid foundation for the economy and impart to each citizen a sense of having a personal stake in society. While this much was achieved in the Baltic states, yet another goal was also realized: the political and economic power of the Baltic Germans was broken.

EARLY EXPERIMENTS IN DEMOCRACY

For each of the Baltic countries, the era between the two world wars can be divided into two distinct periods. The first was a democratic period, during which parliaments held the upper hand in state politics while national institutions were being built. The second period was authoritarian, beginning in Lithuania in 1926, and in Latvia and Estonia in 1934. Fearing the instability of parliamentary politics in the face of internal and external threats, authoritarian figures seized executive power in the name of the greater national good. These regimes, characterized by most Baltic historians as benign dictatorships, lasted until the region's occupation by Soviet forces in 1940.

Before turning to the rule of dictators, however, the Baltic countries were recognized as being among the most democratic states in the world, and their citizens enjoyed universal manhood suffrage (including voting rights for women), equality before the law, and guarantees for the rights of minorities. True to the antiauthoritarian spirit of the early postwar era, the Baltic states adopted parliamentary forms of government, in which executive power was weak. Constitutions were based on the model of Weimar Germany, which provided for proportional representation in the parliament on the basis of party lists. In each of the Baltic countries the result was fragmentation, the proliferation of political parties, and frequent government turnover.

The Republic of Estonia, where there was no independently elected president to balance the power of the legislature, was a textbook example of the sort of instability that plagued the newly created democratic governments of Europe in the 1920s. The Estonian constitution, adopted on June 15, 1920, provided for a State Elder (*Riigivanem*), who was effectively a prime minister, elected by the 100-member State Assembly (*Riigikogu*). Equipped with extensive powers, the *Riigikogu* could dismiss the government at any time without penalty; the *Riigivanem*, however, lacked even the basic power of veto over parliament, which could be dissolved only by popular referendum. Given the legislature's power over the government, the results were unsurprising: Estonian cabinets lasted less than nine months on average.

During the period of liberal democracy, Estonia's politics were generally dominated by three parties. The main party on the left was the Socialist Workers' Party, a noncommunist labor party that was formed in 1923 from a merger of the Social Democratic Party (descended from the Russian Social Democrats), and the Independent Socialists.[7] The center was occupied by several parties, which consolidated themselves into the National Center in the 1930s. Although a true conservative party did not exist at this time in Estonia, the right was occupied by the Farmers' Party, which consisted mainly of those farmers who had acquired land before the country had attained independence. After 1925–26 the Farmers' Party began to converge with the Settlers' Party, whose constituents were mainly those who became property owners as a result of the land reform.[8] Because of their small numbers, Estonia's national minorities received little representation in the *Riigikogu* and consequently carried little political weight in the country.

Despite the emergence of what might be recognized as a three-party system, the existence of many other small parties made coalition-building in the *Riigikogu* a nearly impossible task. Governments frequently fell and prime ministers rotated in office: Konstantin Päts (of the Farmers' and United Agrarian Parties) was head of state five times, while Jaan Teemant (Farmers' and United Agrarian parties) and Jaan Tõnisson (National Party and National Center) each served four times.

During the liberal democratic period, prior to 1934, the political center and right-center tended to dominate the country's politics. Although the noncommunist Socialist Workers' Party was the largest in the Estonian

Riigikogu from 1926 to 1932 (Socialists even headed the government for seven months in 1928–29), the far left's popular appeal was somewhat tempered by extensive land reform in the early 1920s, and its credibility was undermined by an attempted Communist coup on December 1, 1924.[9] Following its failed attempt to seize power, the Estonian Communist Party was banned, and even with new names its successor organizations exercised little influence on the country's political life.

As in Estonia, the Latvian constitution, adopted in February 1922, created a unicameral *Saeima* of 100 members, each elected to three-year terms. Unlike Estonia, however, Latvia had a president, elected by the *Saeima* to a three-year term, but this post was largely ceremonial. Thus Latvia suffered from the same maladies of political division and government instability, demonstrated by the fact that 12 years of parliamentary democracy produced 14 cabinets. Just as unsettling was the corruption that often accompanied cabinet formation.

Despite the extreme fragmentation that characterized the country's politics between 1922 and 1934 (no fewer than 27 parties were represented in the *Saeima* in 1925 and 1928, for example), several blocs were discernible. The left was led by the Latvian Social Democratic Party, a Marxist but noncommunist organization concerned primarily with the interests of trade unions and the urban proletariat. Its influence steadily declined through the 1920s, although it revived somewhat during the economic crisis of the early 1930s. The left-center was dominated by the Democratic Center, a coalition of three parties of the middle classes. Although the Democratic Center elected few representatives to the *Saeima*, it held the delicate balance between the parties of the left and the right. Somewhat further to the right, an Agrarian bloc was led by the Agrarian Union, which promoted farming as the backbone of Latvian economic life. Agrarians were well-represented in all Latvian governments: 3 of the country's 4 interwar presidents and 10 of 13 prime ministers were from the Agrarian Union. Also represented in the *Saeima*, where they often allied with the Social Democrats against the Agrarians, were Latvia's national minorities, including a relatively strong German Party as well as Russian and Jewish parties.

Like its northern neighbors, the Lithuanian system that finally emerged in 1922, after two years of work on the constitution, was characterized by a strong legislature, a weak executive, and a proportional representation system in the *Seimas*.[10] A feature that distinguishes the Lithuanian system from those of its neighbors, however, was the Catholic Church's crucial role in politics. Throughout Lithuania's short period of liberal democracy (until 1926), Christian Democratic coalitions dominated, presided over by Aleksandras Stulginskis (1885–1969), who was one of the party's founders and Lithuania's second president (1920–26) after Antanas Smetona.

Because of its emphasis on the role of the Catholic Church in the national life of the country, the Christian Democratic Party (LKDP) encountered opposition from sectors of society that might otherwise have supported it for its Lithuanian nationalist, anti-Polish, and anticommunist positions. Peasants tended to share these views, but most joined either the Lithuanian Socialist Populist Party or the Lithuanian Peasant Populist Union, which in December 1922 merged to form the Lithuanian Peasant Populist Union (LVLS). Opposed to what they saw as the Catholic Church's excessive influence in education and state administration, Populists nevertheless often worked together with Christian Democrats in government coalitions. A falling-out between the two blocs in 1926 over this issue, however, helped pave the road for the establishment of a nationalist dictatorship in Lithuania.

While the center and right dominated Lithuania's political life in the 1920s, on the far left a small underground Communist Party worked closely with Moscow. Although some Lithuanian leaders were preoccupied by the specter of a Bolshevik-style coup, the appeal of communism in this overwhelmingly rural country was in fact very limited. Indeed, in the absence of a large proletariat, even the more moderate Social Democratic Party (LSDP) lacked a large social base and never won more than 17 percent of the vote (which it did in 1926).

Meanwhile, on the far right margins of Lithuanian political life the influence of the National Progress Party (NP) of Antanas Smetona and Augustinas Voldemaras (1883–1942) was growing. In its early days the NP bucked the tide of popular opinion by opposing land reform, and as a result remained on the political periphery during the early period of independence. In August 1924 the NP formed the Lithuanian Nationalist Union (*Tautininkai*), a movement that was open only to ethnic Lithuanians. While the *Tautininkai*'s ideas about "national unity" resonated with many ethnic Lithuanians, during the parliamentary period it remained an outside critic of government rather than a participant. Its opportunity arrived with the military putsch of December 1926.

AUTHORITARIAN GOVERNMENT

Following the example of General Piłsudski's successful coup in Poland earlier in the year, Lithuania was the first of the Baltic states to turn to an authoritarian solution.[11] For many Lithuanians, exasperated by the continuing animosity between the major political parties and the institutional weakness of executive authority, abandoning liberalism appeared to be the only way to save the country from falling into the hands of extremists. Indeed, the Lithuanian putschists claimed—perhaps spuriously—to have saved the country from a communist coup. Both the Christian Democrats and the Nationalists supported this move—the LKDP because its leaders claimed to fear the outbreak of civil war, and the Nationalists for perhaps more opportunistic reasons. In the end it was the *Tautininkai* who benefited the most, although the LKDP also initially participated in the postcoup government. On December 17, 1926, Dr. Kazys Grinius (1866–1950), elected president earlier in the year, was placed under house arrest and forced to resign in favor of Smetona.

Estonia and Latvia did not succumb to dictatorship until 1934, but the economic decline of the early 1930s provided fertile soil for the growth of extreme nationalist groups, as was true for many European countries. In Estonia, the most popular of these was the protofascist League of Independence War Veterans (*Eesti Vabadussõjalaste Liit*). Founded in 1928 and led by Andres Larka (1879–1943) and Artur Sirk (1900–37), in its early years the League was primarily concerned with the material welfare of the country's war veterans. Loathing corruption, communism, and parliamentary politics, but fond of uniforms, Nazi-style salutes, and street parades, the League began to gain popular support at the expense of the Farmers' and Socialist Workers' parties in the early 1930s.[12]

Sensing the antiliberal mood of the Estonian populace, in autumn 1932 the League proposed the idea of a strong chief executive, independent of parliament with the power to rule by decree. While its opponents alleged that the League intended to create such an arrangement in order to attain power for itself, the League's defenders countered that it was a necessary measure to counteract government instability. As the increasingly unpopular Tõnisson-led government cracked down on the increasingly confident Veterans, constitutional referenda were held in June and October 1933, the results of which overwhelmingly favored the League's proposals. Following this victory, in January 1934 a new constitution went into effect that reflected the League's preferences for a popularly elected president with the power to rule by decree if necessary. Konstantin Päts (United Agrarians), head of the government coalition since the previous October, was made acting president.

The next step in the extinguishing of parliamentary democracy in Estonia came in March 1934 when, alleging a plot by the Veterans to stage an armed coup (they had earlier won local elections in the country's three largest cities—Tallinn, Tartu, and Narva—and their candidate, Andres

Larka, now threatened to win the forthcoming presidential election), Päts declared martial law and prohibited all political activity in the country. The Veterans' League was shut down and hundreds of its leading members were arrested (though Sirk managed to escape prison and fled to Finland), ushering in what Estonians refer to as the "Era of Silence," which lasted until the arrival of Soviet troops in 1940.

In Latvia, it was fear of the left (as in Lithuania), not fear of the right (as in Estonia), that was used to justify an authoritarian coup, but similar conditions—the sharp economic downturn of the early 1930s, growing unemployment, political instability, a loss of confidence in the *Saeima*, the rise of extremist parties with their own paramilitary organizations—militated in favor of an authoritarian solution. Although rumors of an impending putsch had been floating around since 1932, Kārlis Ulmanis, leader of the Agrarian Union, did not act until May 15, 1934, two months after Päts seized power in Estonia. As in Lithuania and Estonia, the Latvian coup, occurring in the midst of a constitutional crisis, encountered little opposition and was essentially bloodless. Alberts Kviesis (1881–1944), who was president at the time of the coup, was allowed to serve out his term to 1936, while Ulmanis governed as prime minister of a Cabinet of National Unity. Ultimately Ulmanis merged the offices of president and prime minister in his own person.

In all three countries, the essential features of authoritarian government were quickly introduced: martial law, press censorship, and strict limitations on political activity. Baltic parliaments were subordinated to a vastly strengthened executive, against which overt opposition could not be expressed publicly. Following the examples of other east-central European countries like Poland, Hungary, and Bulgaria, parliament was ignored or eventually shut down all together. What is striking, however, was how willingly the Baltic peoples surrendered to authoritarianism. Indeed, it would be difficult to argue that ordinary Lithuanians, and then Estonians and Latvians, were not complicit in the extinguishing of democracy in their countries. Political disillusionment, arising from heightened economic insecurity, may help explain the ease with which the former democracies abandoned their constitutions. As Latvian scholar and diplomat Alfreds Bilmanis aptly remarked, "The people came to look upon themselves as grossly betrayed by their politicians, whom they had elected but over whom they had no control in ultra-liberal parliaments. . . . An unfettered executive authority with emergency powers made a strong appeal to peoples confounded by free-for-all politics."[13]

Lithuanian patriots tend to view the country's authoritarian turn as an undesirable but necessary solution to government instability, the dangers of communism, and the threat posed by irredentist neighbors. Under these circumstances, the period of Nationalist rule is usually given a positive evaluation, and Antanas Smetona himself is portrayed as a highly educated philosopher, above the political fray and comfortable in his self-appointed role of national unifier. From the December 1926 coup until the fall of 1928, Smetona worked closely with Prime Minister Augustinas Voldemaras (who headed the fascist *Geležinis Vilkas*—Iron Wolf Association), but then after a power struggle the latter was dismissed in September 1928, leaving Smetona to be the sole dictator.[14] With the adoption of a new constitution in May 1928, the president was no longer chosen by the *Seimas*, but by "extraordinary representatives" of the nation, who reelected him in 1931 and again in 1938.

Of the three dictatorships, Lithuania went the furthest in attempting to establish a unifying nationalist ideology, which drew its inspiration from Lithuanian culture rather than from fascism or Nazism. In this respect, the regime was somewhat successful, for with the exception of some Catholic organizations, there was little opposition to the Smetona regime. However, only the *Tautininkai* and related youth organizations were permitted a great deal of latitude in their operations; unassociated political parties and organizations were either shut down or found their activities sharply circumscribed. The *Seimas* was allowed to function, but it was reduced to little more than a consultative body.

Likewise, shortly after the preemptive coup of Konstantin Päts, all political parties were banned in Estonia, and newspapers that criticized government policy were shut down, including Jaan Tõnisson's *Postimees*. Ignoring the parliament, in March 1935 Päts attempted to concentrate state power by creating the Fatherland League (*Isamaaliit*), a progovernment party that was intended to promote stability and national unity. Little more than a propaganda vehicle for the regime, the Fatherland League failed to capture the popular imagination.

In January 1937 Päts attempted to legitimize his authoritarian approach to government—his defenders say he was in fact dismantling his dictatorship—with the adoption of a new constitution that created a powerful chief executive and divided the *Riigikogu* into a bicameral legislature. The upper house, a 40-member chamber called the State Council (*Riiginõukogu*), was designed as a corporative body to represent the various institutions of Estonian society, such as the army, churches, industry, and local governments. The lower house, called the Chamber of Representatives (*Riigivolikogu*), consisted of 80 delegates elected by popular vote. Despite this government overhaul, no parties were permitted to engage in political activity. By 1938 it appeared to Estonians that the state of emergency was soon to end and democratic rights would be restored, but this failed to take place before the Soviet occupation in 1940.

Like Smetona and Päts, Latvia's Ulmanis portrayed himself as a truly national figure, above the fray of ordinary politics. Convinced of their leader's deep-rooted democratic ideals, many Latvians believed—and still believe—that Ulmanis was motivated less by greed for personal power than by an unswerving commitment to the welfare of his nation in its time of need. Although under his rule all political parties were disbanded (including Ulmanis's own Agrarian Union), there was no terror and no mass imprisonment of the regime's political opponents. Latvia did have a political police and press censorship, but there was in fact little opposition to its leader. Following the example of Mussolini's Italy, Ulmanis attempted to create a corporative form of government in Latvia, according to which a series of newly created councils were to collaborate with their respective government departments.[15] With the government taking a leading role in the economy, Latvia was put back on the track to prosperity—an achievement that earned Ulmanis considerable popular acclaim. Unlike Päts, Ulmanis ended the state of emergency in Latvia in February 1938, well before the country fell under Soviet occupation.

Despite the fundamental lack of political freedoms in Estonia and Latvia between 1934–40 (and in Lithuania since 1926), the Baltic regimes were mild in comparison to many other authoritarian regimes in Europe during the 1930s. The common claims that the Päts regime saved Estonia from the potential tyranny of the League of Independence War Veterans, and that Ulmanis saved Latvia from communism are indeed subject to debate, but there is little doubt that given the ineffectiveness of parliamentary government in the early 1930s, the mild authoritarian governments of Päts and Ulmanis were far preferable to the monstrous totalitarian regimes that would decide the Balts' fate in August 1939.

ECONOMIC DEVELOPMENT

The transformation of the Baltic economies began during the war, when much of the region's industry was destroyed or dismantled, and the Bolsheviks seized power in Russia, which prior to 1917 had been the region's main market. To compensate for this huge loss, the Baltic countries had to expand their domestic markets and find new foreign markets, which in practice meant that the region's trade had to be reoriented toward the West. Within a decade, the Baltic republics managed to develop their agricultural and manufacturing bases while securing a place in the European system. As noted earlier, the parallel with the post-Soviet period, when the Baltic countries once again lost their Russian market and sought to reorient their international trade towards Western markets, is astonishing.

Of the three republics, Estonia emerged from six years of war with the least human and material damage. Its steady economic recovery during the 1920s was aided in part by the 15 million gold rubles paid by the Soviet regime as war reparations, in addition to significant foreign investment, mostly from Britain. Taking 1929 as a base, the top branches of Estonian industry were textiles, foodstuffs, paper, metallurgy, and woodworking. However, with the opening up of the oil shale deposits located in the region between the Gulf of Finland and Lake Peipsi, the chemical industry was given a boost, which helped the economy recover from the depression of the early 1930s.

Blessed with few industrial raw materials, Estonia had to trade for the metals, chemicals, dyes, and paints necessary for industrial growth. Yet Estonia, like the other Baltic states, remained a predominantly agricultural country, with about two-thirds of the working population employed in the agricultural sector. This proportion began to decline only during the industrial expansion of the late 1930s. During the interwar period Estonia's major exports were foodstuffs (butter, meat, and livestock), timber, flax, paper products, and textiles, and its principal trading partners were Germany and Great Britain, followed by Scandinavia, the United States, and Western Europe. However, because the Baltic economies competed against (rather than complimented) each other, the volume of Estonia's trade with its southern neighbors, Latvia and Lithuania, was surprisingly small.

Latvia experienced similar economic development during the interwar period: slow but steady growth in the 1920s, depression in 1929–33, and recovery and industrial expansion during 1933–39. The basis of the Latvian economy was agriculture, which in 1935 employed 60 percent of the Latvian workforce. At the same time, industry, led by metal production and woodworking, as well as food-processing and textiles, employed 13 percent of Latvian workers.

In each of the Baltic republics the state played a leading role in directing the country's economic development through tax, price, and credit policies. Nowhere in the region was the state more active in the private economy than in Latvia during the Ulmanis years, when the government sought to industrialize the country while simultaneously intensifying the country's agricultural development by providing agricultural credits to Latvian farmers and cooperatives. The state also regulated the production and marketing of agricultural produce, with an eye to foreign markets. Latvia's leading exports were butter, bacon, and eggs, as well as fur and flax; timber and wood products were also significant, and later wheat and rye, which in the past had been imported for Latvian consumption. As in Estonia, the biggest customers for Latvian products were Germany, and after the Depression, Britain; however, Latvia continued to import more from Germany. By 1935 trade with the Soviet Union, which had accounted for 25 percent of Latvian trade in 1922, was hardly a factor.

Starting from a weaker base, industrialization and urbanization proceeded more slowly in Lithuania than in Latvia and Estonia. Throughout the first period of independence, Lithuania remained the most agricultural of the Baltic states; more than three-quarters of the Lithuanian workforce engaged in agricultural pursuits, compared to only 6.4 percent in manufacturing as late as 1936. State economic policy was largely responsible for this development—or underdevelopment—as the government was cautious about industrial expansion (perhaps, it has been suggested, partly because many of the larger industrial concerns were in the hands of Germans and Jews rather than Lithuanians) and did little to promote manufacturing. As in Latvia and Estonia, the Lithuanian ideal was the small family farm, and the state did much to promote this vision of rural prosperity by supporting agriculture (a policy that favored ethnic Lithuanians), with particular emphasis on dairy farming.

Despite this policy, during the interwar period Lithuania's industrial capacity more than doubled. However, the products created in the paper, food-processing, and textile-producing factories that were built in the 1930s were oriented principally toward the internal market, not for export. Lithuanian exports were mainly agricultural products, including dairy products, bacon, eggs, processed foods, flax and timber—products that mirrored and competed with those of Estonia and Latvia. Lithuania also had the same buyers for her products: in the 1920s it was mainly Germany, and after 1932, Britain—a consequence of the economic slump and Lithuania's political difficulties with Germany.

NATIONAL MINORITIES

Since the Baltic republics were founded on the basis of the national principle, one of the main social issues confronting each of them was the matter of reconciling their national minorities with the Estonian, Latvian, and Lithuanian majorities. During the interwar period, national minorities shared the goal of securing and maintaining social autonomy in a complex and sometimes hostile national and international environment. In this respect the German, Jewish, Russian, and Polish minorities achieved some successes, gaining representation in Baltic legislatures and exercising at least a modicum of influence on state policies during the early period of liberal democracy. However, enduring prejudices rooted in the region's troubled national-ethnic history did much to undermine relations between the republics' predominant nationalities and the minorities whom they sometimes distrusted. Yet on the whole, conditions for the Baltic minorities were no worse, and in fact were often much better, than those for the national minorities of the other new nation-states of central and eastern Europe.

In the Latvian and Estonian republics, the main nationality issue concerned the Baltic Germans. As the principal objects of the natives' resentment, the Germans were in a precarious position after 1919. In Latvia they constituted 3.7 percent of the population (58,000) and in Estonia only 1.5 percent (26,000). With the ancient *Ritterschaften* disbanded and nobody to support their claims to the land—most of which was expropriated—the Germans who had dominated Baltic society for centuries had little choice but to accept this reversal of fortunes.

Germany, defeated in war and suffering from the stigma of "war guilt," was in no position to help, and was in any event inclined to do little more than support Baltic German cultural organizations and try to maintain economic ties with the Baltic German commercial class. Twenty thousand Baltic Germans had emigrated to Germany during the wars of independence, but with the country's already high unemployment rate it was the Weimar government's policy to discourage more refugees from settling in Germany. Aiming for a recovery of the country's foreign trade, including trade with the Baltic region, the Weimar government hoped to return as many émigrés as possible, and encouraged them to be loyal to their new states. During 1920–21, perhaps half returned to Latvia and Estonia, where they had to settle for positions of formal equality with those they had once ruled.

Under the constitutions of the new governments, Baltic Germans and other minorities were assured cultural autonomy, including the right to set up schools in which education was conducted in the mother tongue. Land confiscation may have destroyed much of the Germans' wealth, but the German bourgeoisie remained strong in Baltic cities. Some Germans, however, found their professional careers blocked (especially in the civil service and army) and in the 1930s chose to emigrate to Germany. Although the situation undoubtedly took some getting used to, Baltic Germans generally accepted parliamentary democracy and were represented in the *Riigikogu* and *Saeima*.

Unlike the Germans, Russian minorities fared poorly in Baltic politics. Russians were the largest ethnic minority in both Estonia and Latvia: in

Estonia they constituted just over 8 percent of the population throughout the interwar period, while in Latvia the number of Russians grew from 7.8 percent of the population in 1920 to 12 percent in 1934. In Latvia, Russian communities were concentrated in Latgale, the least economically developed part of the country, where most were engaged in agricultural pursuits; in Estonia they were more evenly dispersed throughout the country. Organized into a large number of competing splinter parties, Baltic Russians were never able to achieve political representation commensurate with their growing numerical strength. Unlike Baltic Germans or Jews, Russians were also underrepresented in institutions of higher education, perhaps because only a small minority could speak Latvian or Estonian.

Jews were a relatively small but economically vital element of the Baltic population. During the interwar year the Jewish population in Estonia remained steady at a tiny 0.4 percent of the population, about half of whom lived in Tallinn. In Latvia, Jews constituted about 5 percent of the population (just under half lived in Rīga), although Jewish immigration from Soviet Russia added thousands during the early 1920s. In Lithuania, Jews were the largest national minority, comprising 7.6 percent of the population in 1923. Throughout the region Jews continued to play an important role in industry, commerce, and banking, as they had before World War I. Like other national minorities, Jews in each Baltic country were also granted cultural autonomy. Yet conditions for Jews were gradually eroded by the collapse of democracy and the adoption of state policies designed to improve the economic position of the national majorities. Moreover, Jews in Latvia and Estonia were almost entirely excluded from positions in the civil service, leaving them to concentrate on trade, industry, and the professions. While no Baltic government officially sanctioned anti-Semitism, the region's Jews nevertheless endured growing resentment, often fomented by extremist groups.

As the Baltic country that experienced the fewest problems with its national minorities, Estonia was the most tolerant in its treatment of Jews. As one of the four ethnic groups (Russians, Germans, and Swedes were the others) recognized by Estonia's law on national-cultural autonomy (1925), Jews were allowed to establish Hebrew-language educational networks. Yet Jews did not serve in government administration, had difficulty obtaining credit, and with the government's takeover of the grain trade, the large number of Jews employed in this branch of trade were deprived of their livelihoods. By the mid-1930s, Jews in Estonia, as in most of Europe, had become victims of growing anti-Semitism, reflected in a decline in the number of Jewish students at the University of Tartu, which fell from 188 in 1926 to 96 in 1934. The situation was similar for Jews in Latvia, where Jewish autonomy was abolished altogether under the Ulmanis regime.

The census taken in Lithuania in 1923 showed a total of 153,332 Jews in the country, although it is likely that the real number was considerably higher, especially if the lost Vilnius region, restored to Lithuania in 1939, is considered. In larger towns, Jews formed about one-third of the population. Undoubtedly the conspicuous presence of Yiddish-speaking Jews was a source of some irritation to the many Lithuanians who conceived of their country as a nation-state for the Lithuanian people. Nevertheless, from the beginning Jewish autonomy was ensured with the creation of a Jewish National Council, which in conjunction with the Ministry of Jewish Affairs administered Jewish autonomous institutions such as the expanding network of Hebrew- and Yiddish-language elementary and secondary schools.

However, as in the other Baltic republics, Lithuanian state policies effectively undermined the economic position of Jews: by encouraging the growth of cooperatives, which took over the export trade in agricultural products, the policies deprived thousands of Jews, who before World War I had dominated the region's export trade, of their livelihoods. Moreover, the Festivals Law, enacted in July 1924, prohibited labor on Sunday and other Christian holidays; this was particularly injurious to Jews since the Jewish Sabbath fell on Saturday and many Jews worked only half-days on Friday.[16]

Formal autonomy for Lithuania's Jews ended with the closing of the Ministry for Jewish Affairs in 1924. Shortly afterwards, in September, the National Council was dispersed by the police. The situation worsened after the coup of December 1926, which resulted in extreme nationalists, the *Tautininkai*, coming to power. There were no pogroms, as in Poland and Romania; nevertheless, occasional anti-Semitic demonstrations highlighted the growth in the 1930s of an increasingly aggressive attitude toward Jews on behalf of a small but vocal segment of the Lithuanian population. Although Jews managed to retain a modicum of autonomy, including control over the Jewish educational system and a Jewish network of banks, economic discrimination against Jews worsened in the 1930s. As a result the number of Jews engaged in trade, industry, and crafts steadily declined. Because of these conditions, which, it should be noted, were probably no worse than in most of the rest of eastern and central Europe, 30,000 Jews emigrated from Lithuania between 1920 and

1940. Thus over the course of four decades the proportion of Jews in the general population fell dramatically, from 13.8 percent in 1897 to 6.2 percent in 1939.[17]

Poles were the second-largest minority in Lithuania, comprising about 3.2 percent of the population in 1923—although Poles claimed that the accurate figure was closer to 10 percent. Polish national life in Lithuania was complicated by the country's troubled relationship with Poland. Because of this, organized political activity for Poles was circumscribed in Lithuania, although they did elect representatives to the *Seimas*. With official encouragement, Polish-language education gradually declined in the 1920s, and laws enacted in the 1930s restricted such education only to children who had two Polish-speaking parents.

In general, tolerance for national diversity declined under the authoritarian regimes. The demise of the proportional representation systems meant less minority representation in government at a time when national cultural autonomy was being curtailed. While Lithuanian nationalism was directed in particular against the Poles, in Latvia and Estonia, the object of nationalist hostility was the Baltic German community, manifested in language laws passed in 1934–35 that prohibited the use of German names on street signs and allowed for state expropriation of some Baltic German churches as well as the closure of Baltic German agricultural associations. Making the situation worse after 1933 were the subsidies for Baltic German activities being provided by Hitler's Third Reich; with help from Nazi Germany the area's National Socialists came to exert considerable influence over existing Baltic German institutions.[18] Yet, paradoxically, by evacuating Baltic Germans from Latvia and Estonia in autumn 1939, following his agreement with Stalin (see below), Hitler effectively removed German influence in the region for half a century.

SOCIETY AND CULTURE

No longer inhibited by tsarist rule—and yet to be absorbed by the USSR—for two decades national cultures flourished in the Baltic countries. In each case the state played an important role in the organization and finance of theaters, the performing arts, symphony orchestras, radio stations, and other cultural media. While the Baltic artistic world prospered, intellectual life was enriched by an expanding body of literature and the proliferation of newspapers, magazines, and professional, scientific, and scholarly journals.

The basis of this cultural upsurge was an expanded educational system—which also became one of the main agencies for the dissemination of patriotic and nationalist sentiment in the Baltic countries. The emphases on de-Russification and instilling patriotic attitudes were evident, for example, in the Latvian conception of a program called "Native Land Studies," which included lessons on the country's industries, government, and other topics related to the "native land." In all three Baltic countries the native language was elevated to the primary language of instruction, although allowances were made for minority nationalities to use their own languages in separate school networks.

From the time of independence, all Estonian children received free compulsory education, expanded from three to six years, from age eight. Secondary education was voluntary, for which Estonians had to pay a modest tuition. As a result of its vastly expanded educational network, the Estonian literacy rate, already high at the time of independence, approached universal by the mid-1930s. Meanwhile, successes in primary and secondary education were matched at the university level: on December 1, 1919, the University of Tartu, founded as a German institution (University of Dorpat) and then Russified in the late nineteenth century, was reopened as an Estonian institution. Although initially the faculty was composed mostly of Baltic Germans and Russians, by the mid-1930s the curriculum was overwhelmingly Estonian. By 1926, a higher proportion of Estonians (one in 280) attended university than Germans, Swedes, or Finns in their respective countries.[19]

Latvia experienced similar successes. The number of primary schools in Latvia more than doubled between 1920 and 1933, and the number of secondary schools rose from 36 to 96. As a result of these efforts, by 1926 the illiteracy rate was down to 14.3 percent, and dropped still further in the 1930s. Meanwhile, the eastern province of Latgale, which was considerably less developed than many other Baltic regions and whose inhabitants spoke a distinct dialect of Latvian, was the recipient of immense investment, especially in education, in an effort to bring about the full integration of the region into Latvia.

Latvian higher education also made significant advances. Before 1919 there had been no specifically Latvian institution of higher education, since under Russian rule the University of Tartu was to serve all the Baltic provinces. Upon national independence this shortcoming was immediately redressed with the opening of the Latvian State University, in which more than 8,000 students were enrolled by 1933.[20]

As in most areas of national development, in educational matters Lithuania started at a lower base than either Latvia or Estonia. In 1923 nearly one-third of the Lithuanian population was unable to either read or write, but the construction of a vast educational network was designed to correct this aspect of the country's underdevelopment. Between 1919 and 1931 the number of primary schools more than doubled, although compulsory education was not introduced until 1931. With the University of Vilnius having been lost to the Poles as a result of their seizure of the region, an alternative University of Lithuania was set up in 1922 in Kaunas, and in 1930 was renamed Vytautas the Great.

Throughout the independence era, the Catholic Church continued to play an important role in primary education in Lithuania. But the Church's function was not limited to providing spiritual and educational nourishment, for in Lithuania, Catholicism occupied a prominent position in the country's social and political life and was often at the center of the country's most pressing political questions. While Catholicism was the religion of the overwhelming majority of Lithuania's residents, the country's second-most important religion was Judaism. Lithuania also had a substantial Russian and Orthodox minority; many of these were Old Believers whose ancestors, forbidden to practice their religion in the Russian Empire, had arrived in the region in the seventeenth century.

In Latvia, Evangelical Lutheranism was the religion of more than half of the population. However, during the independence era Latvians' attachment to the church appeared to weaken. Although this in part reflected a general European trend toward secularization, it is probably also related to the Latvians' knowledge that Lutheranism was imported by German invaders and that the church had been historically dominated by German clergymen. Thus, during the independence era attempts were made to Latvianize the Lutheran church. While ethnic Latvian clergy became predominant, original Latvian hymns were composed to replace the old German hymns, and the New Testament was translated into modern Latvian. Of the remaining population of Latvia, nearly one-fourth were Roman Catholics, most of whom resided in Latgale. Russians and other Slavs constituted the bulk of Latvia's Orthodox believers (about 9 percent of the total population). Jews, constituting about 5 percent of the country's population, were concentrated in Latvia's largest cities.

In Estonia, Lutheranism continued to predominate. According to the 1934 census, 78 percent of Estonian citizens claimed to be Lutherans. A further 19 percent, mostly Russians, were Orthodox and Old Believers. Estonia also had smaller numbers of Baptists, Evangelical Christians, Roman Catholics, Adventists, Methodists, and about 4,300 Jews.

FOREIGN RELATIONS

The Baltic states began their existence under the most precarious circumstances—they were buffer states between two defeated and resentful pariahs, Germany and Russia. As part of a cordon sanitaire designed to contain Bolshevism to the east and keep their two larger neighbors apart, the Baltic republics' prospects for long-term survival must have appeared grim. Their security was further undermined by their subordinate position to Poland in the cordon sanitaire and the weakness of the League of Nations, which could offer them little protection against irredentist neighbors. Moreover, Baltic leaders showed little foresight by failing to cooperate in a consistent and systematic way on economic, political, and defense issues.

In the early days of the independence era all three republics declared the creation of a Baltic union—one that included Finland, Sweden, and Poland as possible partners—to be a high priority; however, this aim was never fully realized. Instead of a larger Baltic alliance, the links that were developed in the region tended to be bilateral arrangements. Some connections were developed between Estonia and Latvia: in July 1921, Latvia and Estonia signed a bilateral treaty calling for a military and political alliance, which was extended in November 1923. While generally taking neutral positions in their foreign policies, Latvia and Estonia tended to gravitate toward the leadership of Poland, which sought to play the role of a "great power" in the region. As defenders of the status quo, the northern Baltic republics were concerned mostly with their own survival in an uncertain international climate; to avoid being drawn into the struggles of their larger neighbors was the main objective.

Lithuania, however, was dissatisfied with the territorial arrangements that left her deprived of Vilnius, the country's ancient capital, and the Klaipėda territory, which in previous centuries under German rule had constituted part of Lithuania Minor. Due to the simmering conflicts with its neighbors, especially Poland, Lithuania took a more independent course in its foreign policy than did Latvia and Estonia, and it could not be a full partner in any Baltic alliance that included Poland. Meanwhile, Lithuania sought the support of the great powers in the region, namely Germany and Soviet Russia—each of whom bore grudges against Poland.

This conflict of interests made Baltic military and political cooperation difficult and prevented any real alliance from taking shape among the three republics. Only in September 1934 did a narrow "Baltic Entente" emerge; however, even this arrangement made no provisions for a common defense. Indeed, for most of the interwar period the Baltic states were strangers to each other, and their political and economic ties remained weak.

For Lithuania, the main foreign policy questions were the territory and city of Klaipėda and the city of Vilnius. At the Paris Peace Conference Lithuanian delegates made a case for the inclusion of the Klaipėda territory (1,100 square miles) in their new state. Although the proportion of Lithuanian residents who lived in the region was fairly low, Lithuanians believed that they nevertheless had a strong claim: Germany was going to lose territory anyway, and, as peace conference chairman (and French premier) Georges Clemenceau argued, Klaipėda would be Lithuania's sole outlet to the sea. Nevertheless, the peace conference decided to detach Klaipėda and its 140,000 inhabitants from Germany and place the district under French administration for the time being.

In January 1923, after a propaganda campaign warning of an imminent Polish takeover, the Lithuanians organized an insurrection and seized the city with little resistance from the French. They apparently believed that once they had taken over the territory, the world would have no choice but to recognize Lithuania's fait accompli. De facto control, it was believed, would inevitably result in de jure control—which is very much what happened. With the German population of Klaipėda remaining mostly passive, the Weimar government, then preoccupied with problems in the west (the French Army was occupying Germany's Ruhr district to force payment of war reparations), did not object to the Lithuanian seizure, perhaps reasoning that it would be better for Klaipėda to go to Lithuania than to Poland. Ultimately, the Western powers legitimized Lithuania's action by transferring the rights to the Klaipėda territory to Lithuania. Now Lithuania at least had a major port and industrial center, but the Vilnius issue remained.

As discussed in Chapter Four, Vilnius had changed hands several times during the wars of 1914–20, but was ultimately seized by Polish forces in August 1920. Despite Lithuania's claims to its historic capital, the demographic situation did not work to its advantage; indeed, the ethnic Lithuanian population of the city and its surrounding territory was dwarfed by the vastly larger numbers of Poles and Belarussians residing there. Refusing to relinquish the contested city, the Polish administration in Vilnius held elections in January 1922 that produced a provincial legislature that in turn overwhelmingly voted for union with Poland. Lithuania refused to recognize the legitimacy of this act and brought its case before the International Court of Justice in The Hague, but this produced no firm opinion. In an attempt to lay the matter to rest once and for all, the Allies recognized Polish sovereignty over Vilnius in March 1923. Only the Soviet Union recognized Lithuania's claim to Vilnius.

Polish-Lithuanian relations went from bad to worse during the 1920s, and in November 1927 war appeared imminent. Polish authorities in Vilnius restricted activities in Lithuanian schools and institutions, while Lithuanian authorities returned the favor to the country's Polish minority. A heightened sense of nationalism gripped Lithuania, and its Polish minority became an internal enemy. Although direct negotiations between Poland's President Piłsudski and Lithuania's Prime Minister Augustinas Voldemaras took place in December 1927, nothing came of them. The two adversaries were on the verge of trying again in 1935, but the death of Piłsudski aborted this initiative.

Poland may have been Lithuania's main nemesis, but Germany and the Soviet Union—potentially Europe's most powerful irredentist states— were the most significant threats to Baltic independence. Thanks largely to their unusual weakness in the wake of World War I, the danger from Germany and Soviet Russia did not materialize for nearly two decades, and then under very different circumstances. Indeed, while it was clearly in the interests of the Baltic states to pursue cooperative relationships with their more powerful neighbors, the reverse was also true: Germany and the USSR, at least during the life of the Weimar Republic (1918–33), respected the independence of the Baltic republics and attempted to build constructive diplomatic and economic relations with them.

By the mid-1920s, Soviet Russia had turned its energies inward, focusing on building "socialism in one country" rather than actively inciting revolution in foreign lands. During the 1926–33 period the USSR signed bilateral trade agreements and nonaggression treaties with most of its western neighbors. Nonaggression treaties were signed with Lithuania in September 1926, and with Latvia and Estonia in 1932. For the USSR, the agreements were intended to keep the eastern European states divided; for the Baltic states, the objective was to ensure peace and stable relations with the much more powerful Soviet Union. Only after the fall of the Weimar Republic in 1933 was Baltic security seriously threatened by the two major irredentist powers. Concerned by the changed international environment resulting from the Nazi seizure of power and the consequent decline of German-Soviet relations, all three Baltic states belatedly formed an entente in September 1934.

Throughout this period the leaders of the Baltic states were convinced that should the need arise, Britain could be counted on for their defense— the British Foreign Office's formal statements to the contrary notwithstanding. As historians John Hiden and Patrick Salmon wrote, "They [the Baltic governments] suffered from the understandable optical illusion that a relationship which was of paramount importance to them was equally important to Great Britain." Despite the significance of the Baltic trade, Britain refused to commit itself to the defense of these states. Indeed, until the early 1930s, its Foreign Office was convinced that they would ultimately be reincorporated into Russia one way or another.[21]

LOSS OF INDEPENDENCE

That Europe experienced more than a decade of calm was largely due to the anomalous and exceptional weakness of Germany and Soviet Russia during much of the interwar period. Hitler's foreign policy initiatives in the mid-1930s, however, upset an equilibrium that had earlier allowed the Baltic states to enjoy generally peaceful relations with both the Germans and Soviets. As part of the Reich's efforts to reassert its economic influence in the region in the late 1930s, Germany signed trade treaties with the Baltic states that secured access to raw materials such as Estonian shale oil, essential for the German war machine. More ominous still was Nazi support for the claims of dissatisfied Baltic Germans, some of whom felt that their futures would be better secured if the republics were attached to Germany.

With German-Soviet relations worsening after Hitler became Reich chancellor in January 1933, in September 1934 the three Baltic states signed the Treaty of Friendship and Cooperation, which was the basis of a triple entente. However, this Baltic Entente fell far short of a full military alliance, since Estonia and Latvia did not wish to be drawn into Lithuania's unresolved disputes with Poland and Germany over the Vilnius and Klaipėda territories. Even with a potential combined defense force of 500,000 men, the three republics lacked a unified command structure and could not have stopped an attack by any of the great powers. Thus the Baltic states continued to emphasize their neutrality and their desire not to get in the way of Europe's great power struggles.

European stability, and hence the security of the Baltic region, suffered a severe setback with the Munich agreement of September 1938. In an attempt to satisfy Hitler's territorial demands in Europe peacefully, the Western powers acceded to the dismemberment of Czechoslovakia by granting Germany the Sudetenland, an area that contained a large German element whose rights Hitler claimed to be defending. It quickly became clear that the German *Führer* would also demand new arrangements for other areas lost to Germany after World War I, such as Danzig (*Pol.* Gdansk) and the Polish "corridor" as well as Lithuanian-occupied Klaipėda. Soon after German troops marched into Prague in March 1939, Berlin demanded that Lithuania surrender Klaipėda to the Reich. Fearing German occupation of the whole country, Kaunas complied. The Western powers upon whom the Baltic countries relied for their security did little more than murmur a word of protest; indeed, it was not long before Britain, consistent with its policy of appeasing Hitler, granted de jure recognition of Germany's seizure of Klaipėda. It was clear to the leaders of

Lithuania, Latvia, and Estonia that they must either declare their neutral-ity or make a choice between the Soviets and the Germans.

To London and Paris it was Poland's security, rather than that of the Baltic countries, that was the key to maintaining peace in Europe. In the hopes of averting further German aggression, at the end of March 1939 Britain and France gave Poland a joint guarantee; its effectiveness, how-ever, would have required Soviet support. Likewise, from the German perspective, a war against Poland could be carried out successfully only with an assurance that the Soviets would not intervene. Thus both the Western powers and Germany courted Stalin, but for different reasons.

In the end, France and Britain simply had less to offer the USSR than did Germany. For the Western powers, any agreement with the Soviets had to include a guarantee of the sovereignty of the Baltic states (including Finland but not Lithuania, which did not share a common border with the USSR); for the Soviets, however, the ports and naval facilities of the Baltic states were essential for the defense of Leningrad, the country's second-largest city and an important center of military industry.[22] Distrust between the West and the USSR, arising in part from Stalin's resentment of the Munich agreement and in part from the long-standing anticom-munism of the West, prevented the conclusion of an anti-German alliance. The Baltic states thus remained caught between two great powers who appeared to be moving steadily towards war.

Posing as a friendly supporter of Baltic independence, Germany pres-sured Estonia and Latvia into signing nonaggression pacts on June 7, 1939. With Britain and France seemingly powerless to influence events in East-ern Europe, it was clear to Baltic leaders that security lay with either the Soviets or the Germans—and they chose the country that offered them a guarantee. However, the signing of these pacts appeared to imply that Latvia and Estonia had now become part of Germany's security system, which was surely suspicious to the Kremlin. Whereas Latvia and Estonia were coerced into making pacts with Germany, Lithuania tried to main-tain its neutrality, all the while pondering the possibility of regaining Vil-nius in the event that a Polish-German conflict should break out.

Meanwhile, discussions between the USSR, Britain, and France in the summer of 1939 proved fruitless. However, behind-the-scenes negotia-tions between the Soviet Union and Germany resulted in the signing on August 15 of a nonaggression pact, often referred to as the Molotov-Ribbentrop pact in honor of its signatories, People's Commissar of Foreign Affairs Viacheslav Molotov and German Defense Minister Joachim von Ribbentrop. For Hitler, the pact meant insurance against Soviet interfer-ence during the coming German-Polish war. For Stalin, the pact bought time to build up Soviet defenses while offering the USSR something the Western powers could not—a sphere of influence in Eastern Europe. The fate of the Baltic states was decided with the conclusion of a supplementary protocol to the Nazi-Soviet pact on August 23, according to which Poland would be divided between Germany and the USSR; Finland, Estonia, and Latvia would fall under the Soviet sphere, while Lithuania would fall under the German sphere of influence. With the signing of these "secret protocols" and London's refusal to offer the Baltic states security guarantees, the Baltics' option of choosing between German guarantees against Russia or vice versa was removed.

Having succeeded in neutralizing the USSR, on September 1 Germany attacked Poland. Lithuania came under German pressure to attack Poland and occupy Vilnius, but President Smetona, perhaps unconfident of a German victory, instead immediately issued a decree declaring Lithuania's neutrality. Meanwhile, with Soviet forces entering Poland from the east, on September 28 Stalin and Ribbentrop signed a treaty on borders and friendship between the USSR and Germany, according to which Germany would get a larger piece of Poland and Lithuania would be transferred to the Soviet sphere.

After occupying eastern Poland, Moscow pressured the three Baltic states and Finland to conclude "mutual assistance treaties" that would enable the Red Army to occupy strategic bases in Estonia, Latvia, and Lithuania. Acting under duress, the Baltic republics had little choice but to accede to Soviet demands. A Soviet-Estonian treaty was signed on September 28 that allowed the Soviets to establish military bases on Estonian soil and to station 25,000 Soviet troops; similar treaties were signed by Latvia on October 5 and Lithuania on October 10. Significantly, the last of these treaties allowed for the transfer of the Vilnius region (2,569 square miles) with its 457,500 inhabitants to Lithuanian control. Thus the process of incorporating the Baltic countries into the Soviet sphere began. An integral part of this process was the "repatriation" of Baltic Germans to the "homeland" during the winter of 1939–40, including 13,700 from Estonia and 52,583 from Latvia, who were mostly settled in the area of Poland recently taken over by the Reich.[23]

What were Stalin's real intentions in the Baltic region? Was his goal all along to absorb the Baltic republics in an effort to reestablish the western boundaries of the old Russian Empire? Or was he merely trying to draw a defensive line in eastern Europe to protect the USSR against a future German invasion? Or to put the matter another way: if Germany had not attacked in June 1941, would the security arrangements made between the Baltic republics and the USSR in 1939–40 have remained the basis of continued Baltic independence for years or even decades to come? Aggressive Soviet actions in the spring of 1940, a full year before the German invasion of the USSR, suggest otherwise.

NOTES

1. Raun (1987), 90, 129.

2. Artis Pabriks and Aldis Purs, *Latvia: The Challenges of Change* (London and New York: Routledge, 2001), 16; Plakans (1995), 112, 124, 131–132.

3. Eidintas et al. (1997), 16; Georg von Rauch, *The Baltic States: The Years of Independence: Estonia, Latvia, Lithuania 1917–1940* (Berkeley and Los Angeles: University of California Press, 1974), 85.

4. John Hiden, *The Baltic States and Weimar Ostpolitik* (New York: Cambridge University Press, 1987), 36.

5. Although the Estonian government later decided to offer compensation to the landowners whose estates had been expropriated, this amounted to very little—according to one historian, only 3 percent of the real value of the estates. von Rauch (1974), 88.

6. Eidintas et al. (1997), 45–48.

7. Further left was a tiny Estonian Communist Party, a Bolshevik-style organization that worked closely with Moscow.

8. In 1932 the two agrarian parties merged and were reorganized as the United Agrarian Party, but they split again the following year.

9. Sensing that during a period of economic uncertainty it could depend on Tallinn's workers to follow its lead, Jaan Anvelt's Estonian Communist Party, guided by the Comintern (Communist International—a worldwide organization of communist parties), attempted to incite an insurrection. Anvelt, who later died in Stalin's purges, was in Petrograd at the time. The coup leaders anticipated much more support for the putsch in the streets of Tallinn than they actually received, and the uprising was quickly and easily repressed and the ringleaders arrested.

10. The origins of the Lithuanian *Seimas* may be found in the *Seim*, a parliamentary body that gave Lithuanian boyars considerable power and influence in the fifteenth and sixteenth centuries.

11. In May 1926 General Jozef Piłsudksi (1867–1935), a founder of the interwar Polish state, carried out a coup against a government that he believed was incapable of solving the country's most serious problems. The pattern was repeated throughout central and eastern Europe.

12. See Andres Kasekamp, *The Radical Right in Interwar Estonia* (New York: St. Martin's Press, 2000).

13. Alfred Bilmanis, *A History of Latvia* (Westport, Conn.: Greenwood Press, 1951), 357.

14. In 1934 Voldemaras sought to regain power during a coup attempt,

but this failed; after being released from prison in 1938 he settled in France.

15. In 1936 a State Cultural Council (consisting of the boards of the Chambers of Professions and of the Chamber of Literature and Art) and a National Economic Council (consisting of the boards of the new chambers of commerce, industry, agriculture, artisans, and labor) were formed for the purpose of better coordinating the various sectors of the Latvian state and society.

16. Greenbaum (1995), 253.

17. Much of this decline is due to the loss of Vilnius in 1920. However, with the outbreak of World War II in 1939 and the return of Vilnius, 70,000 Jews were returned to Lithuania. Levin (2000), 134–135.

18. Following Hitler's rise to power in Germany in 1933, the Baltic German parties of Estonia and Latvia became Nazified. See Hiden (1987), 36–61.

19. Raun (1987), 134; von Rauch (1974), 128–129.

20. von Rauch (1974), 131–133; Plakans (1995), 138.

21. John Hiden and Patrick Salmon, *The Baltic Nations and Europe: Estonia, Latvia and Lithuania in the Twentieth Century* (London and New York: Longman, 1991), 73–74.

22. Leningrad was known as St. Petersburg until 1915, when its name was changed to Petrograd. In 1924 it acquired the name Leningrad, and then in 1991 it reverted to its traditional name, St. Petersburg.

23. Hiden and Salmon (1991), 115.

6

Soviet Rule, 1940–85

THE FIRST SOVIET OCCUPATION

Although scholars correctly date the formal end of the "independence era" for the Baltic states from June 1940, the fate of Estonia, Latvia, and Lithuania was in fact decided in August 1939 by a secret protocol to the Nazi-Soviet nonaggression pact that divided eastern Europe into German and Soviet spheres of influence. For Stalin, it was a better deal than anything being offered by the hesitant West, as it offered him the opportunity to expand the USSR's strategic presence into those areas of eastern Europe lost to Russia after World War I, including the eastern half of Poland, Finland, Bessarabia (now the bulk of the post-Soviet Moldovan state), Estonia, and Latvia. (Lithuania was transferred to the Soviet sphere in late September.) For their part of the bargain, the Germans received a free hand in western Poland, which they invaded on September 1, just a week after concluding the agreement with Moscow.

The Soviets then occupied their half of Poland, following which they forced "mutual assistance" treaties on the Baltic states. Despite the installation of Soviet military bases within their borders, the Baltic countries were allowed to continue to conduct their domestic affairs without Soviet interference. Finland was also pressured into a mutual assistance treaty,

The Baltic Region before and after World War II. Courtesy of Cartographica.

but balked at the notion of allowing Soviet bases to be set up in its territory. Finnish resistance prompted a Soviet invasion on November 30, and a pro-Soviet puppet government headed by Otto Kuusinen was quickly established.

Approximately 160,000 men were mobilized to defend Finland's 1,200-kilometer eastern border from a Soviet invasion force nearly three times as large. Despite vastly outnumbering its opponents, the Red Army suffered as many as 400,000 casualties during the Winter War, thus demonstrating to the world—and to Hitler especially—the glaring weaknesses of the Soviet military. Nevertheless, by mid-March 1940 the USSR was able to impose a peace treaty upon Finland, which required it to give up 10 percent of its territory but left the country free. Genuinely concerned about a possible assault on Leningrad from the Gulf of Finland, Stalin next turned his attention to Lithuania, Latvia, and Estonia, which he now intended to incorporate into the USSR as Soviet republics.

For more than six months the Soviets had scrupulously observed the terms of the treaties with the Baltic states. Then in the spring of 1940, while the world's attention was riveted on Hitler's triumphs in Denmark, Norway, and France, Moscow began to ratchet up the pressure on its western neighbors. In late May and early June the Kremlin accused the governments of all three Baltic states of unfriendliness and of conspiring together against the USSR. Alleging their inability to carry out the terms of the mutual assistance pacts, Moscow issued ultimatums to each of the Baltic countries, demanding that they form new governments that would be friendly to it and that would be able to fulfill their treaty obligations. The accusations, of course, were false, being merely a pretext to mask the Soviet Union's real intentions of taking over the Baltic states in order to obtain strategic ports and direct access to the Baltic Sea.

Lithuania, which in late May was accused of kidnapping several Red Army soldiers who had strayed from one of the military bases recently occupied by the USSR, was the first to be presented with an ultimatum, on June 14. President Antanas Smetona attempted to clarify Lithuania's good intentions toward the USSR in writing, but the Kremlin ignored his plea. With invasion imminent, Smetona then tried to convince his cabinet and army that Lithuania should at least organize a symbolic resistance to the Soviets and fight, but on the following day he was overruled. Three hundred thousand Red Army soldiers immediately overran the country.

Meanwhile, as the Soviet Union massed additional troops on the Estonian and Latvian borders, on June 16 Soviet Commissar of Foreign Affairs Vyacheslav Molotov issued similar demands to the Latvian and Estonian ambassadors in Moscow. Fully understanding the futility of military resistance, the Baltic leaders had no choice but to accept the USSR's ultimatums. As in Lithuania, Soviet occupation of Latvia and Estonia immediately followed.

The Soviet justification of the occupation, written in history books published in the postwar period, ignored Soviet belligerency in these events, instead emphasizing the "class struggle" then allegedly taking place in each of the Baltic countries. As one Soviet historian wrote of the situation in Latvia:

> In June 1940, a revolutionary situation penetrated Latvia. Outwardly there was a crisis in the internal and external affairs of the dominant class; further, the oppressed classes were absorbed in poverty and disaster. Attempting to maintain power, the fascist government on June 17 enforced a state of siege in the country and intensified a bloody terror against the workers. On this day, the police resumed their fierce punishment of workers in Riga, who went out into the streets to greet part of the Red Army.[1]

The official Soviet claim that the Baltic peoples "voluntarily" consented to their incorporation into the USSR became the legal basis for nearly five decades of Soviet rule. Within weeks, parliamentary elections were organized, the purpose of which was to confirm the voluntary nature of the Balts' acceptance of socialism and their entry into the Soviet Union. To prevent the formation of an organized opposition, the Baltic states were quickly Sovietized. In Rīga the process was overseen by Molotov's deputy, Andrei Vyshinskii, who in the 1930s had organized the Stalinist trials of the "enemies of the people." In Tallinn, Politburo member Andrei Zhdanov took charge, while Deputy Foreign Commissar Vladimir Dekanozov was dispatched to Kaunas. It was their responsibility to pressure the legal cabinets to resign and replace them with Soviet-approved appointees.

With new "elections" scheduled for July 14–15, the occupying authorities immediately carried out purges of noncommunist political organizations and other institutions in each of the Baltic states. In Lithuania, for example, just days before the elections were to take place, 2,000 political opponents were rounded up. Following the sham elections, which despite low voter turnout were overwhelmingly favorable to the recently legalized local communist parties, on July 21–22 each of the new Baltic parliaments issued resolutions in which they declared themselves Soviet republics. Lithuania was admitted to the USSR on August 3, Latvia on August 5, and Estonia on the following day.

As long as Germany was ravaging the continent, Baltic independence was hardly a main concern to either Britain or the United States; nevertheless, on July 23, 1940, the U.S. State Department issued a declaration in which it refused to recognize the USSR's incorporation of the Baltic countries. Under the circumstances, this had no effect on Soviet policy in the region, as the USSR was not yet an ally of Britain and the United States, as it would be from mid-1941 until the end of the war. On the contrary, from August 1939 until June 1941 Stalin and Hitler were partners in the division and subjugation of Europe. However, even as allies of the USSR after the Nazi invasion, Britain and the United States took a pragmatic approach to the region, accepting the de facto, if not de jure, loss of the Baltic states to the Soviet Union.

With Latvia's President Ulmanis and Estonia's President Päts deposed and deported to the USSR along with dozens of other prominent independence-era leaders (Lithuania's Smetona managed to escape to the United States, where he died in 1942), the Baltic countries were given new leaders, chosen from among sympathetic—or opportunistic—natives and cadres imported from the other Union republics.[2] The importation of administrators was necessary partly because few native communists were residing in the Baltic countries on the eve of the Soviet occupation: the Communist Party of Lithuania emerged from underground with about 1,500 members; in early 1940 the Latvian Communist Party could claim about 500 members; tiniest of all was Estonia's Communist Party, with only 133 members in the spring of 1940. Moreover, Baltic communists could not count on the aid of the thousands of Estonian, Latvian, and Lithuanian communists who had spent the interwar years in the USSR, as most of them had been eliminated during the purges of the 1930s. Nevertheless, until the ranks of the local communist parties (now folded into the Communist Party of the Soviet Union, or CPSU) were replenished, the small numbers of communists arriving in the Baltic capitals from the other Union republics (primarily the Russian republic, or RSFSR) in the summer of 1940 were indispensable for the Sovietization of the Baltic states.

The new Baltic governments immediately began to align their policies with current Soviet practices, the basis of which was Marxist-Leninist ideology. The old "bourgeois" societies had to be destroyed so that new "socialist" societies, run by loyal Soviet citizens, could be constructed in their place. The reconstituted parliaments quickly proclaimed the nationalization of large industries, transportation, banks, private housing, and commerce in general. Although land was now considered the property of the people, for the time being the Soviet regime limited itself to expropriating only those holdings comprising 30 or more hectares (about 66 acres); the rest was placed in republic land banks, which then distributed some of the property to landless peasants and farmers with the smallest holdings. By creating large numbers of small, unviable farms, the Soviet regime intended to weaken the institution of private landholding so that later collectivization, a program of agricultural consolidation that was undertaken in the USSR a decade earlier with horrifying results, could be presented as an efficient alternative. Although large-scale collectivization was not yet attempted, the impact of Soviet policies on Baltic agriculture was generally negative: many farmers, afraid of being branded rich peasants (*kulaky,* in the Soviet lexicon) or wanting to avoid the possible expropriation of their sheep, cows, and hogs, resorted to slaughtering their livestock.

With the arrival of the Red Army—which quickly absorbed the military forces of the Baltic states—followed by the Soviet security forces (NKVD), came strict censorship and press control. Perhaps because the Soviet regime was reluctant to antagonize Western opinion, or more likely because it did not want to stimulate local sympathies for Hitler, the antireligious policies that were put into effect in the Baltic states were relatively lenient in comparison to the Bolsheviks' efforts to destroy religious life in the USSR in the 1920s and 1930s. Nevertheless, in each of the new Soviet republics churches and ecclesiastical property were nationalized, religious education and religious publications were forbidden, seminaries and monasteries were seized (often to quarter the Red Army), and many clergymen—considered to be among the most conspicuous enemies of the Soviet regime—were arrested.

The greatest blow to the Baltic clergy, whether Lutheran, Catholic, or Orthodox, was dealt in mid-June 1941, when large numbers of priests and pastors were deported to the Soviet hinterland. This was part of a sweeping deportation simultaneously affecting all three Baltic republics that targeted entire categories of people—rather than just potentially threatening individuals—according to lists prepared by the NKVD. These included former employees of the pre-Soviet Baltic governments, individuals who had been expelled from the communist parties, members of noncommunist parties active during the independence era, former police and prison officials, former large landowners and business owners, heads and active members of labor unions, and former officers in the armed forces.[3] Beginning on the night of June 13–14 and lasting for only a few days, the operation involved the deportation of about 20,000 Latvians, 10,000 Estonians, and 18,000 Lithuanians.[4] Packed into boxcars for a journey of several weeks to northern Russia or Siberia, many died along the way.

OSTLAND

On June 22, 1941, only a week after the Soviets deported much of the Baltic cultural, intellectual, and political elite, Hitler broke the nonaggression pact with Stalin and launched Operation Barbarossa. Despite having stationed hundreds of thousands of soldiers in the recently annexed border areas, the Soviet army, still reeling from the destruction of much of its top brass during the purges of the mid-1930s, was unprepared for this war. German troops quickly advanced through the USSR's western borderlands, reaching Rīga on July 1 and Estonia on July 5. Many Baltic peoples—like western Ukrainians and other inhabitants of the USSR's recently acquired border territories—were at first overjoyed by the invasion, believing that the Germans had arrived as "liberators" from Soviet oppression. Indeed, as one historian has written of the Estonians: "In one year of rule the Soviet authorities had managed to reverse fully a national attitude which had taken several centuries to emerge, from anti-Germanism to anti-Russianism."[5]

By the time the German army (*Wehrmacht*) arrived in the Baltic republics, native groups had already organized, hoping to restore the independence of their countries. In Lithuania, the revolt against Soviet authorities began on June 23, as insurrectionist forces took over police stations and several arsenals in Kaunas. Revolts also broke out in Estonia and Latvia. Everywhere the insurrectionary groups fought the Red Army with the hope that the Germans would recognize the independence of their countries. However, as the officials of the shattered Soviet regimes fled to the Russian hinterland and German forces occupied the Baltic republics, it became clear that the Nazis had their own plans for the region.

German occupation policy was generally muddled, as it was fraught with jurisdictional rivalries and a neglect of political planning. In its bare essentials, however, the goal was to eradicate the Soviet regime and create "living space" (*Lebensraum*) for Germans in the European parts of the USSR. Unlike Ukraine or Russia proper, which were to be merely sources of food and slave labor, the Baltics were awarded a privileged position in the Reich's plans. Joined together with the Belarussian region, they formed a civil administrative unit called *Reichskommissariat Ostland* (RKO) under the rule of Hinrich Lohse in Rīga. Hitler's Minister for the Occupied Eastern Territories was Alfred Rosenberg, a Baltic German and Nazi ideologist. According to Rosenberg's plans, ultimately the Baltic region would be annexed to the German Reich. For the moment, however, the Germans set up native administrations that allowed the Lithuanians, Latvians, and

Estonians a degree of administrative autonomy denied to the other occupied peoples of the Soviet Union.[6]

Since nationalities were to be treated according to racial criteria, the Baltic peoples were spared the genocidal policies directed at Jews, Slavs, and other *Untermenschen* (subhumans). According to Nazi racial theory, ranked at the apex of the Baltic racial hierarchy were the Estonians, whom Rosenberg regarded as largely Germanized. Some Latvians and Lithuanians could be assimilated, but the rest would have to transferred to the Russian hinterland or destroyed. The resulting vacuum would be filled by colonizing Germans, thousands of whom were in fact brought from the Reich to settle on some of the expropriated farms. Reich colonists were joined by thousands of the Baltic Germans who had departed from Estonia and Latvia at the end of 1939.

Of course, at the top of the Nazis' racial agenda in the occupied territories was the elimination of the Jewish population, which was significant in the larger Baltic cities and especially in Vilnius and the Lithuanian cities. This task fell to the *Einsatzgruppen*—the mobile killing units that followed the advancing German army into Soviet territory. However, it should be noted that with the negative image of the "Jewish Communist" reinforced during the year of Soviet occupation (despite the fact that thousands of Jews were among those arrested and deported by the NKVD), *Einsatzgruppe A* received some help from local police battalions and zealous individuals. By January 1942, most of Latvia's 80,000–85,000 Jews had been killed, while another 10,000–15,000 had fled to Soviet Russia. Many of Estonia's approximately 4,500 Jews had been deported by the Soviets or chose to evacuate to Soviet Russia at the start of the German invasion; nearly all the remainder were executed. The horrors were the worst in Lithuania, where about 180,000 Jews—some 80 percent of the Jewish population at the time of the German invasion—were killed by the end of 1941.

In Lithuania and Latvia, the remaining Jews were crowded into sealed ghettos, where they were generally allowed to run their own internal affairs. Many Jews were forced to contribute to the German war effort as slave laborers. Over time, these ghettos were liquidated and their residents executed or transferred to extermination camps in other occupied territories. Although non-Jews, primarily communists who had not fled to the Soviet hinterland, were also killed during the occupation, their eradication was not as systematic as that of the Jews.

This was certainly not the fate that the Balts expected. Indeed, many had greeted the German invaders as liberators from Soviet rule and expected an imminent return to normalcy. However, the occupation authorities failed to live up to this exaggerated hope. While Jews were targeted for extermination, the economic centralization and strict labor policies instituted by the Soviets remained in place: confiscated commercial and industrial enterprises remained nationalized, Baltic workers remained tied to their workplace (and were denied the right to strike), and efforts by former landowners to reacquire their confiscated lands met with little success. In addition, food rations were introduced that favored German administrators over local inhabitants—tens of thousands of whom were deported to the Reich to labor in German industries. As a result of these policies, living standards in the Baltic region continued to decline, and the German authorities quickly squandered the natives' initial goodwill.

While Baltic industries were expected to contribute to the Reich's war needs, Baltic men were needed for the struggle then being waged against Soviet Russia, especially as the invasion's momentum slowed during the second half of 1942. At first, non-German nationalities were recruited on a voluntary basis: an Estonian Waffen-SS unit, called the Estonian Legion, was created in August 1942, but by mid-October could claim only 500 recruits. Turning to forced mobilization when the war began to go badly, the Germans conscripted several thousand Estonian men and sent them to the eastern front in 1943, but perhaps another 5,000 were able to avoid being drafted by fleeing to Finland. Nevertheless, when the Red Army threatened once again to cross the Estonian border in February 1944, Hjalmar Mäe (1901–78), the head of the Estonian civilian administration (and a former propagandist for the protofascist League of Independence War Veterans), was able to conscript 38,000 men to fight a "new war of independence." They were added to the 20,000 Estonians already serving in the German army. German mobilization efforts met with similar success in Latvia and Lithuania: 30,000 Lithuanians volunteered to fight the Soviets (but unlike Latvians and Estonians, Lithuanians did not join the Nazi SS-Legions) and as many as 150,000 Latvians were also mobilized.[7]

While these numbers are certainly significant, they nevertheless suggest that hundreds of thousands of youths were able to resist recruitment—just one of many forms of resistance that the unexpected harshness of Nazi occupation policies inspired in the Baltic region. However, with the pre-1940 elite largely deported or executed, the small underground resistance movements that formed were generally ineffective.

Despite the apparent hopelessness of the situation, as the German war effort began to collapse, some Baltic patriots began preparing for the eventual reinstatement of their countries' independence. Expecting that the western Allies would come to their aid as they had following the First World War, in late 1943 the various Lithuanian resistance forces united to form the Supreme Committee for the Liberation of Lithuania, which managed to publish underground periodicals and organize small military forces. Meanwhile, Latvian resisters formed the Latvian Central Council in August 1943, but its leadership was arrested and deported to Germany in the autumn of 1944. Likewise, the National Committee of the Estonian Republic led a furtive existence in the spring of 1944, but many of its leaders were quickly arrested. Some of those who escaped arrest by German security forces managed to form a provisional Estonian government in September, but by the end of the month they too were arrested—this time by the Soviets.

SOVIETIZATION AND RESISTANCE

The Soviet advance to the west in early 1944 met with fierce resistance by Baltic soldiers, who managed to delay the occupation of their countries until the summer and autumn. By the end of September, however, nearly all of Estonia, Latvia, and Lithuania were overrun by the Red Army. Of course, this feat could not have been achieved so quickly without the efforts of sympathetic natives: just as the Germans were able to recruit locals to fight the Red Army, the Soviet Union also formed national forces, often by compulsory mobilization, between 1941 and 1944. By the end of the war 30,000 Estonians, 50,000 Latvians, and 82,000 Lithuanians belonged to the Red Army.[8]

Having endured a year of Sovietization in 1940–41, most Balts knew just what to expect from a second occupation. Between the summer of 1944 and early 1945 at least a quarter-million people chose to flee westwards rather than live under a restored Soviet regime. These refugees, which included many of the region's intellectuals, property owners, and cultural and religious leaders, were able to escape the mass executions and deportations—ostensibly for having collaborated with the Germans—that followed the Soviet reoccupation of the Baltic region. While many fled, tens of thousands of fighting-age men retreated to the forests, where they continued to resist Soviet authority for nearly another decade.

In addition to the population dislocations that accompanied Soviet reoccupation, the reincorporated Soviet Socialist Republics (SSRs) were forced to accede to generally unfavorable border changes. However, the transfers of territory that took place in the Baltic republics must be seen in the context of the new borders being drawn throughout northeastern Europe. Germany was forced to cede a large portion of East Prussia, now renamed the Kaliningrad *oblast'*, to Soviet Russia. Poland was shifted westward: while absorbing a large amount of eastern German territory, Poland lost its own eastern regions to the Ukrainian, Belarussian, and Lithuanian SSRs.

In comparison to the overhaul which Germany and Poland received, the outlines of the Estonian and Latvian republics were not drastically altered by Stalin's blue pencil. Estonia ceded to the Russian republic (RSFSR) eastern territories located both north and south of Lake Peipsi, including most of the Petserimaa district and all the territory east of the Narva River. These areas constituted about 5 percent of the prewar territory of the Republic of Estonia and were home to about 70,000 residents, mostly ethnic Russians. Latvia was forced to cede to the RSFSR the Abrene region, a thin sliver of territory in the northeast.

Among the Baltic republics, Lithuania experienced the most significant territorial adjustments, as it was enlarged by the incorporation of the Klaipėda and Vilnius territories. Related to these changes was the ethnic homogenization of the country that occurred between 1940 and 1945. Owing to the nearly complete destruction of Lithuania's once-large Jewish community, the repatriation of 52,000 Germans in 1940–41, and the removal of more than 200,000 Poles (as they described themselves) to the new Poland following Soviet reoccupation, the postwar Lithuanian SSR was both territorially larger and, despite (or because of) the catastrophic population losses, considerably more ethnically homogenous than the prewar state.

As a result of the scorched-earth policies of both the Soviets (during the 1941 retreat) and the Germans (throughout 1944), damage to Baltic buildings, industry, and infrastructure was extensive. Estonian cities suffered especially acute devastation: nearly all of Narva's buildings and almost half those of Tartu and Tallinn were destroyed. Moreover, entire ethnic communities were uprooted or destroyed, including the Baltic German and Jewish communities, depriving the Baltic region of much of its ethnic and cultural diversity as well as many of its most educated and socially active individuals. Total human losses are difficult to estimate, but it is likely that the Baltic countries lost about 20 percent of their population during World War II, due to a combination of flight to the West, losses of territory, deportations, and deaths caused by war and occupation.

Since all three Baltic states suffered devastating human losses, the Soviet authorities now faced the challenge of recruiting personnel for the management of the Baltic governments and economies. Most pressing was the matter of the communist parties, which were to resume their leading role in the re-Sovietized republics despite the thinness of their ranks. With most of their leaders wiped out during the war, in late 1944 there were only a few thousand communists in each of the Baltic republics. Once again the importation of cadres from the other Union republics provided a convenient solution.

As a result of this process the ranks of the Baltic communist parties (CPs) swelled with non-natives, mostly Russians. The Lithuanian Communist Party (LiCP) best reflected the results of this policy: only 18.4 percent of its members in 1947 were Lithuanian, rising to 38 percent by 1953. The other republics fared somewhat better: the proportion of ethnic Estonians in the ECP was 48.1 percent in 1946 and following a purge declined to 41.5 percent in 1952; although ethnic Latvians could claim a majority of 53 percent in the Latvian Communist Party (LaCP) in 1949, this number fell dramatically after a decade.[9] Despite the underrepresentation of natives in the early years of Soviet rule, over the following decades the composition of the Baltic communist parties came to reflect more closely the ethnic composition of the republics. In the early years, however, the parties were dominated by Russians and other communists who had spent the interwar period in Soviet Russia. Indeed, while first secretaries were usually Russian-trained natives, throughout the Soviet era the second secretaries in the republics were always Russians.

Since Stalin was unconvinced of the reliability of cadres in the Baltic SSRs—and was even more suspicious of communist authorities in the satellite states of Eastern Europe—the threat of a purge was ever present. The most drastic case among the Baltic parties was the Estonian Communist Party (ECP), from which "bourgeois nationalists" were purged in 1950–51. They were replaced by Estonians—called "Yestonians," a play on the Russian pronunciation of Estonia—whose families had emigrated from Estonia to Russia in the decades before 1920. The Yestonians had made their party careers in the USSR before the war, but with the Soviet absorption of Estonia they saw opportunities for advancement in their old homeland. Most notably, during the purge Nikolai Karotamm (1901–69), ECP first secretary since 1944 (and acting first secretary since 1941), was replaced by Johannes Käbin (1905–99), an Estonian who had been born in his homeland but had risen through the party bureaucracy in Soviet Russia, only to return during the first Soviet occupation.

In Latvia and Lithuania, where homegrown leaders were an even smaller minority than in Estonia, the makeup of the Communist Party leadership showed signs of greater stability. From 1940 to 1959 the first secretary of the LaCP was Jānis Kalnbērziņš, who like Käbin had resided in the USSR before 1940. Even more steady was the LiCP leadership, whose First Secretary Antanas Sniečkus (1903–74) retained his post from the 1930s until his death in January 1974. Such leaders, most notably Sniečkus, have sometimes been credited with defending the interests of their republics, mitigating the harshest aspects of Soviet rule principally by protecting the native cultures from extinction. However, it should be remembered that these very same leaders were also partly responsible for the repressions and deportations of the 1940s, while executing Moscow's policies of collectivization, industrialization, and Russian colonization.

While the Baltic republics were being assimilated into the USSR in the years after World War II, the war against Soviet reoccupation continued to smolder in the forests. It will be recalled how the Baltic states were too weak and disunited to resist the first Soviet occupation in 1940–41. However, three more years of Nazi occupation provided the Balts with time and resources to develop a large-scale resistance to another round of Sovietization. Many resisters had fought in the Waffen-SS legions that were organized as German luck began to run out in 1943. At their peak in 1944–46, anti-Soviet partisans—called "forest brothers"—dominated the Baltic countryside. Although it is difficult to say with any certainty how many guerillas were active at any one time, it is estimated that as many as 30,000 Lithuanians, and smaller numbers of Latvians and Estonians, took up arms against the Soviet authorities.[10] Emerging from their forest hideouts they shot at Soviet uniformed personnel and party cadres while inflicting substantial damage on buildings, especially in rural areas. Encouraging the local populations to resist Soviet rule, the forest brothers also published and disseminated underground literature—and executed hundreds of suspected collaborators.

Despite being vastly outnumbered, undersupplied, and isolated, some partisan bands rejected repeated Soviet offers of amnesty and held out in the forests until as late as 1955, by which time they certainly could not have expected to drive the Soviets out. Many were motivated by the hope that the western Allies would help them restore Estonian, Latvian, and Lithuanian statehood, perhaps following an anticipated Western-Soviet war. Nevertheless, by 1948 the main formations, strongest in Lithuania, were broken. By this time the guerillas had been deprived of recruits and food supplies due to the mass deportations that accompanied the collectivization of the Baltic countryside.

COLLECTIVIZATION, INDUSTRIALIZATION, AND RUSSIFICATION

Although Baltic farmers were spared large-scale collectivization during the first Soviet occupation in 1940–41, the second occupation saw a vigorous application of the devastating agricultural policies that had first been imposed on Soviet farmers in the early 1930s. Since the emphasis in the Baltic republics—Estonia and Latvia in particular—was on rapid industrialization, planners in Moscow accorded a low priority to Baltic agriculture. However, once the situation in the Baltic region stabilized, collectivization would serve several purposes: in principle, the collective farms (*kolkhozy*), supplied with tractors and other equipment normally beyond the reach of ordinary family farmers, would provide Baltic agriculture with economies of scale that would permit the transfer of excess rural labor to the new industrial concerns. However, the political benefits of this policy may have been even more important, as collectivization was also a means of ending partisan resistance in the Baltic countryside.

After a delay of several years, Soviet land reform in the Baltic territories picked up where it had left off in 1940–41. During the 1944–47 period, the Soviets continued to eliminate farms larger than 30 hectares, while expropriating the land, livestock, and property of the *kulaky*—the so-called "rich" farmers. It also nationalized farms formerly belonging to German colonists and native landowners who had fled to the West. Only in 1947 were the first postwar collective farms set up in the Baltic region; by the end of 1948 there were more than 500 *kolkhozy* in both Latvia and Lithuania, but less than half that in Estonia, where collectivization was slowest.

Despite Soviet attempts to encourage the growth of collective farms, most agricultural land remained in the hands of family farmers. Since voluntary collectivization was not working to the desired effect, the regime took more drastic measures, principally raising tax rates on farms to a level where it became impossible for them to continue functioning. This left many peasants little choice but to join the *kolkhozy*. Meanwhile, the *kulaky*—a word that surely carried more political than socioeconomic meaning—were liquidated as a class. Many were sent to Siberian exile, which often meant certain death. In late March 1949, at the height of the collectivization drive, nearly 100,000 rural Estonians, Latvians, and Lithuanians—more than half of them women and children—were deported and dispersed to various locations throughout the USSR.[11]

Collectivization was nearly complete by 1952, and along with this achievement the Soviet regime could rejoice in having nearly completely eliminated the guerilla resistance movements in the Baltic countryside. Meanwhile, as a result of the Soviets' success in abolishing privately held farms, there was by every conceivable measure a catastrophic drop in agricultural production in each Baltic republic between 1948–55—although Baltic farmers did not resort to the large-scale slaughter of livestock as Ukrainian farmers did in the early 1930s. Only in the second half of the 1950s did Baltic agriculture begin to recover.

Because of the region's skilled labor reserve and existing industrial infrastructure, the focus of Soviet economic policy in the Baltic region—and in Latvia and Estonia in particular—was on industrial development. Lithuania was also a target for heavy industry, but since its industrial base was still considerably weaker than that of its northern neighbors, it received less capital investment than did Latvian and Estonian industry. On the whole, however, industry in each of the Baltic republics was developed at a much faster rate than in the rest of the Soviet Union. The objective was to integrate the Baltic republics into the centralized Soviet economic system; they would then serve as a source of energy and a range of industrial and agricultural products for export to the rest of the USSR. First, of course, existing industry had to recover from the destruction it had suffered during the war. This was mostly completed by 1950, partly aided, especially in Estonia, by the use of German prisoners of war as laborers and by the importation of industrial plants dismantled by the Soviets in their occupation zone in eastern Germany.

Latvian industry was concentrated in Rīga, focusing on the production of steel and agricultural machinery, electric motors, and diesel engines. In Estonia, Soviet planners emphasized the expansion of one of interwar Estonia's most successful enterprises—the oil shale industry. Immediately placed under the direct control of the All-Union Ministry of the Coal Industry, Estonian oil shale was to serve as a fuel source for the northwestern region of the USSR. With the construction in 1948 of a pipeline linking the oil shale region of Estonia to Leningrad, Estonia's most important natural resource began flowing to the RSFSR.

For Lithuania, Soviet economic policy during the first postwar decade focused on light industry and food-processing. Intensive industrialization focusing on heavy industry did not take place until after Stalin's death in 1953, thanks in part to the efforts of LiCP First Secretary Antanas Sniečkus. Although a career communist bureaucrat who was intensely loyal to party authorities in Moscow, he is often credited with sparing his republic from some of the negative effects of intensive industrial development and from the kind of massive Russian immigration endured by Estonia and Latvia.

The migration of Russians to the Baltic republics was partly due to the labor requirements of the industrialization drive; however, there was undoubtedly a political motive as well, for the presence of a large Russian-speaking community would reinforce Soviet political control over the Baltic republics. In fact, precisely as large numbers of Estonians, Latvians, and Lithuanians were being deported eastward into the Soviet hinterland during the collectivization drive, thousands of Soviet citizens were moving westward into the Baltic republics to work in the revitalized and expanded Baltic industries. These immigrants included significant numbers of Estonian-Russians and Latvian-Russians who had spent the interwar period in Soviet Russia; however, the lion's share of immigrants were Slavs from the Ukrainian and Belarussian SSRs, and most of all from the Russian republic.

Although the peak influx came during the immediate postwar years, immigration continued for the next several decades, but less intensively than in 1945–47. As the Latvian SSR received more than 500,000 immigrants in 1945–59 (overwhelmingly Russians), the Latvians' share of the republic's population declined from about 84 percent in 1945 to 60 percent in 1953, and declined even further in subsequent decades. Perhaps 4 million people all together passed through Latvia during the Soviet period. However, sheer numbers can be misleading, for in Latvia migration tended to be rotational, with constant migratory movements taking place between the Latvian SSR and the other Slavic republics. Moreover, after Stalin's death in 1953 the Slavic immigrants to the Baltic republics were joined by the tens of thousands of Estonians, Latvians, and Lithuanians who had managed to survive the earlier deportations and were now released from the prison camps of the Soviet east.

Estonia, whose population has historically been about half that of Latvia, received approximately 180,000 immigrants in 1945–47, followed by another wave of more than 30,000 in 1950–53. Among the pioneers of colonization in Estonia were significant numbers of ex-convicts from Russia, most of whom settled in northeastern Estonia and urban centers such as Narva. As a result of this massive immigration, Estonians were pushed out of the country's resource-rich border regions. As in Latvia, the natives' share of Estonia's population dropped dramatically during the decades of Soviet occupation, from about 94 percent in early 1945 (after Estonia ceded regions largely inhabited by Russians to the RSFSR) to 72 percent in 1953, and finally to 61.5 percent in 1989.[12]

As noted above, Russian immigration occurred on a smaller but still significant scale in Lithuania. In 1939 Russians accounted for 2.3 percent of the Lithuanian population, but by 1989 this number had risen to 9.4 percent. As elsewhere, since many of these immigrants were government and party officials, industrial managers, engineers, and professionals, they were accorded priority in the awarding of scarce urban housing, thus contributing to the natives' resentment of the Russian-speaking arrivals and the belief that the Russians were colonizing their homelands.

Rapid urbanization accompanied industrialization and large-scale immigration in the Baltic republics. Estonia and Latvia were among the most urbanized of the Soviet republics from the outset, but the pace of urbanization picked up rapidly after 1945. According to Soviet estimates, from

January 1, 1940, to January 1, 1953, the proportion of the Estonian population residing in urban areas rose from 33.6 percent to 52.5 percent; from
1944 to 1955 the population of the republic's largest city, Tallinn, nearly
doubled. Likewise, the percentage of Latvians living in cities and towns
rose from just over 35 in 1939 to 52 in 1950. In Lithuania the process of
urbanization was slower; it was not until 1970 that its urban population
outnumbered its rural population, by which time Estonia had become the
most urbanized of the Soviet republics, with 65 percent of it population
living in cities. In each of the republics, much of the urban population
consisted of Russian-speaking immigrants, who came to dominate Rīga
and other Baltic cities.[13]

Of course, industrialization, Russification, and urbanization were closely
related processes: the industrialization and Russification of the Baltic republics was planned to serve Moscow's desired economic and political
ends; urbanization was the unavoidable social outcome of these changes.
Also, by creating a surplus of rural labor, the collectivization of agriculture
further contributed to the urbanization of the region. Despite the extended
period of recovery from the negative effects of collectivization, by 1953
the Baltic republics had each become nearly fully integrated into the political and economic structures of the Soviet Union. With no hope for the
restoration of their independence, for the next three decades the Baltic
peoples had little choice but to accommodate themselves to the realities
of Soviet life while attempting to maintain their ethnic identities and cultural traditions.

THE BALTIC COMMUNIST PARTIES

As instruments of control and repression, and as avenues for upward
social mobility, the communist parties were the focal point of political and
economic life in the Baltic republics throughout the Soviet era. The party
imposed service obligations and ideological conformity on its members,
but it also rewarded them with status and career opportunities. While an
individual could usually choose whether or not to join the party, he or
she could not hope to avoid its influence over the most personal aspects
of daily life, ranging from access to higher education, housing, and consumer goods, to matters of ideology, religious belief, and individual
conscience. Led by Marxist-Leninists eager to please Moscow, the local
communist parties were both the Balts' jailers and mediators between
them and the larger CPSU.

Despite the iron grip of the Communist Party, after the passing of Stalin
in 1953 life in the Baltic republics, as in the Soviet Union as a whole,

became somewhat more relaxed. Following a bitter power struggle with his Politburo rivals, by 1956 Nikita Khrushchev (1894–1971) emerged as the new master of the Kremlin. The Khrushchev era was known as the "thaw" (*ottepel'*)—a period of de-Stalinization of intellectual life and de-centralization of the Soviet economy. While the regime's use of terror as an instrument of social control diminished substantially, Khrushchev's distrust of local nationalism meant that political power remained concentrated in Moscow. Despite the preponderance of power enjoyed by the CPSU, the thaw afforded the leaders of the Baltic CPs an opportunity to try to block those policies—namely breakneck industrialization and Russification—that they believed to be harmful to their republics.

In Latvia, intraparty discussions between those pursuing greater republican autonomy and the more orthodox Moscow-oriented officials began in the late 1950s. The autonomists were led by Eduards Berklāvs (b.1914), a secretary of the Rīga party organization (*gorkom*) and deputy chairman of the Latvian Council of Ministers from 1956 to 1958. Kremlin orthodoxy was represented by Arvīds Pelše (1899–1983), a Latvian who had left the country in 1918, matured in the USSR, and then during the Soviet occupation returned to Latvia, where he became responsible for propaganda. While Berklāvs and his supporters passed regulations that restricted in-migration (aimed at Russian-speaking immigrants) and planned to limit the growth of industry that would require labor from outside Latvia, Pelše often spoke of the historic ties enjoyed by Russians and Latvians and criticized such manifestations of local nationalism. The struggle ended after Khrushchev's visit to Rīga in June 1959, following which Pelše was appointed first secretary of the LaCP, replacing Jānis Kalnbērziņš.

Soon afterwards *Pravda* (*Truth*), the official mouthpiece of Soviet policy, accused the Central Committee of the LaCP of promoting local interests over those of the USSR as a whole, thus foreshadowing a massive purge of the party. Over the next two years thousands of members were expelled for being sympathetic to "national communism." (But in this case, unlike in Stalin's purges, such as that in Estonia in 1949–51, the victims were not murdered.) With Berklāvs exiled to Russia, henceforth the LaCP was the most uncompromisingly orthodox of the Baltic party organizations.[14]

As the struggle in the LaCP intensified, the trend toward gradual nativization stalled, and Russians and Russian Latvians continued to dominate the party leadership. By the early 1960s, the proportion of Latvians in the LaCP stabilized at around 35 percent (and never exceeded 40 percent); yet it should be noted that many Latvians—like many Estonians and Lithuanians—residing outside their republic were members of the CPSU.

The nativization of the Estonian and Lithuanian CPs proceeded with greater ease. By 1963 the percentage of ethnic Estonians in the ECP exceeded 50 percent for the first time; and by 1965 the proportion of Lithuanians in the LiCP was up to 61.5 percent (and natives were disproportionately represented in the party's leading bodies, the Politburo and the Secretariat), up from 38 percent in 1953.[15] With the influence of non-native cadres diminishing during the 1960s, the Estonian and Lithuanian parties were left largely in the hands of individuals who had authentic roots in the republics.

In addition to being nativized, the ranks of the Baltic CPs continued to swell, suggesting that by this time many Balts had come to accept not only the permanence of Soviet rule, but also the legitimacy of the Communist Party as a means for achieving career goals. Indeed, with nowhere else to turn for help, Balts were increasingly opting to work within the system rather than against it.

The relative stability of the Estonian and Lithuanian parties in the post-Stalin decades is perhaps best demonstrated by the continuity of their top party leaders: Johannes (Ivan) Käbin remained in charge of the ECP for nearly three decades (1950–78); his successor, Karl Vaino (b.1923), a Russian-born Estonian, headed the party from 1978–88—despite the fact that he never was able to master his ancestral language. Lithuania's Antanas Sniečkus enjoyed an exceptionally long tenure (1936–74), as he loyally served Stalin, Khrushchev, and finally Leonid Brezhnev (1906–82). After Sniečkus's death the top post went to Petras Griškevičius (1924–87), who retained it until his own demise in 1987. In Latvia the party leadership stabilized once the purges ended in 1961. In 1966, following Pelše's promotion to Moscow to head the Party Control Committee (he was also made a full Politburo member), Augusts Voss (b.1916) took the post of first secretary, in which capacity he continued his predecessor's Russophile policy until 1984.

Although Käbin and Sniečkus were unswervingly loyal to Moscow, each exemplified that brand of Soviet republican leader, especially common during the Brezhnev era, who was able to negotiate the treacherous waters of Kremlin politics while providing at least some protection to the residents of their respective republics. Of course, no top leader of any Soviet Communist Party regarded himself as a mouthpiece of his people. Indeed, Sniečkus was no Lithuanian nationalist, and Käbin was far from an Estonian patriot. Nevertheless, each had made peace with the local cultural establishment and each tolerated some nonthreatening manifestations of local national feeling.

CULTURE AND RELIGION

Restrictions on art in the Baltic republics were put in place during the first Soviet occupation in 1940–41. The ideological controls on art are best described by a document received by the Latvian SSR's Administration of Art Affairs in January 1941, which lists 120 themes to which Soviet artists were expected to pay particular attention, including:

> "Theme No. 27: The 1905 Revolution in Russia. A rally. The orator is held high on the workers' hands. Red flags."

> "Theme No. 120: The RK(b)P CC Politburo inspects a large new construction."[16]

No doubt similar directives were again issued after the war.

World War II and Soviet reoccupation devastated Baltic cultural life, as many of the most talented Baltic writers, intellectuals, and other cultural figures of the independence era fled to the West rather than face persecution at the hands of Soviet authorities. Those who remained behind risked accusations of (and punishment for) sins such as "deviationism," "formalism," and "bourgeois nationalism."

The darkest era for national cultures in the region was in 1948–53—Stalin's last years. During this period, strict ideological controls made it impossible to publish anything falling outside the parameters of "socialist realism." Moreover, only politically reliable authors could hope to see their works in print, since in order to publish one usually had to be a party member and a member of the republic branch of the guardian of literary orthodoxy, the Union of Writers. Likewise, artists and musicians also found their creative lives regulated by the Union of Artists and the Union of Composers. On the other hand, Soviet artists were given a guaranteed material existence. Thus, although the occupation was unpleasant for Baltic artists, writers, and composers, as it was for society as a whole, the system provided security for those who went along. And, as Latvian curator and art critic Hēlena Demakova reminds her readers, "those that did go along formed the majority."[17]

For at least a decade after the war, émigré writers were more productive than those who remained in their home countries. Few literary works of high quality were published in the Baltic republics—or elsewhere in the USSR—until the thaw that followed Stalin's death. However, by the late 1950s, with the return, in many cases from Siberia, of many of the writers who had been expelled from the Estonian, Latvian, and Lithuanian writers' unions in the 1940s, Baltic writers began to publish in greater quantity and quality. Perhaps more significantly, Balts were allowed to recover some of their literary past, as thousands of publications from the pre-1940 period, previously banned, were allowed back into print.

Once liberated from the strictest Stalinist ideological controls, Baltic artistic and literary life began a recovery that peaked during the 1960s, only to experience a chill during the conservative 1970s. A significant turning point in the recovery of Baltic literary life was the thaw-era publication of Rudolf Sirge's (1904–70) *The Land and the People* (1956), which described the 1941 deportations. Shortly afterwards, in 1958, Jaan Kross (b.1920) debuted with a poetry collection, *The Coal Concentrator,* which established his reputation as one of Estonia's foremost literary talents. Later, in the 1970s, he turned to writing novels that explored the lives of important Estonian historical figures. Music began its recovery during the 1950s with the revival of Estonia's ancient folksong tradition, while in the 1960s the experimental composer Arvo Pärt (b.1935) began a career that led to worldwide fame.

In Lithuania, as in Estonia, poets led the way during the thaw. Among the best-known was Justinas Marcinkevičius (b.1930), a party member who first attempted to break away from Stalinist rigidity in his 1956 collection *Twentieth Spring.* In the 1960s he turned to writing plays about Lithuanian national history. Among the most significant of these was *Mindaugas* (1968), which examined the life of the founder of the medieval Lithuanian state. By this time Mykolas Sluckis (b.1928) had gained recognition for writing stories that combined socialist realism with experimental forms such as stream-of-consciousness narration. Although Sluckis's work generally focused on the Lithuanian intelligentsia, his 1963 novel *Steps to the Sky* was noteworthy for its tragic portrayal of Lithuanian rural life. A few Lithuanian authors, including Jonas Mikelinskas and Romualdas Lankauska, went beyond socialist realism, but their prose was often coldly received by Soviet critics.

In Latvia, the works of earlier writers such as Fricis Bārda (1880–1919) and the poet Aspāzija (1868–1943) were published in 1956, while some contemporary writers such as Ojārs Vācietis (1933–83) and Visvaldis Eglons-Lāms (b.1923) took advantage of the relatively liberal climate by publishing works that were somewhat critical of the Soviet experience. Following the party purge, Latvian cultural life stagnated for nearly another decade, and the classics by Bārda and Aspāzija were once again banned, only to be republished in 1968 as Latvian intellectual life began to recover. By this time, Alberts Bels (b.1938) had established his reputation as an important writer with the publication of *The Investigator* (1967), a short novel that explored the Latvian national experience during the Stalin era.

Like Baltic literature, the Baltic folksong tradition enjoyed a recovery during the late 1950s and especially the 1960s. A Latvian folksong festival held in Daugavpils in July 1959 involved 5,000 singers and attracted an audience of 70,000. Even larger festivals were held in Estonian cities in 1965 and 1969. These were opportunities for Balts to express national pride in ways acceptable, and sometimes unacceptable, to Moscow. For example, at the 1965 festival in Estonia, an audience of 120,000 demanded a repeat performance of the song "My Homeland is My Love," an unofficial anthem of the Estonian people.

While the post-Stalin years allowed for the recovery, within limits, of intellectual and cultural life, in the religious sphere a brief relaxation of Soviet policy was followed by further repression. In 1954–56, the return home of 130 deported priests (perhaps one-third of the total) contributed to a recovery of religious life, but in 1957 an antireligious campaign that was conducted throughout the USSR resulted in the closing of numerous churches. Only after Khrushchev's ouster in 1964 did the antireligious campaign begin to relax. Although the impact of the Soviet antireligious measures on personal belief is difficult to measure, it was evident that external manifestations of religiosity, such as participation in church ceremonies, declined during the 1960s. This was especially true of Estonians and Latvians, who endured a deficit of functioning churches, Protestant pastors, and bibles. Lithuanians, whose national identity was closely tied to Catholicism, were better able to train young men for the priesthood and perpetuate their religious traditions.

Of course, for the "new Soviet man," religion was an outdated superstition—a relic of the past to be discarded. An individual's Soviet identity—as an effective worker and a defender of communism—was to supersede his religious and national identity. One instrument commonly used for the creation of a Soviet identity was sport. When the Soviet Union participated in international athletic competitions, such as the Olympics beginning in 1956, athletes competed as members of Soviet national teams; thus individual successes by Baltic athletes were seen as successes for the Soviet system. Although the Estonian, Latvian, and Lithuanian republics could not field their own teams for the Olympics or most other international competitions, republic teams did sometimes compete against the national teams of Soviet bloc countries such as Czechoslovakia or East Germany.

SOCIOECONOMIC DEVELOPMENTS

In material terms, life in Estonia, Latvia, and Lithuania in the 1960s and 1970s was better than in the rest of the USSR. Already Latvia and Estonia were the USSR's most industrialized and urbanized republics, and during the 1960s Lithuania was beginning to catch up. Farming had generally recovered by the end of the 1950s and in the Baltics had become relatively efficient by Soviet standards. In most respects, during the post-Stalin era the Baltic republics enjoyed a superior standard of living, with relatively high incomes and better access to consumer goods than was the case elsewhere in the USSR. For Russians and other Soviet peoples, the Baltic republics offered attractive opportunities in industry and education, and hundreds of thousands relocated to the Soviet West.

A main consequence of this immigration, cultural Russification, was further facilitated by the adoption of a new educational system in 1959.[18] Henceforward, the Russian language became a "voluntary" subject in Baltic schools where it was not already the language of instruction. In practice this meant that Balts were pressured to become bilingual—practically unavoidable for those who aspired to higher study or professional careers—while immigrants could continue to speak Russian only. The results of this policy were reflected in the Soviet census of 1970, which showed that while only 18 percent of ethnic Russians living in Latvia—the most heavily Russified of the Baltic republics—could speak the native tongue, nearly half of all Latvians could speak Russian.

An important arena for the intended *sblizhenie* ("drawing together") of the nationalities was the Soviet system of higher education. Students from each of the 15 Union republics were enrolled in more than 500 Soviet universities, academies, and institutes, and thousands of students from other Union republics attended higher schools in Estonia, Latvia, and Lithuania. Likewise, the number of Baltic students studying outside their republics, usually in the RSFSR, was comparable to the number of Balts enrolled in native institutions. In 1974–75, the Estonian SSR had 6 institutions of higher education, while Latvia and Lithuania had 10 and 12, respectively. As was the case throughout the USSR, most institutions of higher education were specialized institutes or academies rather than universities. In addition, each republic had its own Academy of Sciences, which served as the republics' main research centers.

Immigrants (primarily Russians) and natives often chose different educational and career paths. While immigrants tended to concentrate in technological fields such as engineering, Balts were more likely to choose the educational, cultural, and artistic fields, in addition to the study of agriculture and economics. This is indicative of a more general bifurcation of the lives of natives and immigrants in the Baltic republics. As one Russian journalist observed in 1988: "The population was divided along linguistic lines. The Estonians had their own kindergartens, schools, enterprises, and regions. The Russians had theirs." Indeed, in Latvia and Estonia, where the concentration of Russians was higher than in Lithuania, society was split between natives and immigrants, each with its own language, institutions, educational preferences, industrial specialization, and geographical concentration.[19] While the Baltic elites controlled only the weaker and smaller economic sectors, Russians and other Slavic immigrants built, managed, and staffed much of the more powerful all-Union sector of the economy, which benefited from its closer ties with Soviet authorities in Moscow.

During the post-Stalin era, the Baltic republics retained their position as the most modernized and industrialized of the Soviet republics, and were thoroughly enmeshed in an extremely centralized economic network. At the end of the 1950s, however, the establishment of regional economic councils (*sovnarkhozy*) heralded a shift towards economic decentralization. The new policy meant that planners in each republic would enjoy greater autonomy and less interference from Moscow. The consequences of this reform were greatest in Lithuania, where an emphasis on industrial development was only just beginning. Unlike the case in Estonia and Latvia, where breakneck industrialization was coordinated by Moscow for the benefit of the other Union republics, in Lithuania local authorities could plan industrial projects in a way that was consistent with the republic's resource profile. Nevertheless, by 1962 the pendulum swung back to centralized economic planning and within a few years the *sovnarkhozy* were abolished and the power of the central ministries expanded once again.

Although production slowed somewhat during the 1960s, industry in the Baltic republics continued to develop more rapidly than in the rest of the USSR. Baltic economies were also distinguished by the relative importance of light industry and food-processing. To the other republics the Baltics exported energy, machinery, industrial equipment, and some consumer goods and agricultural products. However, with few natural resources, aside from oil shale and fertilizers, the Baltic republics were importers of most necessary industrial raw materials such as coal, iron, and cotton. Despite this disadvantage, the Baltic republics were relatively productive: with only 2.8 percent of the total Soviet population, they were responsible for 3.6 percent of the Soviet gross domestic product by the end of the 1960s.[20]

As a result of this productivity, Baltic—especially Estonian and Latvian—wages and incomes far exceeded the Soviet average. Collective farmers also saw their earnings increase dramatically during the 1960s. By the 1970s rural incomes, which included the proceeds from the highly productive private plots, often exceeded those of urban industrial workers. Although their relatively high incomes translated into superior living standards for Latvians and Estonians, Baltic standards of living remained well below that of Scandinavian and Western European norms—and by some measures even below the levels enjoyed by Balts in 1939. Indeed, even high per capita incomes did not necessarily translate into purchasing power in a Soviet economy that was deficient in the production of consumer goods. Still, Baltic consumers did not fare badly during the 1968–75 period, which was the peak era of Soviet consumerism. Indeed, the prospect of acquiring a car, a summer cottage, a washing machine, quality furniture, or a trip abroad encouraged conformity and only reinforced most Balts' outward acceptance of the existing system.

Balts received additional privileges withheld from most other Soviet citizens. Although most Soviet television programs available in Estonia were in Russian, Estonians could watch Western (Finnish) television and listen to Finnish radio; thousands were able to visit Finland via the ferry line from Tallinn. It has been said that in some ways the Baltic republics were laboratories where experiments, often based on models copied from the West, could be conducted on a small scale before their application in other parts of the USSR. Moreover, the Baltic republics were eager consumers of Western entertainment and fashions, which exerted somewhat greater appeal to them than did Russian culture. As the most westernized areas of the Soviet Union, the Baltic republics were able to enjoy scientific and cultural exchanges with Western partners—which no doubt contributed to the Balts' consciousness of the discrepancies between the quality of life in the West and in the Soviet Union. Cultural exchanges also resulted in the loss of some Soviet talent to the West; one of the most famous Baltic émigrés was the composer Arvo Pärt, who left Estonia in 1980.

Meanwhile, social trends in the Baltic region reflected the perils of rapid modernization and urbanization, aggravated by factors particular to life under Soviet rule. In general, social indicators in Lithuania, like economic development, tended to follow the patterns prevailing in Estonia and Latvia. For example, Estonian and Latvian birthrates had always been among the lowest in the USSR, bottoming out in the mid-1960s; in Catholic Lithuania, which had earlier enjoyed higher birthrates, the decline began in the 1960s and continued steadily thereafter. In Estonia and Latvia, the old tradition of late marriage contributed to this trend, but significant roles were also played by high abortion (legalized in 1955) and divorce rates, compounded by inadequate housing. Having risen substantially during the 1960s, by the end of the 1970s the divorce rate in Latvia was approaching 50 percent; Estonia and Lithuania were somewhat further behind. Meanwhile, given the absence of reliable alternatives, abortion became the most common method of birth control in the USSR. As a result, the numbers of registered abortions in each of the Baltic republics (as in the USSR more generally) well exceeded the numbers of live births.

There were also other negative social indicators: an increase in crime in the 1970s paralleled similar developments in the West, while rising alcohol consumption in the Baltic republics was part of a general Soviet trend. By 1970 Estonians, who preferred hard spirits to wine or beer, consumed 50 percent more alcohol per capita than residents of the RSFSR or the United States. Trends in Lithuania and Latvia were similar, with tragic results: in Latvia, alcohol was a factor in half of all auto accidents, in the majority of drownings and crimes, and was surely a catalyst in the growing divorce rates. To such negative social developments one could add declining productivity at work—a product of chronic absenteeism, drinking on the job, high labor turnover, and theft.

The trend that disturbed many Balts the most, however, was the continuing influx of Russians and other immigrants into the Baltic republics, which naturally contributed to a heightened fear of Russification. Latvia in particular continued to attract immigrants. As a result, by 1970 the Latvians' share of the republic's population had fallen below 57 percent, with Latvians accounting for less than half of all urban dwellers. Likewise, by 1970 natives accounted for just over 68 percent of the population of the Estonian republic, while the corresponding figure for Lithuanians was 80 percent, which held steady through the 1970s.[21] It would appear that the arguments of Lithuanian First Secretary Sniečkus for reduced immigration were considerably more successful than similar arguments by Latvian (or Estonian) leaders, if they were made at all. Yet Lithuania was never much of a magnet for Russians in the first place: since Lithuanian cities were less developed and had never had large Russian communities, they were less attractive to Slavic immigrants than cities such as Rīga and Tartu, each of which had been Russian cultural centers during the tsarist era.

NATIONALISM AND DISSENT

Nikita Khrushchev, it is well known, had little tolerance for nationalism of any kind, including Great Russian nationalism, and worked tirelessly to promote the vision of a truly "Soviet" man. He was removed in 1964, and the nationalities policy of the succeeding Brezhnev regime remained ambiguous for nearly another decade. However, the 50th anniversary of the founding of the USSR, celebrated in late 1972, marked a return to the Khrushchevian line of the *sblizhenie* of nations. Although, Brezhnev now declared, the party opposed forcing this process, it "regards as impermissible any attempt whatsoever to hold back the process of drawing together of nations, to obstruct it on any pretext or artificially to reinforce national isolation."[22]

The formulation of this hard line on nationalities policy coincided with and was a response to growing manifestations of local nationalism throughout the Soviet Union. Among the offenders were the Baltic republics: at least two Latvian underground organizations were uncovered in the early 1960s, and attempts to create an underground Estonian nationalist party resulted in a series of political trials in 1970. Rather than being indicative of a persistent pattern of anti-Soviet resistance, however, such activity was in reality episodic and limited to small groups and individuals.

Nationalism in the Baltic countries, as in Russia itself, was mostly connected to interest in folklore, culture, and local history; political defiance was the exception rather than the rule. Yet as the Soviet state strove to attain international respectability, it was no longer able to terrorize the population into submission as it did in Stalin's day. By 1970 the old methods of shooting or deporting the unreliable had been replaced by imprisonment in psychiatric hospitals and, in some cases, exile abroad. Certainly this decline in the risk factor, combined with rising expectations and an indelible memory of statehood and independence, contributed to the growth of nationalist and dissident movements in the Baltic republics in the 1970s.

The "Prague Spring" in 1968 was a significant turning point for Baltic nationalists and dissidents, as it was for the many communists abroad who opposed the Soviet invasion. The Czechs and Slovaks who tried to create "socialism with a human face" offered what appeared to many to be an attractive alternative to Soviet socialism, but Moscow saw the movement as a threat to its authority in the communist bloc. Indeed, the dispatch of Warsaw Pact tanks to Czechoslovakia was meant to demonstrate to the rest of the Soviet empire that there could be only one path to socialism.[23] Having displayed its will to its satellites in Eastern Europe, the CPSU began a counteroffensive against "nationalist deviations" within the USSR, and in troublesome Lithuania in particular.

After nearly two decades of outward compliance, most Lithuanians had learned to live with the system; nevertheless small-scale dissent took several forms in the late 1960s and 1970s. Many dissidents were defenders of the rights of the Catholic Church and of religious believers in general; some advanced the cause of human rights; and still others demanded national rights and self-determination. Although each of these movements overlapped—indeed, to Lithuanians, Catholicism and nationality are closely related—the religious current in Lithuanian dissent was most powerful.

Dissident activity was usually peaceful. However, the two days of rioting and public demonstrations in Kaunas that followed the public self-immolation of 19-year-old Romas Kalanta on May 14, 1972, showed the intensity of anti-Soviet feeling in Lithuania. But this outburst was exceptional. Since most dissidents sought to force the regime to observe its own laws and international agreements, they usually emphasized legal and nonviolent methods of protest. *Samizdat'* (self-publishing) was a common form of dissident activity, and was used to great effect especially by Lithuanian religious activists, who in March 1972 began to publish *The Chronicle of the Lithuanian Catholic Church* in imitation of the Moscow human rights publication *Chronicle of Current Events*. KGB attempts to repress Lithuanian religious activists, documented in the *Chronicle*, only attracted international attention to the plight of religious believers in the USSR.

Of the other Lithuanian dissident groups to appear in the 1970s, the most successful were open civil rights organizations such as the Catholic Committee for the Defense of Human Rights and the Lithuanian Helsinki Watch Group. Nationalist dissidents, focusing on the restoration of Lithuanian independence, worked underground and, unlike the Catholic movement, suffered from a lack of leadership and organizational structure. Their ideas—ranging from liberal to nationalist, Catholic to secular, anti-Marxist to neo-Marxist—were reflected in publications such as the *Aušra* (*Dawn*, named after a patriotic newspaper published at the end of the nineteenth century), *Varpas* (*The Bell*) and *Perspektyvos* (*Perspectives*). In an echo of the previous century's national awakening, *Aušra* sought to awaken Lithuania from its "spiritual sleep."

For more than a decade, official reaction to Lithuanian dissent vacillated between a relatively soft and a hard-line approach. Arrests were followed by trials rather than deportations or shootings. A KGB crackdown on dissident activity in the early 1980s stifled the voices of many critics, who would have to wait until Gorbachev's *glasnost'* to be heard again. Nevertheless, despite official repression, the Lithuanian church, buoyed by the 1978 election of Karol Wojtyla—a Polish bishop with a history of standing up to communist authorities—as Pope John Paul II, continued to defy the regime and to defend the rights of believers, as guaranteed by the Soviet constitution.

Dissent in Lithuania was more outspoken than in the other Baltic republics, due in part to the predominant role Catholicism played there. Estonians enjoyed a relatively privileged status as a bridge between the

USSR and the West, and it is partly for this reason that oppositional movements in Estonia lacked the virulence of dissent in Lithuania. Rather than having a national-religious orientation, the Estonian movement was better characterized as national-democratic. The Lutheran church, which was completely subservient to the Soviet regime, played almost no role in Estonian dissident movements. As in Lithuania, however, the main weapons of Estonian dissidents were demonstrations, mostly by students, and *samizdat'*. Another method was to draw the West's attention to their country's plight, as did the Estonian Democratic Movement and the Estonian National Front. Their joint appeal to the United Nations, issued in October 1972, listed the abuses of human and political rights and demanded the restoration of Estonian independence.

In Latvia dissident activity was less conspicuous than in Lithuania or even Estonia. Led by trusted Communist Party officials who completely lacked national feeling, Latvia was the most repressed and most Russified of the Baltic republics. The few dissidents there emphasized human rights and circulated their ideas in *samizdat'*, much like their Lithuanian and Estonian counterparts did. The most noteworthy document of Latvian dissent was the "Letter of the Seventeen Communists" (1972), which called on the communist parties of Romania, Yugoslavia, France, Spain, and Austria to help Latvian communists correct the mistakes of the CPSU—foremost among which was the official policy of "Great Russian chauvinism."

Solidarity among dissidents of the different Baltic republics was virtually absent during the Brezhnev era. However, the 40th anniversary of the Molotov-Ribbentrop Pact, on August 23, 1979, did not go unnoticed in the three republics. To commemorate the occasion, a group of Baltic activists, mostly Lithuanians and a handful of Latvians and Estonians, addressed a public appeal to foreign governments, the USSR, and the secretary-general of the United Nations. In the appeal they demanded the pact's publication, along with its secret protocols on the division of Eastern Europe. As will be discussed in the following chapter, this document was a key to the Balts' exit from the USSR.

BALTIC DECLINE?

In 1980 there were few reasons to believe that the Baltic republics would achieve their independence anytime soon, if ever. By this time, a KGB crackdown on dissident activity throughout the USSR had, with few exceptions (notably Lithuanian Catholics), effectively stifled open expressions of nationalist or democratic thought. The presence of more than 150,000 Soviet officers and soldiers in the region further discouraged any misguided thoughts of independence.

While Western countries in general and the USA in particular suffered from oil shortages, economic stagnation, political scandals, and foreign policy setbacks, the USSR appeared strong enough to brook any challenges. The Soviet Union had long ago achieved nuclear parity with the United States. For the moment the communist bloc (excluding, of course, the People's Republic of China and its Albanian ally) remained firm as socialist revolutions struck countries in Africa and Central America. Oil flowed from newly exploited deposits in Siberia, which contributed to the postponement of a reckoning with Soviet economic realities.

Although popular enthusiasm for communist ideology by this time was certainly shallow, Soviet leaders were never more confident of the USSR's global position and the future of the Union. With regional leaders maintaining order in what amounted to personal fiefdoms, the republics were relatively quiet. If the KGB crackdown of 1980 had failed completely to choke dissident activity, a 1983 sweep of all three Baltic republics, under the watch of new CPSU general secretary and former KGB chief Iurii Andropov (1914–84), was somewhat more thorough. To some observers, the creation of a truly "Soviet" people was not a utopian dream but a certifiable fact; the new Soviet man—shorn of an overriding national and religious identity, loyal to the Soviet state, and dedicated to building a communist society—was coming into being. Though his language and culture would be Russian, his worldview would be thoroughly Soviet. In this context, the future of the Baltic peoples as distinct nationalities was in doubt.

In 1978, Hélène Carrère d'Encausse, a respected scholar of Soviet nationalities, proposed three possible destinies for the non-Russian nationalities of the USSR: (1) assimilation, (2) survival and development, or (3) weakness and possible extinction. According to this analysis, among the USSR's European peoples, Belarussians were in the first category, Ukrainians were in the second, and the Baltic peoples—the Estonians and Latvians in particular—were fated to disappear.[24]

The demographic facts appeared to bear out this conclusion. Baltic birthrates were among the lowest in the USSR: in 1980 the combined total of Estonians, Latvians, and Lithuanians living in their native republics barely reached 5 million out of a total Soviet population of 262 million; indeed, most of the population growth in the Baltic republic during the 1970s was the result of immigration. Nevertheless, d'Encausse's sad prediction underestimated the vitality of the Baltic peoples and overestimated the durability of the Soviet Union. While certainly on the defensive, Baltic national communities nevertheless managed to retain the use of their native language and were in fact, countered Lithuanian expert V. Stanley Vardys, "strong, competitive, and very self-conscious."[25]

As the late 1980s would prove, the Sovietization of the Baltic nations was shallow. Having managed to preserve the historical memory of the independence era—two decades during which the Baltic nations were firmly a part of European politics and culture—the Baltic republics remained the most Western of the Soviet republics in heritage and lifestyle. Gorbachev's *glasnost'* would finally provide them with the opportunity to reclaim that heritage.

NOTES

1. D. Y. Stradins, ed., *Istoriia Lativskoi SSR* [History of the Latvian SSR] (Rīga: Academy of Science of the Latvian SSR, 1955), 481, as appears in I. Joseph Vizulis, *Nations Under Duress: The Baltic States* (Port Washington, N.Y.: Associated Faculty Press, 1985), 46.

2. Jews were especially prominent in the Soviet administration in Lithuania—an arrangement that did not go unnoticed by ethnic Lithuanians. Nevertheless, Jewish-owned enterprises were nationalized just as Lithuanian-owned businesses were.

3. The original plans for the deportation of "anti-Soviet" elements were written in October 1939. The document is reproduced in Vizulis (1985), 99–101.

4. The exact figures for these deportations will never be known. The figures cited in the text above are on the conservative side and are taken from a textbook compiled by a team of Baltic historians. See Zigmantas Kiaupa, Ain Mäesalu, Ago Pajur, and Gvido Straube, *The History of the Baltic Countries*, 3rd ed. (Tallinn, Estonia: AS BIT, 2002), 169.

5. Tõnu Parming, "Nationalism in Soviet Estonia since 1964," in George W. Simmonds, ed., *Nationalism in the USSR and Eastern Europe in the Era of Brezhnev and Kosygin* (Detroit: University of Detroit Press, 1977), 118.

6. The classic work on German occupation policy remains Alexander Dallin, *German Rule in Russia, 1941–1945: A Study in Occupation Policies* (New York: St. Martin's Press, 1957).

7. Kasekamp (2000), 138; Romuald Misiunas and Rein Taagepera, *The Baltic States: Years of Dependence 1940–1990* (Berkeley and Los Angeles: University of California Press, 1993), 59.

8. Kiaupa et al. (2002), 176.

9. V. Stanley Vardys and Judith B. Sedaitis, *Lithuania: The Rebel Nation* (Boulder, Colo.: Westview Press, 1997), 6; Raun (1987), 170; Plakans (1995), 153.

10. Though significant, the numbers of anti-Soviet partisans operating in the Baltic countries are often exaggerated. Misiunas and Taagepera write that up to 100,000 people were "involved" in the Lithuanian resistance, and that the Latvian and Estonian forest brotherhoods may have involved as many as 40,000 and 30,000 people, respectively (p. 46). The contributions of Baltic historians in Arvydas Anušaukas, ed., *The Anti-Soviet Resistance in the Baltic States*, 3rd ed. (Vilnius: Akreta, 2001) use the most recent information and together suggest that the figures were somewhat lower.

11. For the 1944–52 period as a whole, Vizulis (1985) claimed that as many as half a million Estonians, Latvians, and Lithuanians were deported (p. 107). However, Kiaupa et al. (2002) present the significantly lower figure of 130,000 deportees for the 1945–52 period (p. 181).

12. Misiunas and Taagepera (1993), 112.

13. Raun (1987), 183; Misiunas and Taagepera (1993), 364.

14. Berklāvs later returned and became actively involved in the Latvian independence movement at the end of the 1980s.

15. Misiunas and Taagepera (1993), 359–360.

16. Helēna Demakova, *Different Conversations. Writings on Art and Culture* (Rīga: Visual Communications Department of the Latvian Academy of Art, 2002), 205–207.

17. Ibid., 207.

18. The Baltic republics retained an 11-year educational program, whereas the Soviet norm was 10 years.

19. Gershon Shafir, *Immigrants and Nationalists: Ethnic Conflict and Accommodation in Catalonia, the Basque Country, Latvia, and Estonia* (Albany: State University of New York Press, 1995), 157, 159.

20. Misiunas and Taagepera (1993), 184.

21. Ibid., 353.

22. *Pravda*, December 22, 1972.

23. The Warsaw Treaty Organization, or Warsaw Pact, was created in 1955 and was the communist bloc's answer to the North Atlantic Treaty Organization (NATO). In 1968, pact forces invaded Czechoslovakia to overthrow an independent-minded regime.

24. Hélène Carrère d'Encausse, *Decline of an Empire* (New York: Newsweek Books, 1979), 267.

25. V. Stanley Vardys, "The Baltic States in the Soviet Union," in Alexander Shtromas and Morton A. Kaplan, eds., *The Soviet Union and the Challenge of the Future.* Vol. 3, *Ideology, Culture and Nationality* (New York: Paragon House, 1989), 440, 451.

7

Reawakening, 1985–91

The general mood of the Baltic populations in the early 1980s was neither hopeful nor desperate, but is perhaps best described as resigned: most Estonians, Latvians, and Lithuanians were resigned to economic stagnation and shortages; resigned to the rising pressure of Russification; resigned, for the foreseeable future, to communist and Soviet rule. Far from addressing the concerns of its dissatisfied citizens, the regime took strong police measures to stifle any popular expressions of discontent in the Baltics and throughout the USSR. The message was clear: Soviet policies were made by the Communist Party alone.

Although suppressed, the voices of civil society were not completely silenced. While an honest public discussion about the Soviet past or the present role of the Communist Party was nearly unthinkable before Gorbachev's accession, during the mid-1980s some outspoken citizens—intellectuals, writers—were able to navigate the tiny gray area between protest and submission in openly addressing quality of life issues. By 1986, concern about ecology, ostensibly a nonpolitical subject, became a cause that united various sectors of Soviet society regardless of their political beliefs, especially in Russia and the Baltic republics. As environmental concerns gave way to national concerns in a more open political atmosphere, the Baltic republics began the process of national rejuvenation.

Fully utilizing the political space granted them by Gorbachev's liberalization policies, the Baltic nations began a political journey that led within a few short but turbulent years to the restoration of their independence.

While the Czechs describe their struggle for freedom in the late 1980s as the "Velvet Revolution," Balts refer to this period as the "Singing Revolution." Reviving a tradition begun during the nineteenth century national awakenings, Balts used their traditional song festivals to demonstrate their unity, resolve, and national patriotism. Long since abandoned were old Soviet anthems such as "Latvians Sing Praise to Stalin" and "May the Land of Soviets Be Glorified," which Latvians were forced to sing at the festival in Rīga in 1948. After the passage of 40 years the atmosphere had been utterly transformed: in September 1988 the estimated 250,000 people (more than one in four Estonians) gathered at the Tallinn Song Festival Grounds delivered a stirring rendition of "My Native Land," the Estonian national anthem which had been expressly forbidden by the Soviet regime. For the peoples of Estonia, Latvia, and Lithuania, revolution came not, to quote Mao Zedong's famous phrase, out of the barrel of a gun, but through peaceful protest—and song.

GLASNOST' IN THE BALTICS

The rebirth of Baltic national life must be understood within the context of the revolution that was taking place in the USSR more generally—a revolution that began with a generational change at the top of the Soviet leadership that brought Mikhail S. Gorbachev (b.1931) to the post of general secretary. In contrast to the dull, aging leaders who came before him—Leonid Brezhnev (1964–82), Iurii Andropov (1982–84), and Konstantin Chernenko (1984–85)—Gorbachev was relatively young, energetic, and charismatic. However, that he would be the last Soviet ruler, the last CPSU general secretary, or even the architect of a radical reform program, was not at all evident in April 1985. Indeed, during the first years of Gorbachev's rule the USSR remained a heavily centralized and intolerant police state.

In an effort both to combat local corruption and consolidate his own position, in his first year in power Gorbachev embarked on the biggest purge of the Communist Party elite since Stalin's day. Conservative Brezhnev-era officials were the first to go. While Lithuania's First Secretary Petras Griškevičius and Estonia's Karl Vaino managed to avoid the initial sweep, the apparatuses of their parties were quickly overhauled. In Latvia, change at the top had preceded Gorbachev: in 1984 First Secretary

Augusts Voss was promoted to the post of chairman of the USSR Supreme Soviet's Committee for Nationalities and was replaced by Boris Pugo (1937–91), a Russian Latvian who had headed the Latvian KGB since 1980.

Gorbachev's long-term plan was unclear during his first two years at the helm. Nearly two decades later it still remains unclear. *Perestroika* ("restructuring"), a word that gained currency in 1987, aimed to reinvigorate the stagnant Soviet economy; beyond that broad aim, however, the parameters of *perestroika* were ill-defined. Indeed, *perestroika* was a largely improvised policy that began as an attempt to unleash the energies and talents of the Soviet people but ultimately took on a life of its own. To overcome the bureaucratic resistance to restructuring, a policy of *glasnost'* ("openness" or "publicity") was articulated that aimed to encourage criticism of entrenched elites. *Glasnost'*, in its narrow conception, was the necessary corollary to *perestroika;* however, it was not long before *glasnost'* too exceeded the designs of its architect. As Anatol Lieven, a journalist who was based in the Baltic republics in the early 1990s, observed: "Glasnost was inevitably going to bring a new honesty about the past; but since the entire Communist claim to leadership was based on lies, this honesty would sooner or later bring down the whole system."[1]

Russian nationalist intellectuals were the first to seize the opportunity provided by *glasnost'*, as they dominated public debate during much of the first two years of the Gorbachev era. At first their main concern was ecology—in particular Soviet plans to embark on a massive project to divert several northern and Siberian rivers to arid Central Asia, which was halted in August 1986 after a vigorous debate in the official Soviet press. This victory, occurring in the wake of the Chernobyl disaster the previous spring, encouraged the efforts of Latvians who were concerned about the possible environmental impact of a proposed hydroelectric complex, to be built at Pļaviņas on Latvia's largest river, the Daugava. Popular protest in the form of letter-writing, led by the Environmental Protection Club, successfully pressured the authorities to halt construction in November 1987.

Likewise, throughout 1987 Estonian intellectuals discussed their concerns about the potential environmental impact of intensive phosphate excavation in Kabala-Toolse—a plan that would also require the immigrations of tens of thousands of laborers. The Estonians' pressure ultimately forced the Soviet leadership to abandon the project in October. In Lithuania, the environmental debate focused on the Ignalina Atomic Energy Station, a Chernobyl-type installation that was located only 80 miles from Vilnius. Opposition to its planned expansion was one of the first causes to mobilize the Lithuanian masses in the spring of 1988. Balts, and soon afterwards other Soviet nationalities, were quick to grasp the potential for change in this new, more tolerant atmosphere.

By mid-1987, Gorbachev's attempt to produce guided reform from above had the unintended affect of inducing challenges to Soviet policies, which in the Baltic republics metamorphosed into national protests. Latvians were the first of the Baltic peoples to confront Soviet authorities openly. On June 14—a date that coincided with the Soviet occupation in June 1940 and the massive deportations of June 1941—thousands of Latvians took part in a demonstration near the Freedom Monument in Rīga, organized by the tiny human rights group "Helsinki '86." Following the success of this demonstration, others soon followed. On August 23, 1987, the anniversary of the Nazi-Soviet Pact of 1939, crowds gathered in all three Baltic capitals, most notably in Rīga. However, the largest of these 1987 demonstrations occurred on November 18 (also in Rīga), the anniversary of Latvia's declaration of independence in 1918.

The Kremlin's response to these implicit challenges to the legitimacy of Soviet rule was uneasy: central authorities tried to downplay the significance of these events and discouraged press coverage of them. Yet Moscow opted not to pursue a persistent campaign of repression against the protesters. Thus the communist parties of the Baltic republics found themselves in a quandary: a permissive policy would only encourage more political activity, yet repression would be inconsistent with Moscow's line on *glasnost'* and could jeopardize their own legitimacy. As a result of this ambivalence, the local communist parties began to split.

THE COMMUNIST PARTIES AND BALTIC POPULAR MOVEMENTS

At the heart of the Baltic challenges to Moscow was the matter of historical truth. While the official line (discussed in Chapter Six) claimed that the Baltic republics voluntarily joined the USSR in 1940, most Balts regarded their republics as occupied territories. Under the conditions of *glasnost'*, for the first time it became possible to address the dark history of Soviet rule in the Baltic—the occupation and annexation of 1940, the deportations of 1941 and afterward, the drive for collectivization.

Intellectuals in the Latvian Writers' Union—an organization whose main purpose hitherto had been to censor and control Latvian writers—were among the first to challenge the standard Soviet interpretation of the events of 1940. On June 1–2, 1988, the issue was debated at a Latvian Writers' Union plenum, and the speeches were subsequently published for the reading public. Among the plenum's numerous resolutions were that Stalin forcibly annexed Latvia to the USSR; Latvian ought to be the state language of the republic; political and taxing authority should be devolved to the republican and local levels; and the secret protocols of the Molotov-Ribbentrop Pact should be published.

Having moved decisively to the side of reform, the Latvian writers were instrumental in the creation of the Latvian Popular Front (LPF) in the weeks ahead, following the creation of analogous organizations—each ostensibly in favor of *perestroika*—in Estonia and Lithuania. Not long after the formation of the LPF, a group of former political prisoners, human rights advocates, and environmental and cultural activists announced their intention to create the Latvian National Independence Movement (LNIM), a considerably more confrontational organization than the LPF. With the Communist Party maintaining its monopoly of power, Latvia did not by any means enjoy full political liberty; however, the activities of the LPF and the LNIM, and indeed the fact of their very existence, indicated that a Latvian "reawakening" was in full swing by mid-1988.

In 1987–88, however, it was in Estonia that the boldest challenges to Soviet orthodoxy took place. In the fall of 1987 establishment reformers in Estonia, emboldened by their success in getting Soviet authorities to halt projects for new phosphate mines, published a plan for the republic's economic autonomy. This group recommended that enterprises and resources presently managed by Soviet authorities be placed under Estonian jurisdiction, and that market principles and prices be introduced in inter-republic and foreign trade. The idea was in effect to turn the Estonian republic into a "self-managing economic zone." The demand for economic autonomy—rejected by the ECP—proved popular and anticipated the growth of a massive nationalist movement. By the spring of 1988 the national flag of the prewar Estonian state reappeared at demonstrations throughout the country.

Responding to Gorbachev's encouragement of the creation of "informal" groups for the support of *perestroika*, in April 1988 Estonian reformers, including establishment Communists and intellectuals, created a "Popular Front for the Support of Restructuring in the USSR," which soon became the Popular Front of Estonia (PFE). Edgar Savisaar (b.1950), a signatory of the economic plan introduced the previous fall, proposed the Popular Front's creation and emerged as its leader. Although the PFE's members were overwhelmingly ethnic Estonians, membership was not based on nationality, but rather on common goals, including economic sovereignty for Estonia, greater concern for the environment, and limits on immigration.

ECP First Secretary Karl Vaino soon fell victim to the changing mood in Estonia: on June 17, 1988, he was dismissed (over 100,000 people went out the next day to celebrate) and replaced by a native Estonian, Vaino Väljas (b.1931), a moderate advocate of the PFE platform. Väljas hoped that the ECP and the PFE could work together to bring about the necessary changes in a controlled manner acceptable to Moscow. Following the lead of Estonian society, by the autumn of 1988 the entire leadership of the ECP was on the side of the reformers. Although the party was indeed transforming itself, it continually lagged behind the Popular Front, which by November was calling for an overhaul of the federal structure of the USSR, with the goal of assigning greater rights to the republics.

By this time other more radical Estonian organizations, such as the Estonian Heritage Society (dedicated to restoring pre-Soviet monuments) and the Estonian National Independence Party, were making an even bolder demand: they wanted the reestablishment of the Estonian state that existed before 1940. That popular opinion was on the side of this revolution was undeniable. On September 11, 1988, more than 250,000 people gathered on the Song Festival Grounds in Tallinn, where slogans calling for democratization were displayed alongside those calling for the restoration of the country's independence.

This event marked the pinnacle of the Baltic republics' "Singing Revolution" of the summer of 1988, but the autumn brought further success. On November 16, 1988, the Estonian Supreme Soviet—an increasingly pro-Estonian body—declared the republic's sovereignty (which in fact was already guaranteed by the Soviet constitution) and its right to veto USSR laws that violated that sovereignty. This declaration, though far short of a full declaration of independence, was to set the precedent for later sovereignty declarations in other parts of the Soviet empire.

At this stage of the revolution, Estonia was well ahead of its more cautious Baltic neighbors. In Lithuania, which was led by the Brezhnevite First Secretary Petras Griškevičius until his death in November 1987, and then for another year by the orthodox Ringaudas Songaila (b.1929), the situation had stagnated until the birth on May 23, 1988, of a new mass organization called the Lithuanian Movement for Restructuring, later known simply as *Sąjūdis* ("Movement"). Before long this organization would emerge as the most popular force for Lithuanian nationalism.

At the beginning, *Sąjūdis* was a movement that united various strata of Lithuanian society, including nationalists from Kaunas, liberal intellectuals from Vilnius, and communist reformers. Independent from the LiCP but at first not necessarily inimical to it, *Sąjūdis* quickly gained mass legitimacy as it called for a meaningful definition of "sovereignty," economic independence, and a discussion of Stalinism and the Molotov-

Ribbentrop Pact of 1939. Still bolder demands were put forward by another Lithuanian nationalist movement, the Lithuanian Freedom League (LFL), which unlike the more cautious *Sąjūdis* sought outright independence from the USSR and was unwilling to cooperate in any way with the Communist Party.[2]

At this early stage of the Lithuanian national reawakening, the LiCP leadership failed to collaborate with the reform movements, and instead attempted to contain undesirable manifestations of *glasnost'*. Unlike in Estonia, where the party leadership strove to accommodate the Popular Front, in Lithuania relations between the party and *Sąjūdis* grew tense, especially as nationalist demonstrations began to draw growing crowds in the summer of 1988. This policy of noncooperation cost the party dearly, as it appeared to be recalcitrant and unresponsive to popular feeling, and as a result the LiCP found itself increasingly marginalized. Indeed, it was *Sąjūdis*, rather than the LiCP, that would define the republic's political agenda for the remainder of the Soviet era.

Leaders of the Lithuanian and Latvian CPs soon realized that they could not depend on help from the Kremlin, where Gorbachev too was caught between conservative elements who sought to roll back *perestroika* and radicals who urged him on. Despite the more liberal atmosphere of the time, there was still considerable uncertainty about the future: one could not be certain that *perestroika* and *glasnost'* were not just the latest whim of the latest Soviet tsar. Nevertheless, reformers in Moscow tolerated and often even supported the popular fronts and *Sąjūdis* in the belief that they could be useful allies against hardliners within the CPSU.

In an attempt to clarify the present party line, in August 1988 Gorbachev sent his Politburo ally, Aleksandr Yakovlev (b.1923), to Lithuania and Latvia to deliver the message that Moscow would not support unconditionally those who refused to adapt to the changing circumstances. The Baltic communist parties, Yakovlev suggested, should work with the nationalists in the republics in a common effort to implement the goals of *perestroika*. At the same time, the Kremlin also held firmly to the line that Baltic ideas about independence were simply senseless dreams: the USSR was a single interdependent economic system, not to be taken apart.

Yakovlev's visit was followed by an effort to co-opt the new mass movements while maintaining pressure on the Baltic CPs. *Sąjūdis* was even given access to the official media, which naturally increased its public visibility. By the end of September, following the scandalous suppression of an LFL-organized popular demonstration in Vilnius that was intended to mark the anniversary of the Molotov-Ribbentrop Pact, *Sąjūdis* became emboldened in its dealings with the LiCP. Demanding an investigation of the incident, for the first time *Sajūdis* made common cause with the more radical Lithuanian Freedom League. Meanwhile, hardliners in the LiCP were made to understand that they had lost the support of Moscow. On October 20 First Secretary Ringaudas Songaila was pensioned off and replaced by the more flexible Algirdas Brazauskas (b.1932), a popular figure who since June had been the party's liaison to *Sajūdis*. Henceforth the LiCP would find itself responding to the demands of *Sajūdis* rather than initiating changes itself.

Similar if less profound changes took place in the party leaderships of the other Baltic republics. Despite his attempts to accommodate popular positions and thereby ensure his own political survival, Latvia's First Secretary Boris Pugo was unable to keep up with the Kremlin's shifting reformist line. On October 4, 1988, he was transferred to Moscow to head the Party Control Commission and was replaced by a compromise candidate, Jānis Vagris (b.1930), a native Latvian. Anatolijs Gorbunovs (b.1942), by now one of the LaCP's leading reformers, took the post of Chairman of the Supreme Soviet of the Latvian SSR. Although with these changes at the top the Baltic CPs were clearly moving in the direction of reform, they could not hope to keep up with the pace being set by the popular fronts, *Sajūdis*, and other, often less compromising organizations such as the Latvian National Independence Movement, the Estonian National Independence Party, and the Lithuanian Freedom League.

In October 1988 *Sajūdis* and each of the Baltic popular fronts held founding congresses. Although they held no formal power, by this time they had eclipsed the communist parties as the leading political forces in their republics. As noted earlier, at first Moscow tolerated the fronts, as Kremlin reformers viewed them as potential allies in the struggle for *perestroika*. However, as the fronts became disillusioned with the slow pace of *perestroika* and began to take more radical stances—including, eventually, independence for the Baltic republics—Moscow's support for them evaporated. Even the moderate demands made by the popular fronts at their founding congresses—such as economic autonomy and, in the case of the PFE program, the USSR's transformation "from a formally federal state into a union of actually sovereign states based on the confederal principle"—exceeded what Gorbachev was willing to concede.[3] For Gorbachev and the CPSU, the point of *perestroika* was to strengthen the empire, not to destroy it.

Likewise, at the republic level, as the demands of the popular fronts grew more radical, hardliners in the communist parties became less willing to cooperate with them. Some fell under the influence of new political organizations founded by the Russian-speaking populations of the Baltic republics, including the International Movement of Workers in the Estonian SSR (later called the Intermovement), formed in July 1988, and a Latvian counterpart, called Interfront, which was created in October. Russian-speakers in Lithuania founded *Edinstvo* (Unity) in November. Fearing that the rise of national movements in the Baltic would encroach upon Russian interests, these organizations called for "internationalism" (meaning Soviet rule) and firm support from the CPSU in Moscow.

Indeed, the reawakening of local nationalism in the Baltic republics, as in other Soviet republics, often asserted itself in ways that were threatening to non-native settlers. Initially one of the main concerns of the Russian-speaking population was the question, raised by Baltic nationalists, of declaring the indigenous languages the state languages of the Baltic republics. This of course would jeopardize the traditional primacy of the Russian language—the only language most of the settlers knew. Lithuania passed a language law in November 1988, followed by Estonia in January 1989 and Latvia the following May. In some ways these laws were rather rigid, and if fully implemented would have resulted in the exclusion of many Russian immigrants from full citizenship. Estonia's law, for example, mandated that all sessions of governmental and administrative bodies, as well as judicial proceedings, be conducted in Estonian. Moreover it differentiated levels of proficiency in Estonian required of people in six occupational categories; complete fluency would be required of government and party officials as well as factory directors.[4] The Latvian and Lithuanian language laws were somewhat less stringent, and the Estonian law was eventually loosened.

Naturally, the Russophone organizations vehemently opposed the passage of these laws. Some of their leaders even took a "Great Russian chauvinist" stance: seeking safe harbor in the empire, they called for the restoration of Moscow's firm control over the republics. The battle cries of the Russian-speaking organizations grew ever more shrill as the popular fronts—their principal adversaries—began to endorse the idea of independence. Convinced that if the Baltic republics seceded from the USSR then the Russians who lived there would suddenly find themselves a vulnerable minority in a hostile environment, the Interfront, the Intermovement, and *Edinstvo* each made common cause with hardline elements in the KGB and the CPSU. It should be noted, however, that these organizations probably did not represent the majority of Russians who lived in the Baltic republics—many of whom actually supported the goals of the popular fronts—but only the most conservative and frightened among them.

SOVEREIGNTY OR INDEPENDENCE?

An important turning point in the Baltic republics' drive for sovereignty came with the election in March 1989 of a new USSR Congress of People's Deputies (CPD). In creating the congress, Gorbachev's intention was to establish an institutional counterweight to an intractable CPSU. Although one-third of its 2,250 seats were reserved for public organizations such as the Communist Party and its Youth League (Komsomol)—thus ensuring the body's essential conservatism—the remainder went to representatives of the regions and districts, who were elected by popular vote.

While the Communist Party dominated the elections (87.6 percent of the seats were awarded to its members), the popular fronts and *Sąjūdis* heavily influenced the selection of Baltic representatives. Of the 42 elected Lithuanian deputies, 36 had been nominated by *Sąjūdis*. In Latvia First Secretary Jānis Vagris was nearly defeated by a candidate from the Latvian National Independence Movement, which was the largest popular movement in Latvia by the fall of that year. To the leaders of these organizations, their successes doubtless confirmed the correctness of their increasingly confrontational approach; for the Baltic communist parties, however, the elections confirmed that they were losing control of the situation in their republics.

For the Soviet Union in general, the CPD was a forum for a more open discussion of both all-Union and local problems; for the Baltic deputies, however, the CPD provided a medium through which to articulate their demands for sovereignty within the USSR. Most joined the Interregional Group of Deputies, a democratic faction that supported *perestroika* but challenged the congress's conservative majority. Aside from the demand for economic autonomy, another issue the Baltic deputies frequently raised was the history of the Baltic states' incorporation into the Soviet Union— the matter upon which the legitimacy of Soviet rule depended. Even LiCP First Secretary Algirdas Brazauskas, a moderate who was concerned that *Sąjūdis* was moving too quickly, could not avoid addressing the issue, stressing at one of the congress's early sessions (May 31) that the Soviet government's vagueness on the matter weakened his own party.[5]

Under pressure from the Baltic delegates, a commission under the CPSU Central Committee was created to study the question. By the time its report—which confirmed the existence of the Molotov-Ribbentrop Pact's secret protocols—was adopted by the congress in December 1989, the Soviet government had developed a new line on the issue: even if the pact had been a violation of the sovereignty of the Baltic states, it ran, the incorporation of these countries into the USSR had been accomplished through the voluntary actions of their parliaments. The pact and the incorporation of the republics, the Kremlin now claimed, were two different matters.[6] As Gorbachev said on September 19, there were "no grounds to question the decision by the Baltic republics to join the USSR and the choice made by their peoples."[7] Thus throughout 1989 the Soviet government and the Baltic republics were increasingly working at cross-purposes: as the former struggled to strengthen a reformed union of sovereign socialist republics, the goal of nearly all indigenous Baltic organizations had become the restoration of unfettered independence.

Unlike the 1930s, when the Baltic states failed to cooperate with each other in any meaningful way, from 1989 onwards Baltic nationalists saw cooperation as a vital component of their effort to break free of Soviet rule. They made contacts with the other republics of the Soviet empire, with the West, and with each other, thereby lessening the likelihood of a violent crackdown on their movements of national liberation. The Baltic Council of Popular Fronts, formed in July 1989, met on a regular basis to discuss and coordinate their activities. Most famously, the popular fronts organized the "Baltic Way" demonstration of August 23, 1989, in which up to two million people held hands to form a human chain running through Tallinn, Rīga, and Vilnius. Perhaps more than any single act, this demonstration of solidarity drew the world's attention to the plight of the Baltic republics and their struggle for freedom. Moreover, demonstrations such as this (as well as the song festivals attended by hundreds of thousands of Balts) induced a dramatic transformation of consciousness not only among the Baltic masses, but also among their leaders, many of whom now became aware of their own latent nationalist sentiments.

Of course, the Baltics were not the only aggrieved Soviet satrapies, and their aspirations to national independence should be viewed within the context of the more general struggle of the republics against the dictates of the "center" (Moscow) that began to unfold at the end of the 1980s. In contrast to the relatively peaceful situation in the Baltics, in Alma-Ata, the capital of the Kazakh SSR, rioting occurred in December 1986 when its first secretary was replaced by a Russian; and in April 1989, a peaceful demonstration was suppressed by the Soviet army in Tbilisi, Georgia, with more than 20 killed. Worse still was the civil war that threatened to break out between the Armenian and Azerbaijan republics over the disputed Nagorno-Karabakh region, an Armenian enclave in Azerbaijan. Challenges from the Belarussian, Moldovan, and Ukrainian republics followed. Meanwhile, beyond the USSR's western border, by the end of 1989 a "velvet revolution" had swept through Eastern Europe, toppling communist regimes and obliterating the military and economic structures that linked the USSR to its former satellites. It was the latter route—the non-violent one taken by Poland (exemplified by the nonviolent tactics of the Solidarity movement), Hungary, and Czechoslovakia—that Baltic leaders intended to take as they moved toward the goal of independence.

Indeed, the successful revolutions of Eastern Europe emboldened the separatists in the Baltics and other Soviet republics to take decisive action. Their efforts were further encouraged by the repeated assertions of Gorbachev and other Politburo members throughout 1989 that Moscow would not use military force to resolve its disputes with Baltic nationalists. However, in contrast to his magnanimous treatment of the former satellites of Eastern Europe, Gorbachev was unwilling to preside over the disintegration of the "inner" empire. The Union, the Soviet president insisted, must be preserved. Thus, in the unfolding struggle of the Soviet "periphery" against the "center," Gorbachev took a middle position, advocating both strong republics *and* a strong center. This notion was captured by the CPSU's draft program on "The Party's Nationalities Policy in Present-Day Conditions," issued on August 17, 1989. "Without a strong union," the draft said, "there cannot be strong republics. And without strong republics, there cannot be a strong union."[8] For the Baltic republics such a formula was increasingly unacceptable.

Following the lead of the popular fronts and other new movements, by the end of 1989 the Baltic communist parties found themselves in the paradoxical position of endorsing independence, albeit in a gradual and controlled manner, for their republics. They also found that if they did not distance themselves from the CPSU, they ran the risk of appearing out of touch with the mood of the people. Concerned about the prospect of losing in the local elections planned for early 1990—free, multiparty elections that would determine who controlled the Lithuanian government—the Lithuanian Communist Party (LiCP) was the first to seek a divorce from the mother organization. First Secretary Brazauskas first informed Gorbachev of this plan on December 1, 1989, less than a week before the Lithuanian Supreme Soviet voted to eliminate the Communist Party's monopoly on power. The LiCP's separation from the CPSU, Brazauskas reasoned, was the only way for his party to retain enough popular support to succeed in the elections. Sensitive to the charge that the Communist Party had not changed during *perestroika*, Gorbachev hoped that his Lithuanian comrades could be convinced to remain in the CPSU while a new program was prepared for the party congress, scheduled for the following spring.

Despite Gorbachev's pleas, on December 20 the overwhelming majority of the LiCP delegates to the local party congress in Vilnius voted in favor of their organization's independence from the CPSU. The rest, about 160 of the 1,033 delegates, decided to remain aligned with the CPSU, retaining the CPSU's program and forming their own central committee to rival the one headed by Brazauskas. (An analogous split in the ECP occurred in March 1990 and in the LaCP the following month. However, the majority of Latvian Communists, who in fact were mostly non-Latvian, remained loyal to Moscow and elected the hardline Alfrēds Rubiks to the post of first secretary.)

Gorbachev, still convinced that the breach in the party could be healed and that most ordinary Lithuanians truly supported the Soviet system, rejected Brazauskas's argument and in January went to Vilnius (he was the first and only CPSU general secretary to do so) to plead his case. Addressing both wings of the LiCP, he promised "big changes in the operation of the Party [CPSU]." The party, he declared, "will deliberate, work at its plenums and Congresses, decide on Union affairs, political questions, how *perestroika* should be developed, and meanwhile Comrade Brazauskas will be reading newspapers to learn what we have decided and what the fate of Lithuania should be in this connection."[9] For Brazauskas, however, the withdrawal of the LiCP was irrevocable.

While in Vilnius, Gorbachev also took his case to the Lithuanian people. Speaking with factory workers, Gorbachev emphasized the political, economic, and defense ties that bound together all the Union republics, and warned Lithuanians of the dangers of ethnic strife and even bloodshed should they continue their secessionist course. "At present," he insisted, "no republic can live without the other republics. . . . We're all tied together now." Despite his assurances that progress was being made toward the creation of "a full-fledged federation with sovereign republics and a unified CPSU as a mighty integrating political force under conditions of democratization and decentralization," Lithuanians refused to accept his argument.[10] Contrary to Gorbachev's intentions, his visit to Lithuania exposed the vast gulf that had emerged between his way of thinking and that of ordinary Lithuanians, who increasingly sided with the pro-independence movement headed by *Sąjūdis*.

Although the popularity of the independent LiCP recovered for a time, it was a radicalized *Sąjūdis*, then approaching the height of its popularity, that dominated the local elections of early March 1990: *Sąjūdis*-supported candidates won 98 of 141 seats in the parliament, while most of the rest went to members of the independent LiCP.[11] The chairman of the new Lithuanian Supreme Soviet (the Russian word "Soviet" was quickly replaced by "Council") and head of state was Vytautas Landsbergis (b.1932), a musicologist and a leader of *Sąjūdis* since November 1988. An outspoken

Lithuanian nationalist, Landsbergis was convinced that there was no time to waste: Lithuania must declare its independence immediately, before Gorbachev, soon to be elected president of the USSR, accrued additional powers that would allow him to prevent the secession of the republics.[12] Thus on the same day as Landsbergis's election, March 11, 1990, the legislature declared the Republic of Lithuania's exit from the USSR. Although the right to secede was guaranteed in the existing Soviet constitution, officials in Moscow, including many liberals, insisted that the Lithuanian government had violated the constitution and thereby perpetrated an illegal act.

As in Lithuania, elections were held in Latvia and Estonia in February and March. Candidates who supported both the Latvian Popular Front (LPF) platform and independence easily carried the day in Latvia, securing just over the necessary two-thirds majority required to control the Supreme Soviet. Hardliners in the LaCP were effectively excluded from power. Although supporters of independence constituted the overwhelming majority of the 101 deputies elected to the Supreme Soviet of the Estonian SSR, the Estonians, split between radicals (independence now) and moderates (independence later), were well aware of the harsh Soviet response to Lithuania's declaration and therefore considered it necessary to compromise. Thus on March 30 the Estonian legislature, renamed the Supreme Council of the Republic of Estonia in early May, declared the republic to be "in a transition phase toward independence." Likewise, on May 4 the Latvian Supreme Soviet endorsed the goal of restoring the independence of the Republic of Latvia following a transitional period. Gorbachev quickly pronounced the decisions null and void.

By May 1990 all three Baltic republics had formally declared their intention to achieve independence from the USSR, but with one important difference between them: whereas at this stage Estonia and Latvia still approached independence as a matter to be negotiated with Moscow, Lithuania treated its independence as an accomplished, irrevocable fact.

STALEMATE

Following the local elections in the spring of 1990, Arnold Rüütel (b.1928) was elected chairman of the Estonian Supreme Soviet—the ceremonial head of state—thus retaining a position he had held since 1983.[13] Likewise, the incumbent chairman of the Latvian Supreme Soviet, Anatolijs Gorbunovs, was retained for the top post in the Supreme Council. Although both Rüütel and Gorbunovs favored sovereignty for their republics, each had risen through the ranks of the Communist Party—each had been a career Soviet apparatchik. Lithuania, unlike its northern neighbors, chose a more confrontational course: despite the tremendous personal popularity of LiCP First Secretary Brazauskas, in March 1990 the Lithuanian Supreme Council chose as head of state Professor Vytautas Landsbergis—a man who had never been a member of the Communist Party.

To many ordinary Lithuanians he was an arrogant academic—in contrast to the "man of the people" image cultivated by Brazauskas—but in the eyes of the Lithuanian intelligentsia, Landsbergis was untainted. As journalist Anatol Lieven, a perceptive observer of the Baltic scene during this period, wrote, "Much of the Lithuanian intelligentsia identifies passionately with a national cultural vision of Lithuania. They love Landsbergis because he is the perfect symbol of that identification."[14] Landsbergis's great-grandfather had fought the Russian Empire during the 1863 rebellion; his grandfather, a writer, had played a role in the founding of the modern Lithuanian state; in 1941 his father had been appointed a minister in a Lithuanian Provisional Government composed of anti-Soviet rebels. Standing up to Moscow as his ancestors had before him, Vytautas Landsbergis was, in the spring of 1990, the living embodiment of Lithuanian patriotism.

Landsbergis and the Communist Party had been on a collision course ever since November 20, 1988, when upon becoming president of *Sąjūdis* he declared that "Only Lithuania can decide and execute its own laws."[15] Three months later he called for the full restoration of Lithuanian sovereignty—a first step toward the country's independence. "We long ago decided that this is something we must do, to fight for our independence," Landsbergis declared in August 1989, in response to a warning from the CPSU. "We're not extremist and we are not violent, but we are determined."[16] Little more than six months later the Supreme Council of the Republic of Lithuania, which he now chaired, declared its full independence from the USSR. The decision was based partly the result of the mistaken belief, encouraged by émigré contacts in the United States, that U.S. President George H. W. Bush would provide the country with diplomatic recognition.[17] Although many deputies were uncomfortable with a declaration of immediate secession, the principle of independence had already won out in Lithuania; few were willing to vote against it.

The Vilnius declaration provoked a strong reaction from Mikhail Gorbachev, who immediately called it "invalid and illegal." Some observers, including Brazauskas and Estonian president Rüütel, believed that the Soviet president's denunciation was only for public consumption, and that his private views regarding Lithuania's eventual independence were somewhat more flexible. Whatever the case, Gorbachev made it clear to the Soviet public (and to his critics in the Kremlin) that he intended to prevent Lithuania from pursuing this course.

Until this time, and for perhaps even longer, Gorbachev sincerely believed that the people of the Baltic republics did not really want to break from the Soviet Union. Convinced that the Balts understood that they could not survive economically if they left the Union, the general secretary was certain that they could be dissuaded from doing so. Like many Russians, Gorbachev was also certain that nobody benefited more from the Soviet economic system than the Baltic republics, and that it was mostly Russians who paid for the Balts' relatively high standard of living. Indeed, it was precisely this notion—that the empire was bleeding Russia white— that convinced many Russians to rally around Boris Yeltsin's (b.1931) call for *Russian* sovereignty in the spring of 1990.

However, as the Baltic drive for independence picked up steam, Gorbachev began to grasp more fully both the precariousness of his own political position and the potential domino effect on the other republics about which his hardline colleagues had been warning him for months: first Lithuania would leave, then Estonia and Latvia. Not only would the extensive Soviet military deployments along the Baltic be lost—thus compromising the USSR's ability either to defend itself or project its forces into Europe—but the precedent set by the Baltics would ultimately trigger the collapse of the entire empire. Lithuania, Gorbachev concluded, had to be stopped.

To force Landsbergis to rescind the declaration of independence, the Soviet president applied steady pressure on Lithuania. Soviet military planes and helicopters began unscheduled maneuvers over the republic; buildings were seized from the independent Lithuanian Communist Party by Interior Ministry troops and handed over to the pro-Moscow loyalists. Meanwhile, a new law on secession began to be worked out in the USSR Congress of People's Deputies, and was passed on April 7, 1990. According to this plan, Lithuania, like any other Soviet republic, would have to jump a series of legal hurdles before it could attain its independence: a referendum would have to be held, and a five-year waiting period would be necessary while the details were sorted through. While Gorbachev claimed to have created a constitutional mechanism for secession, the real purpose was to prevent the Soviet republics from defecting.

Despite Gorbachev's maneuvers, Landsbergis maintained his conviction that Soviet law did not apply to Lithuania, an illegally occupied country. Thus in mid-April, an exasperated Gorbachev resorted to imposing a partial embargo on the vulnerable republic, thereby cutting off much of its energy supply. While Brazauskas and Lithuanian Prime Minister

Kazimiera Prunskienė (a reform communist and also a *Sąjūdis* leader) urged compromise, Landsbergis refused to give in. Even as the popularity of *Sąjūdis* and its leader began to decline, most of the Lithuanian public continued to support his policy of resistance to Moscow.

Although Landsbergis refused to rescind the declaration of independence, at the end of June he and the Supreme Council agreed to suspend its implementation for 100 days while Vilnius and Moscow worked to negotiate a settlement. With the Lithuanian parliament approving the moratorium, Gorbachev agreed to lift the sanctions. By this time, however, Gorbachev had to deal with another, potentially more threatening crisis: on June 8, 1990, the RSFSR Supreme Soviet, chaired by Boris Yeltsin, declared Russia's sovereignty and gave its laws precedence over the laws of the USSR, thereby setting into motion a "parade of sovereignties" in the other Union republics. In the process, Yeltsin, embroiled in a bitter political rivalry with Gorbachev, had agreed that his government would cooperate with Lithuania. The enemy of my enemy, Yeltsin surely reasoned, may prove to be a valuable friend.

As Yeltsin cultivated allies in the Baltics—establishing bilateral relations between the RSFSR and each of the Baltic republics—negotiations between Moscow (Gorbachev) and the Lithuanian government went nowhere. The same was true of the Soviet government's negotiations with the other Baltic republics: each side repeatedly set out its positions, but proved unable to find common ground. The struggle between the republics and the "center" had reached an impasse.

Meanwhile, the Baltic rebellion had spread to the military. The spring military draft was a disaster in the Baltics and in other rebellious regions such as the Caucasus republics and western Ukraine. With the active help of pro-independence parties, Baltic soldiers had even begun deserting. With the army falling apart and the Union threatening to fracture along national lines, more than ever Gorbachev was facing strong pressure from his hardline colleagues to take control of the situation.

Thus in the fall of 1990, Gorbachev's ruling style took a sharp authoritarian turn. In November the Soviet president acquired new emergency powers, and placed known reactionaries at the head of the ministries of interior and defense. The Soviet program for accelerated economic reform, called the Shatalin (or "500 Days") Plan, was dropped. As for the Lithuanian problem, Gorbachev would work with the republic's Soviet loyalists, such as Mykolas Burokevicius (appointed to the Politburo in Moscow the previous summer), rather than with Landsbergis and Brazauskas.

Still, to this point Gorbachev had refused to allow the matter to be settled by means of force, as the hardliners who surrounded him often urged him to do. Although the Soviet army had been used to quell demonstrations in April 1989 in Tbilisi, the capital of the Georgian SSR, and to stop ethnic fighting in Azerbaijan's capital, Baku, in January 1990, Gorbachev, unlike his predecessors, was averse to the application of brute force. Moreover, the Soviet leader was keenly aware that a crackdown on Lithuania would provoke a backlash in Washington, which in turn would jeopardize his entire reform program—and his political survival. As Soviet Minister of Defense Dmitri Yazov told an American official in the spring of 1990: "If one republic secedes, Gorbachev is through. And if he has to use force to prevent one from leaving, he's out too."[18]

THE COLLAPSE

While Gorbachev had long been under pressure from his colleagues in the Politburo to do something about the situation in the Baltics, it was the Moscow loyalists in the rump LiCP who finally convinced him that a show of force was necessary. In early January 1991, as the pro-empire *Edinstvo* group (which after the split of the LiCP in December 1989 was an arm of the pro-Moscow organization) led a series of demonstrations against the nationalist government in Vilnius, Soviet troops began to occupy strategic buildings. The Prunskienė government's dispute with Moscow over prices only aggravated the tense situation in the streets. With Vilnius engulfed in a crisis atmosphere, on January 10 the Prunskienė government resigned. Taking advantage of the political disarray in Lithuania, pro-empire forces quickly went into action.

The situation turned violent during the night of January 12–13, when a mysterious "National Salvation Committee" claimed to have seized power in Lithuania. At the same time, Soviet paratroops and members of the KGB Alpha unit attacked the Vilnius television tower, which was then surrounded by thousands of young Lithuanians. Fifteen were killed and hundreds were injured. Convinced that this was a prelude to an attack on the parliament, Landsbergis called upon Lithuanians to gather at Independence Square to defend their government; they would greet any assault with passive resistance. Despite the fact that international attention was otherwise focused on the conflict in the Persian Gulf, television viewers around the world witnessed scenes of brutality and heroic resistance in Vilnius. Indeed, it was likely this factor—world opinion, along with the presence of Western journalists—that prevented Moscow from launching a final, lethal assault.

Meanwhile, in Rīga, where a similar attack appeared imminent, hundreds of thousands gathered in the streets, surrounding key public buildings with hastily constructed barricades. Five Latvians were killed on January 20 when Soviet special forces attacked buildings belonging to the Ministry of Internal Affairs. As in Lithuania, a "National Salvation Committee" appeared during the crackdown, led by party First Secretary Alfrēds Rubiks and supported by the Latvian Interfront. Russian democrats, fearing that the RSFSR was next, organized demonstrations in Moscow and demanded the Soviet president's resignation.

Gorbachev, not wanting to tarnish the liberal image he had carefully cultivated for Western consumption, denied responsibility for both the attack in Vilnius and the deaths in Rīga. Meanwhile, on January 13, immediately after the Vilnius attack, Boris Yeltsin, then conducting his own struggle against the Soviet "center" (and in this sense realizing that his fate was entwined with that of the Baltic leaders), flew to Tallinn to offer his support. Upon his return to Moscow he appealed to Russian soldiers serving in the Baltics not to fire on the people. While the immediate crisis passed, for several months afterwards Moscow continued a policy of low-level harassment in both Latvia and Lithuania.

None of the three Baltic republics was dissuaded from pursuing its course. With Landsbergis at the height of his popularity, on February 9 a referendum was held in Lithuania on the matter of independence: 90 percent of voters were in favor. Likewise, on March 3, referenda were held in Estonia and Latvia, where 78 percent and 74 percent voted "yes." Planning to conduct referenda of its own in mid-March, the Soviet leadership refused to acknowledge the legitimacy of those held in the Baltic republics.

With such an overwhelmingly positive response to the question of independence, it is evident that even many non-Balts living in these republics had voted in favor. Indeed, an often-overlooked aspect of this period was the often-positive response of the non-native, usually Russophone, segment of the Baltic populations to the question of Baltic independence. A poll taken in December 1990 in Latvia found that 47 percent of non-Latvians supported independence (including 59 percent of those non-natives who had been born in Lithuania); perhaps 30 percent of non-Estonians voted in favor of independence in the March referendum.[19]

By this time Gorbachev had shifted tactics once again, abandoning the hardliners—who no longer trusted him—to pursue a more flexible position that was more favorable to republican sovereignty. The Soviet president now planned to hold an all-Union referendum on the question of voluntarily preserving the USSR "as a renewed federation of equal sovereign republics." The referendum was held on March 17, but the Baltic republics, now regarding themselves as independent states, refused to participate. Throughout the spring of 1991 Moscow negotiated the terms of a new Union treaty with the leaders of the republics; but the three Baltic republics—as well as Georgia, Armenia, and Moldova (formerly Moldavia)—refused to participate.

Having reached agreement with the governments of the nine participating republics, the new Union Treaty was set to be signed on August 20, 1991. On August 4, Gorbachev left Moscow for his annual vacation on the Crimean shore. Exactly two weeks later, a group of Soviet hardliners arrived at his vacation house, where they tried to persuade the president to endorse their plans for the introduction of a state of emergency. Refusing to go along with their plot, Gorbachev was confined to house arrest in Foros, while the self-proclaimed State Committee on the State of Emergency—a coalition of forces from the KGB, military, Ministry of the Interior, and the party apparatus—announced its takeover early on the morning of August 19. They expected no serious opposition.

Yeltsin's resistance in Moscow was heroic—and marked the summit of his career as an anticommunist rebel. Managing to elude arrest, he declared the takeover an illegal coup d'etat and galvanized popular resistance to it. While the commander of the Baltic military district announced that he was taking control of Estonia, Latvia, and Lithuania, the three Baltic governments threw their support to Yeltsin and called for a general strike. As the coup collapsed—the putschists had no stomach for the large-scale violence that would have been required to pull it off—Estonia and Latvia declared their full independence, on August 20 and 21 respectively. Despite a few casualties in Lithuania—which had regarded itself as independent since March 1990—Soviet military units quickly retreated to their barracks.

Throughout the USSR the bungled coup attempt completely destroyed whatever popular legitimacy the Communist Party had enjoyed before August 19. When Gorbachev returned to Moscow on August 21, he was the president of a state that for all practical purposes no longer existed. As the remaining Soviet republics declared their independence one by one, on September 6 the USSR formally recognized the independence of Estonia, Latvia, and Lithuania. Eleven days later the Baltic states were admitted to the United Nations. While in the formal sense the empire lingered on for several more months, Russian President Boris Yeltsin (he was formally elected RSFSR president in June 1991) and the leaders of Ukraine and Belarus decided officially to end the Soviet Union on December 31 and create in its place a looser Commonwealth of Independent States (CIS). The Baltic states, now completely independent and recognized as such by the international community, opted not to join. Their destiny, they concurred, was with the West.

NOTES

1. Anatol Lieven, *The Baltic Revolution: Estonia, Latvia, Lithuania and the Path to Independence* (New Haven and London: Yale University Press, 1993), 222.

2. The Lithuanian Freedom League was a dissident movement that first appeared in the late 1970s, then faded from view until reemerging in 1987. It soon became a main rival to the more moderate *Sajūdis*.

3. Walter C. Clemens, *Baltic Independence and Russian Empire* (New York: St. Martin's Press, 1991), 99.

4. Shafir (1995), 175.

5. Rolf H.W. Theen, ed., *The U.S.S.R. First Congress of People's Deputies, Vol. 1* (New York: Paragon House, 1991), 244.

6. After initially defending the pact, Aleksandr Yakovlev, who chaired the commission, on December 24, 1989, revealed the text of the documents and denounced the secret protocols and Stalinism. Yet he still separated the issue of the pact and the illegal annexation of the Baltic states.

7. Clemens (1991), 235.

8. Ibid., 232.

9. TASS, January 14, 1990.

10. *The Current Digest of the Soviet Press* 42:2, (February 14, 1990): 3.

11. Two bodies were elected in each republic: first the new Congress of People's Deputies (CPD), and then the existing legislatures, called Supreme Soviets. Unlike the larger lower houses, the smaller Supreme Soviets of the Estonian, Latvian and Lithuanian SSRs were standing bodies able to pass legislation.

12. Gorbachev was elected president by the USSR CPD on March 14. The post would allow him to declare a state of emergency and thereby obstruct any Soviet republic's quest for independence. Moreover, the new secession law proposed by Gorbachev would hinder Lithuania's move toward independence, not facilitate it.

13. The real head of state in Estonia was Prime Minister Edgar Savisaar, who formed a PFE government.

14. Lieven (1993), 25.

15. Richard J. Krickus, *Showdown: The Lithuanian Rebellion and the Breakup of the Soviet Empire* (Washington and London: Brassey's, 1997), 64.

16. Clemens (1991), 126, 195.

17. Providing Lithuania with diplomatic recognition, Washington believed, would result in Gorbachev's ouster, which would be a setback to reform in the USSR and the improved international climate. Moreover, the State Department claimed that it had recognized the Lithuanian state in 1922 and had never withdrawn that recognition.

18. Michael R. Beschloss and Strobe Talbott, *At the Highest Levels* (Boston: Little, Brown, 1993), 195.

19. Shafir (1995), 183.

8

The Post-Soviet Baltic States

In 1918, when they first declared their independence from Russia, the Estonian, Latvian, and Lithuanian peoples were little known outside their homelands. Occupied by Soviet forces in 1940, the plight of the tiny Baltic republics was barely noticed by Western countries as Europe struggled with Nazi aggression. Even after the war's conclusion, the place of these three "Soviet Socialist Republics" within the USSR was hardly questioned in the West, although émigré organizations attempted to keep hope alive by keeping up pressure in Washington and London. For Britain's Winston Churchill, however, the Baltic countries' Sovietization was an unfortunate but nevertheless acceptable price for the wartime alliance with Stalin. Although the USA never legally recognized the Baltic states' incorporation, Churchill's realist perspective ultimately prevailed, and for more than four decades the USA's Soviet policy was predicated upon the assumption that Estonia, Latvia, and Lithuania were permanently tied to Moscow.

By 1989 the situation had changed dramatically: as the Iron Curtain fell, the Soviet claim of the Balts' "voluntary" incorporation into the USSR was exposed for the sham that it was. Never before in their history had the Baltic peoples so effectively attracted the world's attention as they did during their struggle for independence in 1988–91. The euphoria quickly faded, however, as the Estonians, Latvians, and Lithuanians began to confront the myriad political, social, and economic problems facing their countries.

Most importantly, the political structures of the Baltic states, designed in Moscow for the purpose of maintaining the republics' subordination to the Kremlin, had to be remade to conform to the resurgent values of national sovereignty, personal liberty, and democracy. Likewise, the heavily centralized economies of the Baltic states, also created and regulated by planners in Moscow for the benefit of the USSR, needed to be revamped, reinvigorated, and reoriented to serve national needs rather than Soviet ones. Furthermore, as each Baltic country reasserted its identity as a *nation-state*, requirements for citizenship in that state needed to be determined—a controversial issue for countries that had experienced decades of foreign occupation and massive immigration of Russians and other Slavic peoples. Finally, the Baltic states needed to take security measures to protect their newly won independence; for each this meant the building of native defense forces, the withdrawal of the remaining Soviet/Russian troops on their territory, and the new states' integration with European and international institutions.

POLITICS AND GOVERNMENT

Latvia

On August 21, 1991, as the coup by Soviet hardliners unraveled in Moscow, the Latvian Supreme Council seized the moment and declared that the constitution of February 15, 1922, was the law of the land, with no revisions or amendments. The political system of the new Latvian state was to be based on that which existed before Soviet annexation in June 1940: the parliament (*Saeima,* so named to emphasize the restored Latvian government's continuity with the prewar Latvian state) would consist of 100 representatives elected for three-year terms by all citizens aged 18 or over on the basis of proportional representation. A president was to be elected by the *Saeima* for a term of three years. (In 1997 terms for representatives and the president were extended to four years.) The president's responsibilities include the appointment of a prime minister, who in turn nominates other cabinet ministers.

Since elections did not take place until June 1993, the structure of the Latvian government remained the same for nearly two years after the parliament's declaration of independence. Much of the old *nomenklatura* (the Soviet state and party elite)—with the exception of the banned pro-Moscow Latvian Communist Party—remained in power, where they shared the task of governing with reformers, anticommunists, and young, ambitious people who had remained outside of government during the tumult of 1988–91.

Unsurprisingly, once the main goal of independence was achieved, Latvian politicians were divided as to how to proceed with the rebuilding of their country. On both the political "left" and "right" there was general agreement on the need for political and economic reform, but differences emerged over the pace and the details. While the Latvian "left," composed largely of ethnic Russians, had by 1991 jettisoned much (but far from all) of Soviet-style socialism, it sought a gradual approach to economic reform while advocating full legal and economic protection for the Russophone minority. The "right" tended toward Latvian nationalist positions as it sought the restoration of Latvia as a nation-state; it distrusted communists in general and Russians in particular, and favored a strong defense, but was initially unable to come to a consensus on the matter of economic reform. Like the left, the right generally favored a strong state role in the economy and the retention (or creation) of state welfare programs.

On June 5–6, 1993, while the country was at the nadir of a devastating economic crisis, elections to the Fifth *Saeima* were finally held, despite the fact that the absence of a citizenship law deprived many non-Latvians of the right to vote. The election process was strikingly different from that which existed in Soviet days: instead of a single communist party, whose candidate one could either vote for or against in the meaningless Soviet elections, by 1993 there were more than 20 parties or coalitions, representing diverse constituencies and interests, contending for seats in the *Saeima*.[1] The leading vote-getter in the first post-Soviet election was Latvia's Way (36 seats), a moderate, centrist party. Lacking an absolute majority, however, it had to form a coalition with the Agrarian Union (12 seats), a right-wing party that sought to protect the interests of Latvia's rural communities. By this time the Popular Front, a decisive force in Latvian politics between 1988 and 1991, had fallen apart and failed to pass the 4 percent threshold required for representation in the parliament.

Thus the Latvian government that ruled from June 1993 to July 1994 was a right-of-center coalition that nevertheless demonstrated unmistakable continuity with the communist past, as shown by the fact that 33 representatives elected to the *Saeima* had also been deputies in the old Supreme Council. Anatolijs Gorbunovs (Latvia's Way), the Latvian head of state since 1990, was elected presiding officer of the *Saeima*. The *Saeima* in turn elected to the presidency Guntis Ulmanis (b.1939), a grandnephew of Kārlis Ulmanis (prewar Latvia's last president) and a leader of the Agrarian Union. Ulmanis chose as prime minister the anticommunist Valdis Birkavs (b.1942) of Latvia's Way.[2] However, in July 1994 the entire cabinet resigned after three of its members were forced out on corruption charges.

With the debate about citizenship rights for non-Latvians inflaming passions in both the Russian and Latvian communities, in the mid-1990s Latvian politics veered in an unmistakably nationalist direction: local elections held in May 1994 resulted in a landslide victory for nationalist parties, largely at the expense of Latvia's Way. Likewise, parliamentary elections in the autumn of 1995, in the wake of the collapse of Latvia's largest bank, showed a striking rise in popular support for parties of the far left (such as the Peoples' Harmony Party and the Latvian Socialist Party) and the nationalist right (principally the bloc formed by the merger of For Fatherland and Freedom with the Latvian National Independence Movement Union).

By 1998, however, with the divisive issue of citizenship for non-Latvians seemingly settled and Latvia's recovery from its economic doldrums well on its way, politics shifted back toward the moderate center. Following the parliamentary elections of October 1998, a new centrist coalition took shape that included the Fatherland Front, Latvia's Way, the New Party, and the Latvian Social Democratic Alliance.[3]

With more than 40 officially registered political organizations in the country in the year 2002, the Latvian political scene remains fragmented, and attempts to create a stable government are fraught with difficulties. Between 1998 and 2000 alone, Latvia had no fewer than four prime ministers (Guntars Krasts, Vilis Kristopans, Andris Skele, and Andris Berzins). One of the major achievements of Latvian politics, however, was the Seventh *Saiema*'s election in June 1999 of the first woman president of central and eastern Europe, Vaira Vīķe-Freiberga (b.1937) of Latvia's Way. Born in Latvia and for many years employed as a professor at the University of Montreal, where she wrote books on Latvian folklore, one of Vīķe-Freiberga's first actions upon being elected president was to reject a bill that would have completely excluded the Russian language from Latvia's public life.

Lithuania

In attempting to create a new democratic state, Lithuania faced many of the same problems and obstacles as its northern neighbors. Unlike Latvia, however, Lithuania chose not simply to resurrect its prewar constitution, but instead elected to create a new constitution that would reflect the experiences of democratic countries such as the United States, France, and postwar Germany, while retaining some elements of Soviet-style government—including the combining of some legislative and executive functions, as well as providing guarantees of social rights such as free medical care. After two years of acrimonious debate in the Lithuanian Supreme Council, the new constitution was approved by a voter referendum on October 25, 1992.

As during the prewar period, the legislature is the *Seimas,* a popularly elected body consisting of 141 members, 70 of whom are chosen on the basis of proportional representation (selected from party lists), with the remainder elected from single-member districts on the first-past-the-post principle. The executive branch consists of a popularly elected president, who serves a five-year term, and a prime minister, who is chosen by the president with the approval of the *Seimas.* The president's role is largely ceremonial and consultative in regard to domestic affairs, but the office has considerable power to shape foreign policy. Although the judiciary is independent of the other branches, the president may influence it by appointing justices to the Supreme Court and Constitutional Court.

Until the constitution went into effect, Lithuania was governed by the old *Sąjūdis*-dominated Supreme Council, headed by Vytautas Landsbergis. However, by the time parliamentary elections took place in October 1992, Landsbergis and the *Sąjūdis* movement had become deeply unpopular, as the government had failed to deal effectively with the negative effects of the economic collapse, including runaway inflation, a decline in living standards, and unemployment. While Landsbergis's zealous anticommunism and moralizing seemed excessive to many Lithuanians, his advocacy of a strong presidency and apparent unconcern for the rights of national minorities alienated many others.

Like other postcommunist governments in Eastern Europe, the one headed by *Sąjūdis* ultimately became a victim of heightened—and frustrated—expectations and its own lack of experience in governing. For many Lithuanians, the experienced and pragmatic Algirdas Brazauskas provided hope. The Lithuanian Democratic Labor Party (LDLP) he headed was the successor to the reform wing of the Communist Party, but had discarded Soviet-style socialism in favor of a social democratic platform. With the resurgence of the LDLP in 1992, politics in Lithuania was soon defined by the struggle between the conservative Lithuanian nationalism of *Sąjūdis* and its successors on the right, and the left-leaning but conciliatory LDLP, with the latter popularly viewed as the party with the experience necessary to alleviate the distress of economic collapse. Reorganizing itself and consolidating support in rural areas and small towns, the LDLP carried the October 1992 elections, winning a majority (73) of seats in the

Seimas. The elections put an end to a two-year period of government instability in Lithuania, during which time five prime ministers formed governments.

In the presidential election that followed on February 14, 1993, the broadly popular Brazauskas defeated the diplomat Stasys Lozoraitis Jr. (1924–94), who, having spent many years in exile, was portrayed by his opponents as a "foreigner" who knew little of the affairs of his own country. For the post of prime minister Brazauskas selected Adolfas Šleževičius (b.1948), a former deputy minister of agriculture. Among his main tasks were the implementation of Lithuania's political and economic reforms and improvement his country's soured relations with Russia, upon which Lithuania still depended for fuel.

To many observers, especially Landsbergis, the victory of the former communists was astounding, and appeared to signal a retreat from democracy and economic reform. It was the beginning of a pattern that would soon become familiar to the other former communist countries of Eastern Europe: disenchanted with the parties and movements that had led them to independence, Polish voters returned socialists to power in 1993; likewise, Hungarian socialists won the 1994 parliamentary elections. Yet the Lithuanian socialists, like their counterparts in Poland and Hungary, had moved toward the political center and proved to be committed to democracy, the development of a market economy, and gradual privatization. The LDLP successfully guided Lithuania through the most difficult years of its transition and held onto power until November 1996, when it was defeated in parliamentary elections by Homeland Union/Lithuanian Conservatives (an offshoot of *Sąjūdis*'s right wing), following a major banking scandal that had implicated Prime Minister Šleževičius and resulted in his removal earlier in the year.

Thus in 1996 the pendulum had swung back to the Conservatives, who occupied 70 seats—just one short of an absolute majority. Their recovery was propelled by a populist campaign that focused on strong social welfare programs, higher pensions for the elderly, and speedy integration into the European Union (EU) and the North Atlantic Treaty Organization (NATO). Right-wing and center parties were also aided by a low voter turnout (54 percent in the first round of the elections); it is likely that most of the abstainers were disillusioned supporters of the LDLP. Nevertheless, perhaps owing to the profoundly negative impact on Lithuania of the Russian crisis of August 1998, the LDLP rebounded again in the October 2000 elections, winning 51 seats and forming a coalition government with the New Union, a party of social liberals.

In recent years Lithuanian presidents have been firm supporters of economic reform. The February 1998 presidential contest resulted in a victory by the émigré Valdas Adamkus (b.1926), supported by the parties of the center and right, over the LDLP's Artūras Paulauskas.[4] Adamkus, who had fled the Soviet invasion of Lithuania in 1944, was a former administrator of the U.S. Environmental Protection Agency and an activist in émigré politics. In 1992 he obtained Lithuanian citizenship and headed the failed presidential campaign of Stasys Lozoraitis. While refraining from allying with the forces of either left or right, for a time the dynamic Adamkus enjoyed considerable popularity as he repeatedly affirmed his commitment to the country's integration into European political and economic institutions.

By the time Adamkus left office in January 2003, when he was unseated by former prime minister and mayor of Vilnius Rolandas Paksas (b.1956), Lithuania, along with Estonia, Latvia, and several other former Soviet satellites, had been invited to join both NATO and the European Union. The much younger Paksas, a businessman and stuntpilot, is seen as a radical economic reformer and has vowed to stay the course with regard to Lithuania's integration into Europe.

Estonia

As in Lithuania, Estonia began its new life as an independent country without a constitution. The governing document that finally came into force in July 1992, after nearly a year of discussion, was based on the principles of the 1922 version, whose emphases included democratic freedoms and protection for ethnic minorities. An important difference, however, was the new constitution's provisions for a clear separation of powers, which was lacking in the earlier version. The four sets of parliamentary elections that have been held thus far (1992, 1995, 1999, and 2003), and the smooth transfers of power that have followed, testify to the durability and widespread acceptance of the new constitutional order.

At the time of the Soviet collapse, Estonia's politics were dominated by Edgar Savisaar's People's Center Party, based on the core of the pro-independence Popular Front. With the restoration of statehood, however, Estonia's political scene quickly fractured. By the time elections to the 101-member *Riigikogu* (which like Latvia has a proportional representation list system) were held in September 1992, the Center Party's popularity had slipped, and Estonian politics had fragmented so thoroughly that no fewer than 38 parties participated in the elections. Since most Russians lacked citizenship rights at this time and therefore could not vote in national elections (as in Latvia), it is unsurprising that the result was a 100-percent ethnic Estonian parliament and a vehemently nationalist ruling coalition led by the conservative Fatherland Party (*Isamaa*), the Estonian National Independence Party, and the Moderates. On October 5 the *Riigikogu* elected Foreign Minister Lennart Meri (b.1929) of Fatherland to a five-year term as the country's new president—a largely ceremonial post. Meri in turn appointed the youthful Fatherland chairman Mart Laar (b.1960), a historian and activist in the Estonian Heritage Society in the late 1980s, to be the country's prime minister.

The election of Meri, who had been deported to Siberia for five years under Stalin, to the country's presidency represented a true changing of the guard in Estonia, as he, unlike the leaders of the transitional governments such as Edgar Savisaar and Tiit Vähi, was free from association with the old ruling authorities. Indeed, for the new right-of-center Estonian government, the key to future prosperity was rapid de-Sovietization—meaning the introduction of democratic rule of law to replace a system that was based predominantly on personal relationships and backroom deals. The Meri government was also committed to pursuing an aggressive free market economic policy.

Of the three Baltic states, Estonia acted most decisively in pursuit of legal and economic reform. However, the life spans of Estonian governments have been short, which suggests that the government's commitment to rapid reform has not always been shared by the general population.[5] Indeed, the parliamentary elections of 1995 witnessed a distinct shift to the agrarian parties and parties of the left—a typical pattern in postcommunist eastern and central Europe—largely at the expense of Fatherland.

By the time the 1999 elections were held, there were fewer active political parties than there had been in 1992, but the Estonian political scene was hardly less fragmented. Despite its precipitous drop in popularity, Fatherland was able to form a right-center government coalition with the Moderates and the probusiness Reform Party. However, the popularity of each of these parties was surpassed by that of Edgar Savisaar's resurgent Center Party (28 seats in the 1999 elections), which remained out of the government until January 2002, when it formed a left-center coalition with the Reform Party. Meanwhile, Lennart Meri remained a source of stability, serving as the country's president from 1992 to 2001. In 1999 he was named "European of the Year" for his efforts to forge closer ties with European institutions. Constitutionally barred from seeking a third term, the popular Meri was replaced by Arnold Rüütel following the October 2001 presidential elections.

A feature common to all of the Baltic governments during the first post-Soviet decade is the trouble they have retaining popular support for any duration. Although frequent scandals, endemic corruption, and unpopular political and economic decisions resulted in recurrent changes in the cabinets of each of the Baltic states, the political contestants—including the refashioned communist parties—have continued to demonstrate their commitment to democratic principles.

CITIZENSHIP AND NATIONAL MINORITIES

One of the most divisive issues facing the Baltic states during the 1990s was the matter of citizenship for their non-native, principally Russian-speaking, minorities. The Estonian citizenship law passed in February 1992 appeared to herald an uncompromising approach to the country's immigrant community, as it declared the principle that immigrants living in Estonia were not automatically citizens of the restored state; this right belonged only to those who were citizens of the prewar republic and their descendants (including 80,000 ethnic Russians). Immigrants and their descendants—more than half a million people, constituting about 30 percent of Estonia's population—would have to be naturalized on the basis of specific language and residency criteria, and would have to take an oath of loyalty to the Estonian Republic. With fewer than one-third of the immigrants prepared to meet the language requirement, which was based on the Citizenship Law of the Estonian Republic of 1938, most Russians were not able to vote in September 1992 parliamentary elections.[6]

During this period of uncertainty many Estonians wished that the Russian immigrants would simply "go back to Russia." From 1992 onwards the Estonian government even offered financial assistance to people wishing to resettle in Russia. In the summer of 1993 the *Riigikogu* forced the issue by passing the Law on Aliens, which demanded that all noncitizens be registered and that they obtain temporary residence permits or face deportation. By this time tens of thousands of Russophones had left for Russia and other former Soviet republics; the remainder were at last forced to decide: would they become Estonian or Russian citizens? With the pressure of a two-year deadline, most Russians opted for Estonia, and since then many have managed to meet the requirements for Estonian citizenship. By early 1999, about 30 percent of legal non-Estonian (in the ethnic sense) residents were citizens of Estonia, 20 percent were citizens of a foreign state (usually Russia), and the remainder were "stateless." Although the number of applications for naturalization has risen sharply since 1999, by 2003 there remained in Estonia about 170,000 stateless people.

Like Estonia, the Latvian government had two basic choices on the citizenship question: it could grant all current residents of Latvia citizenship immediately—the so-called "zero option"—or it could require Soviet-era immigrants to go through the naturalization process. In Latvia, however, the demographic situation was even more threatening to natives than in Estonia: whereas in 1989 about 62 percent of Estonia's residents were ethnic Estonians, Latvians constituted only 52 percent of their republic—and only 39 percent of Rīga's population. Thus Latvia adopted the basic model implemented by Estonia: the citizens of the preoccupation Republic of Latvia and their descendants were declared citizens; the remainder would have to await the adoption of naturalization requirements to apply for citizenship.

In the meantime, the absence of a citizenship law during the first two years of Latvian independence meant than most non-Latvians were unable to vote in the first parliamentary elections. By this time, tens of thousands were leaving Latvia each year to resettle in other areas of the former Soviet Union.[7] Only in August 1994 did the *Saeima* adopt a new Law on Citizenship, but like the Estonian law it was complicated and restrictive. A quota system limited naturalization to about 2,000 people per annum, but Western pressure forced the Latvian government to reconsider the scheme and in 1995 it adopted a less restrictive five-year residency requirement. Although about 53,000 non-Latvians were naturalized from the law's passage until the summer of 2002, more than 500,000 Latvian residents, mostly Russians, are "stateless."

The Lithuanian government was the most conciliatory of the three in regard to its ethnic minorities—perhaps an unexpected outcome given the acrimonious state of relations between Lithuania and Moscow in 1989–91. Part of the reason for Lithuania's more inclusive approach lies in the relative proportion of natives to minorities in the Baltic states: unlike Latvia and Estonia, where natives believed their national cultures were jeopardized by never-ending waves of Slavic immigrants during the Soviet era, in Lithuania the proportion of natives held steady at around 80 percent through the 1970s and 1980s (Russians constituted just under 10 percent); consequently, Lithuanians felt less threatened than their neighbors did by Russification.

On November 29, 1989, nearly two years before the world recognized Lithuania's independence from the USSR, the Lithuanian Soviet Socialist Republic adopted a Citizenship Law that introduced the "zero-option," which allowed all members of national minorities living permanently in Lithuania to apply for Lithuanian citizenship, regardless of nationality and without any language requirements. This law subsequently was amended by a somewhat more restrictive citizenship law adopted in December

1991, when *Sąjūdis* was running the government; in 1995 the law was amended again by the more flexible LDLP government.[8] By early 1993 more than half of Lithuania's ethnic Russian, Polish, Belarussian, and Ukrainian inhabitants had received citizenship; 40,000 others, however, chose to emigrate, thus reducing Lithuania's Russian population to just over 300,000, or 8.5 percent of the population.

Unlike Estonia and Latvia, the Lithuanian government opted for an inclusive and territorially based approach to citizenship, and as a result there has been relatively little external criticism of Lithuania's record on citizenship. Nevertheless, the emigration of tens of thousands of Russians underlines their sense of alienation and unfair treatment by the authorities—a feeling that was common especially during the more difficult early years of Baltic independence. Concentrated in the industrial sector, Russians were often the first to find themselves unemployed. Moreover, Baltic privatization schemes were more favorable to citizens than noncitizens.

In Latvia the plight of Russian-speakers is exacerbated by what they feel has been a systematic government attack on the use of the Russian language. Although Russian is the only language used in some towns and villages, and is used by the majority of Rīga's inhabitants, Russian has been banned on street signs and businesses. However, Russian may be found in other places—museums and restaurant menus, for example. In an attempt to limit Russian influence on Latvia, broadcasting companies are required by law to limit the use of languages other than Latvian to 25 percent of their total daily broadcasting time. However, Russian-speakers in Latvia, as in the other Baltic republics, have the advantage of receiving cable television channels based in Moscow and St. Petersburg.

It should be noted that despite continued ethnic tensions between Russophones and natives—a problem that has been exploited by nationalist politicians in all three Baltic states—the Russian populations have not been a source of instability in the Baltics.[9]

In addition to the "Russian question," Lithuania, uniquely among the Baltic states, also has a "Polish question." Ethnic Poles constitute about 7 percent of Lithuania's population, and are concentrated in the southeast and around Vilnius—an area that belonged to Poland during the interwar period. Unlike the Russian immigrants, most Poles are natives, having lived in the region for centuries. As Lithuania reasserted its national identity in 1988–91, many Poles sided with Moscow and joined the ranks of protesting Russian-speakers. Poles were understandably unhappy that Lithuanian names were being used for their towns and villages; moreover, many believed that they were the victims of discrimination during the land privatization process after 1991, as many were unable to provide proof of their claims to ownership during the prewar period. Like the Russians, Poles tended to remain politically passive during this transition period. But whereas Russian immigrants had the option of leaving, Lithuania's Poles unanimously regard the region as their homeland.

As noted in earlier chapters of this book, Lithuania once had a large and vibrant Jewish community. However, 90 percent of Lithuania's Jews were killed during the Holocaust. After 1989, more than half of the remainder chose to emigrate, leaving only a small and declining community of about 5,000 by 1993.

ECONOMIC REFORM

By the time the Baltic states gained their independence in the summer of 1991, their economies were in free fall: production had declined dramatically while inflation ate away at the Balts' relatively high living standard. Once part of an integrated economic system geared largely toward Soviet needs rather than local ones, the Baltic states needed to overhaul their economies: this meant reconstructing their banking networks, substituting "hard" local currencies for the inconvertible Soviet ruble, replacing the system of centralized planning with market mechanisms, privatizing state-owned properties and enterprises, and reorienting foreign trade to the West while attracting Western investment.

That the old Soviet command economy had to be destroyed was never in question. The debate centered not on the desirability but the pace of the transition to a market-based economy. "Shock therapists" argued for the most rapid economic reform possible, believing that reintegration with Europe, upon which the Balts' future prosperity and security depended, had to be achieved quickly. Gradualists urged a more measured approach to the transition, as many feared that the negative short-term effects of shock therapy would undermine political reform and cause unnecessary suffering. Eager to join NATO and the EU, Latvia and especially Estonia followed the advice of the International Monetary Fund (the IMF, upon which all three Baltic states depended for economic aid) and adopted the neoliberal path of rapid economic reform, while Lithuania was initially reluctant to pursue this approach. Although the early phase of the transition produced misery and hardship in all three Baltic countries, the reforms were bearing fruit by the end of the 1990s.

For most of those who lived through this painful economic transition, which of course was worst for families with children, disabled people, and pensioners, 1992 and 1993 were the most difficult years. As unemployment steadily rose, inflation in all three countries approached or exceeded 1,000 percent in 1992, destroying whatever savings people had managed to accumulate, while making even the most basic foodstuffs, as well as rent and services, prohibitively expensive. Only after the introduction of local currencies in 1992 (Latvia and Estonia) and 1993 (Lithuania) did inflation decrease substantially, reaching the single digits in 1994. By 1995, the economies of each had turned the corner: having fallen 30 to 40 percent in 1992 (and even more in Lithuania), in 1994 the growth in the Gross Domestic Product (GDP) for all three Baltic countries was positive for the first time since 1989.

Estonia carried out its economic reforms first and most resolutely, with the aid of massive investment from Scandinavian countries. As a result, Estonia demonstrated the swiftest progress: adopting a tight monetary policy, Estonia limited government expenditures (including, unfortunately, pensions for the elderly) and subsidies while cutting excessive taxation. By 1994 the Estonian GDP was growing at a rate of 5.0 percent per annum and continues, with the exception of 1999, to expand at high rates into the early years of the twenty-first century. Although oil and natural gas continue to be imported mainly from Russia, thus perpetuating Estonia's economic dependence on its eastern neighbor, by 1993 Estonian trade had begun significantly to reorient itself toward Western markets. An encouraging aspect of this shift is the fact that most Estonian exports are processed goods, based mostly on timber, textiles, and food rather than heavy industry. (This is unlike the case in Latvia or Lithuania, where agriculture and natural resources remain the basis of foreign trade.) East-West transit trade between Russia and Europe has also proved profitable for Estonia. Ranking with the Czech Republic, Hungary, Poland, Slovakia, and Slovenia as among most advanced reforming countries of the former Soviet bloc, Estonia is generally regarded as a success story in the postcommunist transition, and by the beginning of the twenty-first century its citizens enjoyed a significantly higher standard of living than those of Latvia or Lithuania.

Whereas Estonian governments pursued reform quickly and persistently, Lithuania initially chose to change through partial and phased reforms, and as a result lagged well behind Estonia. Economic indices were almost entirely negative for the first few years of the post-Soviet era as the Lithuanian standard of living plummeted. Nevertheless, the LDLP governments of 1993–96 complied with IMF recommendations while trying to avoid abrupt changes, and by 1995 the country appeared to have turned the corner. Between 1995 and 1998 GDP growth rates hovered between 3.5 and 7.4 percent per annum, before dropping sharply during the 1999 recession that followed Russia's currency collapse. Although

Lithuania remains the most dependent of the Baltic states on Russian markets, it too managed to reorient its trade toward the West, sending more than a quarter of its exports to Germany and Latvia in 1999. Like its northern neighbors, Lithuania remains dependent on Russia for oil and natural gas; yet it is home to the only petroleum refinery (Mažeikiai) in the Baltics and appears to have a large reserve of oil—perhaps 12 million barrels.

Like Lithuania, Latvia did not make its choice about the pace or extent of economic reform right away; however, under IMF pressure Latvia had by the mid-1990s moved toward rapid, determined reform. In the past decade it has undergone a profound structural change, developing a dynamic service sector to offset the decline of its manufacturing base. Although the market now determines the prices of most goods and services, public concern about the disparity between high world market prices and relatively low salaries has forced the state to maintain a prominent role in managing certain sectors of the economy. As Artis Pabriks and Aldis Purs note, in Latvia "there are administratively determined prices on state housing, energy, transportation, telecommunications, public utilities, and medical services."[10] The same can be said of Lithuania and to a lesser extent Estonia. In foreign trade, Latvia continues to move steadily closer to its European and Scandinavian neighbors while drawing away from Russia and the other CIS states. However, because Latvian manufactured goods, hitherto made for export to the Soviet republics, are unable to compete in Western markets, its main exports are raw materials—principally lumber and wood-based products.

A key to Latvia's turn, as for that of all the Baltic states, was the privatization of businesses and property that during Soviet times had been owned and run by the state. In all three countries, small enterprises and farms were privatized first, while medium-size and larger enterprises were privatized afterwards, generally after 1994. Once again, Estonia moved most resolutely, with more than half of all registered enterprises placed in private hands by August 1993. In Latvia and Lithuania, political opposition arising from public concerns about corruption and insider dealing, compounded by the sheer complexity of the process, discouraged the sort of rapid privatization that was achieved in Estonia; the result was a slower and more tortured transition to private ownership in these countries.

In all three Baltic states there were two main methods of privatization: cash sales of enterprises to core investors, which many saw as the most efficient way of restoring economic viability, and voucher systems, whereby residents received shares in enterprises based on certain criteria, such as (as in the Estonian system) their years of active employment and service in the economy. The system adopted by Latvia, however, illustrates one of the problems of voucher-based privatization: launched in May 1993, the Latvian plan called for all residents to receive one certificate for each year of residence in Latvia, plus 15 additional certificates if they could prove Latvian citizenship prior to June 1940. Russians naturally saw this as discrimination.

Indeed, in all three countries, the process brought forth charges of discrimination, favoritism, and collusion. A common charge, often true, during the early stage of privatization was that managers and former senior Communist Party officials were able to purchase shares at a discount and thereby retain control of the firms they had run during the Soviet period. Moreover, with privatization came the pain of streamlining and rising unemployment as well as the psychological difficulties of adjusting to the "risk and reward" mentality of the private sector. Many firms drifted under the new conditions, with the managers often expecting that losses would be smoothed over with government subsidies, as was common during Soviet days. More successful was the transfer to private owners of smaller enterprises such as restaurants, small shops, and services, where the smaller scales of operation facilitated innovative approaches to management.

As with the privatization of enterprises and apartments, the issue of land reform was an enormous challenge for the new governments, as a mechanism had to be worked out to return farmland to its pre-collectivization owners. In 1991 each of the Baltic governments made this one of their highest priorities: the old collective farms immediately began to disintegrate as much of the land was transferred to private hands. However, the transition was far from smooth, as claims exceeded the acreage available and the plots transferred to private owners were often too small to be economically viable. Meanwhile, competing claims to the same properties and the lack of proper official documentation in many cases held the process up for several years.

Despite (or because of) the breakup of the collective and state farms, agriculture's share in Baltic economies declined dramatically after 1991. This is explained in part by the desire, often born of necessity, of many rural inhabitants to seek opportunities in other more dynamic sectors of the economy. As a result thousands of acres of suitable farmland lie fallow. However, small farms also lacked the necessary equipment (such as expensive tractors) and infrastructure (access roads, private transportation) to adjust to the requirements of small-scale agriculture.[11] The Estonian government's commitment to neoliberal economic policies has further aggravated its agricultural sector, as Estonian farmers have been deprived of the protective tariffs and state subsidies common in EU countries.

The Baltic banking systems illustrate some of the costs and benefits of economic reform in the region. Certainly the economic recovery of the mid-1990s would not have been possible without the construction of banking networks in each of the Baltic countries. Yet the frequent scandals associated with that system undermined public and investor confidence. The most notorious case was the collapse of Latvia's largest commercial bank, Baltija Bank, in May 1995, which caused thousands of depositors to lose their savings and nearly brought down the entire Latvian banking system. Likewise, at the end of the year, two of Lithuania's largest banks were declared insolvent. As a result, Prime Minister Adolfas Šleževičius, who was reported to have used inside information to withdraw his savings before the suspension of operation, was ousted by the *Seimas*.

Even more harmful to the Baltic economies, at least in the short term, was Russia's financial crisis in August 1998. With the devaluation of the Russian ruble and the consequent collapse of Russia's demand for imports, Baltic industrial and agricultural exports to Russia fell dramatically. As a result, in 1999 the GDP growth rate was negative in each of the Baltic states. As in Russia, a recovery followed in 2000, but Baltic investors, including the banks (especially the heavily exposed Latvian banks), nevertheless suffered permanent damage as their moneys were irretrievably lost in Russia.

SOCIAL AND ENVIRONMENTAL CONCERNS

With the collapse of the old economic system and uncertainty about the future, during the 1990s the Baltic states suffered from a variety of disturbing social and demographic trends, including an explosion of often violent criminal activity (peaking in 1991–94); a rise in alcoholism, drug abuse, and suicide rates; a decline in the already low birthrates; and a sharp drop in life expectancy.[12] All of these trends were paralleled in the other former Soviet republics of Eastern Europe. While the recovery of religious life has helped some to cope with the trauma of the transition, the revived churches proved unable to eradicate the ill effects of unemployment, unmet material needs, and general hopelessness.

In the early years of the transition, Baltic governments could do little to help. Acting on the advice of the IMF and other international financial institutions, they adopted tight monetary policies and consequently were unable to provide much of a cushion for those who were worst affected. Pensioners, whose numbers in the Baltic countries are proportionally twice as large as in Western Europe, found government austerity measures to be especially painful. Moreover, with state subsidies for research, education, and cultural activities sharply reduced, Baltic universities and institutes, orchestras and theaters, and journals and libraries had to slash their budgets while searching for alternate sources of income.

Of course, many of the problems faced by Baltic peoples since 1991 are products of the fifty-year Soviet occupation. Perhaps nowhere is this more obvious than in the ecological challenges facing Estonia, Latvia, and Lithuania. Soviet planners had notoriously little regard for environmental concerns, building large, sprawling industrial complexes with little thought about pollution and waste disposal. This disregard for ecology left the populace acutely sensitive to the dangers of pollution and mindful of the need for ecological conservation, as demonstrated by the prominence of ecology-minded organizations in the nationalist movements of the late 1980s.

One of the main offenders was the Soviet military, which had installations throughout the Baltic region. As they withdrew from the Baltic states in the early 1990s, Soviet/Russian armed forces left thousands of hectares of territory in ruins. In Estonia, for example, the Soviet military improperly disposed of toxic chemicals and dumped hundreds of thousands of tons of jet fuel into the ground, damaging the underground water supply and much topsoil. At one base, an Estonian cleanup crew reportedly found a sixteen-square-kilometer area covered with a layer of petroleum one centimeter thick. Other major sources of pollution included the Estonian phosphorus and oil shale mining industries, as well as major industrial centers such as Narva in Estonia and Daugavpils and Liepāja in Latvia.

Although each of the Baltic countries, and Estonia in particular (with considerable financial resources donated by wealthier neighbors), has made environmental cleanup a top priority, many rivers and ground waters remain polluted by industrial wastes, pesticides, and fertilizers.

THE SOVIET PAST

While environmental cleanup has generally been a popular cause in the Baltic region, issues related to dealing with the past—and in particular the matter of punishment for past collaboration with Soviet security forces—have been more divisive. All three Baltic governments barred former KGB agents from standing for parliament and obtaining high positions in the state administration, but it is in Latvia that the approach to past collaboration has been most confrontational. Contributing factors have included the Latvian Communist Party's activities during the 1991 coup, the critical ethnic situation in Latvia, and the fact that after 1991 Russians still held important positions in the state and government.[13] In Latvia there was even a proposal to forbid former Communist Party officials and members from running for parliamentary seats, but this was rejected.

A series of legal proceedings drew much attention to the matter of Latvia's Soviet past, as high-profile war crimes trials have been held for several former members of Soviet security forces, including Alfons Noviks (found guilty of genocide for his role as the director of the deportations in Latvia in 1949) and Mikhails Farbtuh (found guilty in 1999 for the deaths of 31 deportees). The fact that none of the alleged war criminals tried thus far were associated with Nazi atrocities has not gone unnoticed in Latvia—or in Russia.

In Lithuania, dealing with the past was no less sensitive, especially in the early 1990s. The political careers of former Prime Minister Kazimiera Prunskienė and *Sąjūdis* founder Vagilius Cepaitis were damaged because of allegations of collaboration with the KGB. However, in general few steps were taken to uncover past misdeeds (although several Nazi war criminals have been tried), perhaps owing in part to the LDLP's hold on the presidency and parliament during the critical mid-1990s.[14] In 1998 the parliament approved a bill sponsored by Vytautas Landsbergis that would restrict the rights of former KGB employees, but it was vetoed by President Adamkus on the grounds that individuals would be condemned not for their specific crimes but rather on the basis of guilt by association. In November 1999 another law was passed that offered amnesty to those who admitted past collaboration with the KGB by August 5, 2000 (about 1,400 did so); however, processing the cases of the thousands of collaborators who failed to register would take the court system many years, and it is likely for this reason that the Lithuanian government has not aggressively pursued this course.

Despite persisting ethnic tensions, Estonians have been amenable to reconciliation. This was possible in part because the old Soviet/Russian elites were completely removed during the country's first years of independence, thus ensuring the confident control of Estonian nationalists. Because questions of indigenous control were less acute in Estonia, it became easier to achieve national consolidation and consensus there than in Latvia—and as a result there has been a less confrontational atmosphere regarding the Soviet past than has been the case in Latvia.[15]

WOMEN AND FEMINISM

Since the collapse of communism, Baltic women have seen little improvement in their situation. In comparison to Scandinavia and Western Europe, where social and legal equality for both sexes is widely supported, Baltic attitudes lag behind. In part this is the legacy of five decades of Soviet rule, in which generally conservative attitudes toward women and the family were prevalent.

Although during the Soviet period equal rights were legally guaranteed, this did not translate into real equality. The majority of women worked full-time outside the home, but women were still largely relegated to their traditional roles of wife and mother—which included the time-consuming task of daily shopping under conditions of chronic queues and shortages. In addition to full-time work, women were also expected to do the majority of the housework. State child care facilities were available to alleviate some of the burdens of child-rearing, which to some extent liberated women from dependency on men. In Soviet times, women also enjoyed opportunities to pursue higher education and professional careers: women were especially prominent in fields such as health care and education, for example. However, salaries and opportunities for advancement were limited for most women in comparison to their male counterparts.

Contrary to expectations, the end of the Soviet regime did little to improve the position of women in the Baltic countries. In the post-Soviet era, women in all three Baltic countries demonstrate higher percentages of higher education and academic excellence than men, yet there has been a growing gap in the salaries of men and women. Because persistently retrograde attitudes about proper male and female roles at home and in the workplace continue to force women into secondary positions, women have little chance of competing with men for the most lucrative positions. Moreover, the transition to a market economy has meant that women suffer from unemployment in greater proportions; indeed, economic discrimination against women is commonplace. Meanwhile, throughout the region the number of child care centers—viewed as part of the Soviet legacy—has shrunk drastically. Thus many women have experienced the double blow of losing their income while trying to raise children at home, which in turn complicates their efforts to find work. Perhaps most disturbing of all, at least to the foreign observer, has been the proliferation of beggars, most of whom are elderly women, on the streets of the larger Baltic cities.

Prior to independence Baltic women had little experience in organizing to defend their rights and advance their interests. As women's groups were becoming active in the USA and Western Europe in the 1960s and 1970s, the Baltic countries were still under Soviet rule, where such activity was strictly forbidden. Thus, aside from the traditional temperance movements and women's leagues, there have never been any women's movements to advance the cause of gender equality in the Baltic countries. The new freedoms of the *perestroika* era, however, made it possible for women to organize and create organizations to advance their causes. As a result, by 1995 there were about 30 women's organizations in Lithuania and 15 in Latvia. While some of these associations had grown out of the broad independence movements of the late 1980s, others were revived or reestablished pre-Soviet organizations, such as the Latvian Association of Academically Educated Women and the Lithuanian University Women's Association.

Despite the new opportunities for women to organize in defense of their rights, feminism has enjoyed only limited success in these countries. Indeed, some feminists believe that throughout the Baltic region an antifeminist agenda dominates public discourse; discussions of feminism and women's issues remain confined to universities, academic journals, and conference halls, where there is little hope of influencing still quite conservative public attitudes. Although Soviet realities helped to preserve the traditionally conservative attitudes, contemporary antifeminism is also partly explained by the rise of nationalism and nostalgia for tradition in the Baltic countries. In Lithuania in particular there has been a renewed emphasis on women's roles as the reproducers of future citizens (hence there is a movement under way, absent in Latvia and Estonia, to outlaw abortions in Catholic Lithuania). It is a perspective that relegates women to a secondary role in civil life.

In politics, the record for Baltic women has been mixed since 1990. Before this time, Soviet attempts to realize gender equality could be seen in the Communist Party and the Supreme Soviet, where representation for women was high. However, in none of these institutions did women enjoy any real power, as few women were positioned at the top levels where real decisions were made. Although representation for women contracted substantially with the creation of new democratically elected parliaments in the early 1990s, the trend began to reverse itself in the latter half of the decade. For example, in 1996 11 percent of the deputies to the Estonian parliament were women; the corresponding figures for Latvia and Lithuania were 8 and 17 percent, respectively. By 2000 these figures had grown to 18, 17, and 18 percent—a far cry from Norway's level (41 percent), but still a considerable advancement toward gender equality. Nevertheless, the fact that women are rarely placed into the leading positions of their parties' voting lists (and very few women are in leadership positions in Baltic political parties) makes it difficult for women to enter the parliaments.

Despite these persistent obstacles, some women have held important positions in the governments of the three countries. Lithuania's prime minister from March 1990 to January 1991 was Kazimiera Prunskienė, and the country's first post-Soviet government was also headed by a woman prime minister, Aleksandras Abisala. While in Latvia there were no women in the first two post-independence governments, the situation has changed since 1994 and women have occupied several important posts. Most significantly, in July 1999 Vaira Vīķe-Freiberga was elected Latvian president.

In discussing feminism's failure in the Baltic countries, it should be remembered that although Baltic societies remain dominantly masculine and antifeminist in nature, in this regard they do not necessarily fare poorly in comparison to some other Western countries. One will recall that the USA, unlike Latvia, has never had a woman president—nor as of this writing even a woman candidate nominated by a major party.

RELATIONS WITH RUSSIA

Even before the disintegration of the Soviet Union, the Russian republic (which became the Russian Federation) recognized the Baltic states' independence and signed bilateral treaties with them. Nevertheless, the divorce was mostly a one-sided affair, and numerous aspects of the settlement were not immediately resolved. Contradictory signals from Russia, combined with nationalist Russophobia emanating from Estonian, Latvian, and Lithuanian quarters, were contributing factors to the sometimes tense relations between the Baltic states and their giant neighbor during the 1990s.

For several years after independence, the relationship between Russia and the Baltic states was defined by two main, often linked, issues: the Balts' treatment of their Russian minorities (the citizenship question) and the large contingent of Russian troops on Baltic territory. While Russia repeatedly complained that the stringent citizenship policies pursued by the Estonian and Latvian governments constituted a violation of human rights, Estonia and Latvia, as well as Lithuania, regarded the continued presence of Russian troops as a threat and called for their removal. For Russia, however, the withdrawal of these forces was not quickly or easily accomplished. Where, the Russian government asked, were these soldiers to be housed? What was to be the fate of the tens of thousands of retired military officers (and their families) now living in the independent Baltic countries? Moreover, there was a dispute over ownership of military equipment: the Baltic states regarded military installations and equipment to be the property of the territory on which they were located, whereas the Russian government considered these to be the property of the Russian Federation. (In the end, as they withdrew from the Baltic region, the Russians stripped the military installations of anything of value.)

There were also territorial issues. From the outset, Latvia and Estonia insisted that the peace treaties of 1920, and the territorial provisions contained within, should be the basis of present-day relations between themselves and Russia. Thus Latvia has reason to claim the region of Abrene, which was transferred to the RSFSR in 1944. Many Estonians would like returned to them the 2,000 square kilometers of territory taken from them by the RSFSR in 1945. However, the fact that Russians now inhabit those areas almost exclusively has made these claims difficult to press, and the Latvian and Estonian governments have chosen not to make such demands. To counter potential Estonian claims, Russians have put forth their own claims to Narva in northeastern Estonia, although this demand is not official and is not taken seriously by anyone at present. Moscow has, however, made claims on Latvia, insisting that the radar base at Skrunda was an integral part of its antimissile early warning system. In its dealings with the Baltic states, Russia had the advantage of the Balts' dependence on its cheap oil and natural gas, the supply of which Russian leaders occasionally threatened to choke off in 1992–93.

After years of discussion, the Estonian-Russian border dispute was ultimately resolved in favor of the status quo in a 1996 border protocol, yet a formal treaty has not been signed and ratified. Russia and Latvia were also unable to conclude a formal border treaty; however, an agreement was reached on the Skrunda facility in April 1994. Latvia agreed to lease the radar station to Russia for five years, at the conclusion of which it was dismantled. In return, Russia agreed to hasten the withdrawal of its troops from the Baltic region, finally completing the process in August 1994. For their part, the Baltic countries agreed to grant residence permits and other guarantees for tens of thousands of retired ex-Soviet and Russian military officers.

Unlike Estonia and Latvia, Lithuania did not lose any territory as a result of its annexation to the USSR. In fact, due to Soviet manipulation in 1939, Lithuania gained Vilnius. Although unlike the other Baltic countries it did not share a common border with Russia proper, in the early days of independence it was Lithuania, led by *Sąjūdis* and Landsbergis, that had the worst relations with Moscow. The subsequent LDLP government, however, pursued a more pragmatic and conciliatory relationship.

As noted earlier, Lithuania's policy toward its Russian minority was the most generous of the Baltic states; moreover, its military installations were probably the least important to Russia. With the Russian military withdrawal from Lithuania completed a year before this was done in Latvia and Estonia, Russia's relations with Lithuania developed more amicably than with the other Baltic countries. Nevertheless, important issues remained, including the matter of NATO expansion into the Baltic region and Russia's continued access to the Kaliningrad district, each of which is discussed below.

In general, Russia's policy toward the Baltic states since 1992 has been inconsistent. As discussed earlier, during the Baltic struggle for independence Boris Yeltsin had been a firm ally of the Baltic leaders against the Soviet "center." In the years that followed, however, many Russians living in the Baltic states felt betrayed by the Yeltsin government, which failed to act resolutely to defend the interests of the Russian diaspora. Of course, with Russia considerably weakened and facing its own myriad internal problems, it was hardly in a position to do so. Occasional pressure coming from Russian nationalist quarters, notably the bombastic Vladimir Zhirinovskii—who once threatened that if elected president he would use gigantic fans to blow radioactive waste into the Baltic states—forced the Russian government to take a stronger stance in its dealings with the "near abroad," for which it claimed special responsibility. Fortunately Moscow's harsh rhetoric never resulted in concrete action. Russian military personnel were removed from the region in 1994 and, bogged down in two wars in Chechnya, Russia has shown little inclination to use the threat of military force to defend its interests (or the interests of Russian-speakers) in the region. Moreover, despite Moscow's occasional (and waning) protests, Russia could do little to prevent the expansion of NATO into the region.

KALININGRAD

The Kaliningrad region (pop. 950,000) is a source of tension for Russia and the future EU states, namely Poland and Lithuania, that surround it. Before 1945, Kaliningrad was part of German East Prussia, and the city of Königsberg was its capital. After the war ended, however, East Prussia was annexed and divided between Poland and Russia, with Lithuania also getting a small section. The German population was removed and Russian, Polish, and Lithuanian settlers populated the area. Although separated from the RSFSR by Poland and Lithuania, Kaliningrad (as the area was now called) became a district (*oblast'*) within the RSFSR. After the

Soviet Union's demise, Kaliningrad became an enclave of the Russian Federation; but, unlike the rest of Russia, Kaliningrad still shares a long border with Lithuania.

As during Soviet times, the district is heavily urbanized and militarized. Until 1994, the Baltic Sea Fleet was still headquartered in Kaliningrad, at which time about half of its population were soldiers or associated personnel. To the Lithuanians, Kaliningrad poses a military threat, and after freeing itself from the USSR, Lithuania refused to grant Russia transit rights to Kaliningrad through the country, fearing that this could be a future pretext for Russian occupation. Eventually an arrangement was concluded according to which Russians were allowed to pass in and out of the region without a visa; at the border crossing they only needed to show an internal Soviet passport (which is still possessed by many Russians even at the dawn of the twenty-first century!) with a paper identifying Russian citizenship. However, Lithuania's hopes of soon becoming a member of the EU and thus joining the European visa-free zone made it impossible for Lithuania to continue to hold to this agreement, since it is commonly believed that after EU enlargement (in 2004) Kaliningrad could become a source of crime, disease (especially HIV), and illegal immigration, and thus pose a serious danger to European security.

Although Russia had long insisted that its citizens be able to travel freely between Kaliningrad and "mainland" Russia, the EU pressed for the introduction of visas for those traveling by automobile or train through Lithuania. Since many Russian citizens do not carry passports for foreign travel and therefore cannot obtain visas, this has placed an additional strain on Russia's recent relations with both Lithuania and the EU. Finally, in November 2002 Russia and the EU reached an agreement whereby Russian citizens from the mainland who wish to travel to Kaliningrad by land must acquire "facilitated travel documents," issued by Lithuanian officials at the border.

Another problem associated with the Kaliningrad territory is Lithuania's accession to NATO. Lithuanian membership in that organization allows NATO direct access to Vilnius and, from the Russian perspective, the encirclement of Kaliningrad by NATO member states. As discussed above, the Russian government understandably sees this maneuver as threatening. In sum, the future status of Kaliningrad as a Russian exclave in Europe is not entirely certain.

RELATIONS WITH THE WEST

Upon attaining independence, one of the main goals of each of the Baltic states was the cultivation of close political, military, and economic relations with their western neighbors, including Poland and the Scandinavian countries. Although from the outset the Baltic countries recognized the need for good neighborly relations with Russia as well, their fear of continued political and economic dependence on the Eurasian giant—Russia still had soldiers stationed in the Baltics and controlled the region's energy supply—compelled the Baltic countries to assume a Western orientation as quickly as possible. Their "return to Europe," however, could not be complete without membership in those Western institutions that they believed would provide them with internal and external security. Thus by the mid-1990s most political parties throughout the region agreed that real security could come only with membership in the EU and NATO.

Among the Baltic republics, Estonia had the closest relations with Western countries during the Soviet period. Its language is closely related to Finnish, and Estonians were able to watch Finnish television and listen to Finnish radio. By the 1960s, thousands of Estonian tourists were able to enjoy the short ferry trip from Tallinn to Finland, and even more Finns were able to visit Estonia. This close cultural affinity to Finland and the ties that were cultivated during the Soviet era has helped Estonia to attract significant Finnish foreign investment. By the mid-1990s Swedish investment was even more substantial, with the bulk of it going to Tallinn. Although trade with Russia is still significant, Finland has emerged as Estonia's largest market and greatest source of imports. By cultivating such ties with its northern neighbors, Estonia has sometimes portrayed itself more as a Scandinavian than Baltic country in an attempt to "sell" itself to the West. Unfortunately, this tendency at times has irritated some Latvians and Lithuanians.

Although they have not succeeded to the same extent as Estonia, Latvia and Lithuania have also attempted to reorient their economies away from Russia and toward the West. While Russia remains Latvia's single largest trading partner, by the year 2000 the majority of Latvia's trade was with the countries of the EU. Unlike its Baltic neighbors, however, Latvia does not allow foreigners to own land and buildings, thus making it difficult to attract foreign investment.

In this regard, Lithuania has experienced somewhat greater success than Latvia, with the leading sources of foreign investment being Denmark, Sweden, and the USA. However, for comparative purposes it should be noted that foreign investment in Lithuania (and Latvia) is much lower per capita than in neighboring Poland, a country that has managed the transition from a planned economy to a market-based one with considerable success. Lithuania's growing economic ties with the West during the 1990s are illustrated by the increasing volume of trade it conducts with EU countries: by the year 2000 nearly 16 percent of Lithuania's exports went to Germany (followed by Latvia with 12.6 percent); however, Russia remained the largest source of imports (nearly 20 percent), followed by Germany and Poland.

For all three Baltic countries, the ultimate goal is full economic and political integration with Europe. By the end of 1995, following the implementation of a free trade agreement between the EU and the Baltic states earlier in the year, each had applied for full EU membership. Since the main criteria for accession to the EU include democratic governments, stable borders, the rule of law, respect for human rights, and a functioning market economy, the Baltic countries have had to conform to Western European standards in these spheres. Latvia and Estonia in particular have come under pressure to resolve their minority issues by revising their stringent language laws and citizenship requirements. In Latvia, this has resulted in the abolition of Latvian language proficiency requirements, seen by many as undemocratic, for candidates in general and local elections. Although critics would argue that Estonia and Latvia have some way to go to meet the standard on human rights, in all other areas each of the Baltic countries has made considerable progress since 1991.

Although questions have been raised about the Baltic states' ability to meet the strict criteria and standards necessary for entry into the EU, Estonia, Latvia, and Lithuania were nevertheless among the 10 states to whom invitations were extended in December 2002. Once the accession treaty is ratified, these new member states will join the EU on May 1, 2004, thereby fulfilling the Balts' decades long quest to return to Europe.

Meanwhile, throughout the 1990s the Baltic governments intensively lobbied for inclusion in NATO, which one should not forget (certainly the Russians have not) was formed in 1949 as an anti-Soviet alliance of European states, led by the USA. All three Baltic countries joined the Partnership for Peace (PfP) program when it was launched in 1994. This allowed them to participate in joint planning, training, and exercises with NATO military forces, including NATO peacekeeping operations in Bosnia and Kosovo. With NATO expanding its membership in 1999 to include some of the former Warsaw Pact countries, namely Poland, Hungary, and the Czech Republic, the Baltic countries saw the opportunity to join an arrangement that they believed would provide them with security from an unstable and unpredictable neighbor.

The prospect of the Baltic countries joining NATO caused considerable uneasiness in the Kremlin, which objected to the inclusion in the alliance of *any* former Soviet republic. Indeed, one argument against the Baltic countries' accession to NATO was that it might antagonize Russia and therefore contribute to the destabilization of the security situation in Europe. Another obstacle to joining NATO was the matter of what these small states would bring to the alliance: would the Baltic countries simply be consumers of security or would they be able to make substantial contributions to the defense of the alliance? Moreover, NATO countries spend on average about 2 percent of their GDP on defense: would the Baltic states be able to reach and maintain this standard?[16] Pro-NATO advocates in the Baltic countries pointed out that they could contribute units with specialized skills such as minesweeping.

Although doubts remained about the Baltic states' ability to make a serious contribution to a common European defense, their goal of being admitted to the alliance was finally achieved with the second round of NATO expansion, which took place in November 2002. At this time formal invitations to join the alliance were issued to Estonia, Latvia, and Lithuania, as well as to Slovakia, Slovenia, Romania, and Bulgaria. Thus with the inclusion of the Baltic countries the NATO alliance has expanded up to the borders of Russia proper; moreover, the Kaliningrad region is completely surrounded by NATO states. While Russian President Vladimir Putin has not exactly welcomed this development, his government nevertheless has attempted to accommodate itself to the new geopolitical realities of northeastern Europe and recognizes the right of any sovereign state, including the Baltic countries, to join international organizations.

Strangely enough, given the organization's anti-Soviet origins, NATO's eastward expansion has raised the question of Russia's potential membership in the alliance. Since succeeding the unpredictable Boris Yeltsin in 2000, Putin has consistently emphasized Russia's solidarity with the West while downplaying Moscow's role as defender of Russian minorities in the "near abroad." More recently, as Russia wages a war against Chechen separatism, it has sought to portray itself as a reliable partner in the common struggle against terrorism. Russia now enjoys a form of associate partnership with NATO, and the prospect of it actually joining the alliance as a full member is not as utterly fantastic as it might have seemed just a few years ago. Paradoxically, the Baltic countries may find themselves militarily allied with the same bear which they believe poses the gravest threat to their existence.

BALTIC COOPERATION

Increased Baltic cooperation, which Western countries see as offering better prospects for the region's strength and stability, has been one of the conditions of EU and NATO membership. Although in the early 1990s each of these states was mainly engaged in many independent activities—including the creation of new constitutions and formation of new governments, solving questions connected with citizenship, enacting reform policies, and pursuing the path of economic recovery and development—the Balts' common political aspirations since the end of the 1980s have contributed to a sense of solidarity.

Indeed, wary of the power of their potentially powerful eastern neighbor and sharing the common goal of integration into Western institutions, the Baltic countries have had little difficulty finding common ground on matters related to security and foreign affairs. In November 1991 they formed a Baltic Assembly, composed of 20 representatives from each of the Baltic parliaments. Initially the assembly was created to discuss security concerns and foreign affairs, but its scope gradually widened to include issues related to energy, finance, economic development, education, and culture. The assembly has also actively pressed for EU membership while working to harmonize the legislation of Estonia, Latvia, and Lithuania with the goal of meeting EU requirements. Another coordinating body is the Baltic Council of Ministers, based on the 1934 Treaty of Good Understanding and Cooperation (see Chapter Five), which was set up in June 1994 for the purpose of coordinating trilateral political, economic, and cultural concerns. Its highest body consists of the three Baltic heads of state, who meet about every six months to discuss the main foreign policy issues of common interest.

Despite such cooperation—and despite joining NATO—the Baltic states are militarily vulnerable. In the year 2001 the combined active armed forces of Estonia (5,000) and Latvia (5,400) was about equal to the total armed forces of their Lithuanian neighbor, thus leaving the Baltic countries fewer than 21,000 combined active soldiers and border guards to maintain their security. Since the withdrawing Russian soldiers removed anything of value as they dismantled the Baltic bases, the local armed forces also lack equipment. Until very recently, Latvia's army and navy, for example, were equipped with second-hand items provided by their neighbors, including artillery from Sweden, patrol boats from Norway, and three tanks from the Czech republic.

Given their small size and individual weakness, the Baltic countries have found it sensible to pool their political and military resources. In 1995 a joint peacekeeping battalion, the Baltic Battalion (BALTBAT), was established as part of the Partnership for Peace program, and has since participated in several international peacekeeping operations. The following year the Baltic Naval Squadron (BALTRON) was created. Later, in 1998 they combined efforts to create Baltic Defense College (BALTDEF-

COL), a joint military educational institution for training senior officers. The same year the Baltic states created BALTNET, an air surveillance network that uses brand-new USA-supplied equipment to monitor planes over the Baltic Sea and much of western Russia; in the future it will likely be connected with NATO air surveillance systems.

All of these defense projects are rooted in the Partnership for Peace initiative, and their implementation is based on NATO standards and regulations. What makes these projects unique, aside from the close cooperation of the three Baltic states, is the extensive support and assistance they receive from the international community, including Belgium, Denmark, Finland, France, Germany, Iceland, the Netherlands, Norway, Poland, Sweden, Switzerland, the United Kingdom, and the USA. Nordic countries have taken particular interest in developing ties with the Baltic states. Denmark's initiative in creating the Council of Baltic Sea States (CBSS) in 1992 has provided the region with a forum for cooperation on environmental protection, regional security issues, energy, crime, and other international issues. Thus the CBSS functions as a point of contact not only between the Baltic states and the other countries of northern Europe but also between Estonia, Latvia, and Lithuania themselves.

Despite their outward show of unity and the tendency to treat them as a single unit, there have been some tensions between the Baltic countries. Estonia, for example, had shown concern about Lithuania's slow transition to a market economy, fearing that this would act as a brake on Baltic membership in the EU. Likewise, Lithuania and Latvia resent of Estonia's apparent strategy of selling itself to Europe as a Scandinavian rather than a Baltic state. Moreover, many Latvian and Lithuanian businesses view the successful operation of Estonian businesses in their midst as unfair competition. There also remain disagreements about territory in the Baltic Sea, including the Latvian-Estonian dispute over fishing rights in the waters around the Estonian island of Ruhnu. Likewise, it took several years for Latvia and Lithuania to come to an agreement over disputed oil reserves in the Baltic Sea.

Despite the irritants common to all neighbors, the Baltic countries have made significant progress in the development of common policies and institutions. They have learned the lessons of the 1930s, when their failure to cooperate contributed to their loss of independence. But more importantly, the Baltic governments are finding their place in Europe, which itself has been undergoing a gradual process of economic unification since the end of World War II. Having survived a half-century on the other side of the Iron Curtain, the Baltic countries, like many other states in east central Europe, are being encouraged to become full partners in an integrated European continent, where coordination and cooperation are seen as the keys to peace and prosperity.

CONCLUSION

The Baltic countries entered the new millennium as the success stories of the former Soviet Union. Whereas poverty and dictatorship have been the hallmarks of many of the new states that emerged from the rubble of the Soviet Union—one need only look at nearby Belarus, a country seemingly frozen in the Soviet past, to find a suitable European contrast—the Baltic countries are democratic and economically vigorous. Indeed, they are more appropriately compared to the central European states of Hungary and Poland, whose fate they share as functioning democracies and as fellow members of NATO, than to the Ukraine or Uzbekistan. Nevertheless, to fully appreciate the progress made by the Baltic countries it may be useful to compare them to another small former Soviet republic, Moldova.

In size (similar to Maryland) and population (a dense 4.3 million), Moldova, most of which was part of Romania prior to World War II, is generally comparable to the Baltic countries, with which it shared the fate of Soviet occupation following the infamous Molotov-Ribbentrop Pact. Moldova also shares the ethnic diversity of Estonia and Latvia: about 64 percent of its inhabitants are Moldovans, who speak a Romanian dialect, while most of the country's other inhabitants are Russian-speaking Slavs. Whereas the Baltic countries have experienced ethnic tensions but have been able to defuse them peacefully—if not always to the satisfaction of the Russian-speaking populations—national conflict, sometimes violent, has been a feature of the Moldovan state for more than a decade. As the republic attained its independence from the USSR in 1991, Slavs on the east bank of the Dniestr River immediately proclaimed the existence of a "Transnistria" republic. A civil war followed, with the Russian Fourteenth Army aiding the separatists against Moldovan forces. Meanwhile, the Moldovan economy went into a tailspin from which it has yet to recover. Vowing to end the country's endemic poverty, Vladimir Voronin, an unreformed communist, was elected to the presidency in 2001. While the government claims that the economic situation has improved somewhat, the ethnic problem has worsened as the government attempts to reinstate the Russian language—a language that Romanian-speakers, like the Balts, largely identify with Soviet occupation—and draw closer ties to Russia.

The situation in the Baltic countries could hardly be more different. Lithuania, Latvia, and especially Estonia have in the fullest sense returned to Europe; the return to power of any party that frankly calls itself "communist" is as inconceivable as the prospect of willingly returning to the Russian orbit. But the Baltic states' size, geographical location, and long history of victimization at the hands of larger neighbors ensures that maintaining that independence will not always be easy. Indeed, by joining the West and its institutions, some Balts grumble that they have exchanged one form of foreign domination for another. Moreover, the demographic situation, especially in Latvia and Estonia, is not promising, even if these countries manage fully to assimilate their large Russian-speaking populations. While joining NATO will arguably make the borders of the Baltic countries more secure (while perhaps bringing few benefits to the alliance's incumbents), in decades to come there will be fewer natives living in these countries.

Joining the EU will bring a new set of challenges to the Baltic countries. Like their neighbors to the west, the prosperous (and therefore attractive) Baltic states will have to begin accepting immigrants and refugees, which may result in the sort of cultural and racial tensions common to the Netherlands, France, and Germany. One wonders how the racially homogenous (if ethnically diverse) Baltics will cope with the need to accommodate and tolerate the cultural diversity that future immigration will surely bring. While Estonians, Latvians, and Lithuanians are rightly proud to be citizens of their respective countries, can they be good *European* and global citizens? Although most Balts embrace the economic and security benefits of integration with Europe, their willingness and ability to shoulder the responsibilities of membership in this community are largely untested. As this concluding chapter has shown, the Baltic countries' treatment of the Russian-speaking "colonizers" gives their European neighbors reasons to be both optimistic and guarded.

More troubling still is the widespread apathy common to each of the Baltic states. Although thousands of Balts joined together to work for shared goals during the *perestroika* years, civil society remains weak throughout the region, with few people demonstrating a strong and sustained interest in politics, religion, or even environmental issues. On the positive side, however, surveys indicate that by the end of the 1990s many Lithuanians and to a lesser extent Estonians (but not Latvians) were demonstrating growing confidence in their political institutions. Yet the fact that in the 1998 and 1999 presidential elections, Lithuanians and Latvians selected candidates who had spent their entire adult lives in North America is surely indicative of a substantial degree of dissatisfaction with politics.[17] While it is difficult to make any accurate generalizations regarding the Balts' attitude toward their new elites and political institutions, it is clear that few wish to return to the Soviet past.

NOTES

1. The Communist Party was declared illegal after the August putsch and was not allowed to participate in the June 1993 elections. Its members found new homes in the many new parties that emerged in 1992–93.

2. Three of the government's 13 ministers were representatives of the Latvian diaspora, and 18 of the 100 deputies in the *Saeima* were also western émigrés.

3. The alliance consisted of the Latvian Social Democratic Party and the Latvian Social Democratic Workers' Party, which in May 1999 merged to become the Social Democratic Workers' Party under the leadership of Juris Bojars.

4. Brazauskas had chosen not to run in the elections, citing his age and the institutional weakness of the presidency. However, he cancelled his plans for peaceful retirement when he returned to the government as prime minister in the summer of 2001.

5. Despite the continued popularity of President Meri, Prime Minister Laar lasted for only two years and he was ultimately removed by a parliamentary vote of no confidence in September 1994. He returned to the post from 1999 to 2002. Taken together, between 1992 and 2002 six different men held the prime minister's position—some several times—thereby replicating the experience of the interwar Republic of Estonia.

6. The Estonian Constitutional Assembly later gave noncitizens the right to vote in local elections under terms of the new constitution.

7. The peak of emigration from Latvia was 1992, when nearly 47,000 people left the country. Emigration sharply declined in subsequent years. Pabriks and Purs (2002), 87, n. 21.

8. Immigrants arriving, principally from Russia, after December 1991 would not be granted automatic citizenship but would have to meet certain requirements, including language and residency (10 years) requirements.

9. Sociologist David Laitin suggests that Russian nationalism is not a threat in most of the Russian "near abroad," including the Baltic region. According to Laitin, the "Russian-speaking population" in the Baltic lacks a well-developed sense of Russian national identity; most accept their situation and have chosen to assimilate. See David S. Laitin, *Identity in Formation: The Russian-Speaking Populations in the Near Abroad* (Ithaca: Cornell University Press, 1998).

10. Pabriks and Purs (2002), 99.

11. A team of Estonian and Finnish researchers examining the impact of decollectivization in southeastern Estonia has concluded that the project was conceptually misguided and poorly implemented. They argue that the agendas of Estonian politicians, who tied the goal of independence to that of returning the land to its former owners, conflicted with

the desire of the country's farmers to maintain large-scale agriculture. With the abolition of price controls and the dissolution of the *kolkhozy*, which were "the most important social institution[s] in the countryside" (but which political leaders regarded as bastions of communism), agricultural production collapsed and rural hardship followed. "A very few individuals have made a fortune, some have been able to maintain a moderate standard of living, but for the majority of people the process has been more or less tragic." See Ilkka Alanen, Jouko Nikula, Helvi Põder, and Rein Ruutsoo, eds., *Decollectivization, Destruction and Disillusionment: A Community Study in Southeastern Estonia* (Burlington, Vt.: Ashgate Publishing Co., 2001), pp. 97–98, 390.

12. The population decline in each of the Baltic states is partly due to the outmigration of tens of thousands of Russophones, but the main reason for attrition is the Balts' low birthrates. From 1989 to 2001 the Estonian population fell from 1.56 million to about 1.42 million; from 1993 to 2001 Latvia's population fell from 2.6 million to 2.42 million. In Lithuania, which has historically enjoyed a somewhat higher birthrate than Latvia and Estonia, the population has risen slightly, from 3.67 million in 1989 to 3.69 million in 2000.

13. Former LCP First Secretary Alfrēds Rubiks was sentenced to eight years of imprisonment for his role in the August 1991 coup.

14. Also controversial has been the matter of responsibility for the murder of more than 200,000 Jews in Lithuania during World War II. Although it is true that the Nazis were overwhelmingly responsible for the Holocaust, as a nation Lithuania has yet to come to terms with the atrocities committed by Lithuanians, and few war criminals have been brought to justice. Evidence of this "blank spot" in Lithuanian history may be seen at the Genocide Museum in Vilnius. The exhibit depicts the horrors of Soviet rule in Lithuania since 1940 but barely acknowledges the actions taken by some Lithuanians against their Jewish neighbors.

15. Anton Steen, *Between Past and Future: Elites, Democracy and the State in Post-Communist Countries: A Comparison of Estonia, Latvia and Lithuania* (Brookfield, Vt.: Ashgate Publishing Co., 1997), 93–107.

16. In 1999, defense expenditures constituted about 1.5 percent of Estonia's GDP. For Lithuania this figure was about 1 percent, and for Latvia less than 1 percent. Per capita defense outlays were $48 for Estonia, $28 for Lithuania, and $24 for Latvia—compared to $1,000 for the United States and $600 for Sweden. Walter C. Clemens, Jr., *The Baltic Transformed: Complexity Theory and European Security* (Lanham, Md.: Rowman & Littlefield, 2001), 208.

17. Ibid., 77–82.

Notable People in the History of the Baltic States

Barons, Krišjānis (1835–1923), leading figure of the Latvian national awakening and collector of Latvian folk songs; an editor of *Pēterburgas avīzes*, one of the first Latvian-language newspapers.

Basanāvičius, Jonas (1851–1927), priest, physician, and editor of the Lithuanian-language newspaper, *Aušra* (*The Dawn*); leader of the Lithuanian national awakening; played a prominent role in the establishment of an independent Lithuanian state in 1918.

Brazauskas, Algirdas (b.1932), transformed the Lithuanian Communist Party into the Lithuanian Democratic Labor Party in 1991; served as president of the Republic of Lithuania from 1993 to 1996; Lithuanian prime minister since 2001.

Faehlmann, Robert (1808–50), folklorist and founder of The Learned Estonian Society.

Gediminas (c.1275–1341), Lithuanian grand duke and one the country's last pagan monarchs; attempted to establish cultural, political, and economic contacts with the Christian West in the first half of the fourteenth century.

Hurt, Jakob (1839–1907), theologist and collector of folk songs; ideologist of Estonia's national awakening.

Jannsen, Johannes (1819–90), schoolteacher, journalist, and editor of the Estonian newspapers *Perno Postimees* (*The Pärnu Courier*) and *Eesti Postimees* (*The Estonian Courier*).

Jogaila (1348–1434), Lithuanian grand duke (1386–92) and king of Poland (1392–1434); accepted the offer of a dynastic union with the Polish crown; his acceptance of Christianity in 1386 ended Lithuania's status as the only remaining non-Christian country in Europe.

Käbin, Johannes (1905–99), Russian-born Estonian First Secretary of the Estonian Communist Party from 1950 to 1978.

Kalnbērziņš, Jānis (1893–1986), First Secretary of the Latvian Communist Party from 1936 to 1959; victim of the 1959 purge that targeted "bourgeois nationalists."

Koidula, Lydia (1843–86), poet, playwright, and newspaper editor; inspirational figure during the Estonian national awakening.

Kreutzwald, Friedrich (1803–82), activist during the Estonian national awakening; compiler of the Estonian national epic, *Kalevipoeg* (*Son of Kalev*).

Kross, Jaan (b.1920), Estonian novelist and poet who rose to prominence during the post-Stalin "thaw."

Landsbergis, Vytautas (b.1932), musicologist, anticommunist, and head of *Sąjūdis*, the movement which spearheaded the drive toward Lithuanian independence; Lithuanian head of state from 1990 to 1993; continues to play a significant role in the country's politics.

Lozoraitis, Stasys, Jr. (1924–94), Lithuanian diplomat who in exile worked for international recognition of Lithuania's plight during the Soviet occupation.

Marcinkevičius, Justinas (b.1930), Lithuanian poet and playwright who gained prominence during the post-Stalin "thaw."

Meri, Lennart (b.1929), president of the Republic of Estonia from 1992 to 2001.

Mindaugas (?–1263), the first Lithuanian monarch to accept Christianity; unified the Lithuanians in defense against the attacks of German knights in the thirteenth century.

Päts, Konstantin (1874–1956), one of the founders of the first Estonian Republic; headed an authoritarian government from 1934 to 1940; deported to Soviet Russia during the Soviet occupation.

Pumpurs, Andrejs (1841–1902), wrote *Lāčplēsis* (*The Bear-Slayer*), an epic poem loosely drawn from Latvian mythology.

Savisaar, Edgar (b.1950), a leading figure in the Estonian independence movement in the late 1980s and early 1990s; Estonian Prime Minister, 1990–92.

Sirk, Artur (1900–37), a leader of the extreme right-wing League of Independence War Veterans during late 1920s and early 1930s.

Smetona, Antanas (1874–1944), one of the founders of the Lithuanian Republic; head of an authoritarian government from 1926 until the Soviet occupation.

Sniečkus, Antanas (1903–74), First Secretary of the Lithuanian Communist Party from 1940 to 1974. Although faithful to Moscow, he is sometimes credited with mitigating the worst aspects of Soviet occupation that were experienced by Latvia and Estonia.

Stulginskis, Aleksandras (1885–1969), president of the first Lithuanian Republic from 1920–26; arrested by Soviet authorities during the occupation and sentenced to 25 years in the Soviet camps; allowed to return to Lithuania in 1956.

Teemant, Jaan (1872–1941), prominent politician during the first Estonian Republic; arrested and shot by Soviet authorities during the occupation.

Tõnisson, Jaan (1868–1941?), editor of the first Estonian daily, *Postimees* (*The Courier*) in the late nineteenth century; later was one of the founders of the Estonian Republic and became one of its most prominent political figures.

Ulmanis, Guntis (b.1939), first post-Soviet president of Latvia, holding the post from 1993 until 1999.

Ulmanis, Kārlis (1877–1942), one of the founders of the Latvian Republic; head of a popular dictatorship from 1934 until the Soviet occupation in 1940.

Valančius, Motiejus (1801–75), Bishop of Samogitia and active promoter of temperance among the Lithuanian peasantry, he oversaw his clergy's research on Lithuanian history during the early years of the national awakening.

Valdemārs, Krišjānis (1825–91), economist and editor of *Pēterburgas avīzes*, one of the first Latvian-language newspapers during the national awakening.

Vīķe-Freiberga, Vaira (b.1937), Latvian president since 1999; the first woman president of any Baltic state.

Voldemaras, Augustinas (1883–1942), leader of the Lithuanian Nationalist Union (*Tautininkai*) and later the Iron Wolf Association; key figure in the 1926 coup that resulted in the dictatorship of Antanas Smetona.

Von Buxhoevden, Albert (c.1165–1229), Bishop of Livonia and the founder of Riga; he was a leading figure of the Baltic Crusade in the early thirteenth century.

Voss, Augusts (b.1916), Brezhnev-era First Secretary of the Estonian Communist Party from 1966 to 1984.

Vytautas (1350–1430), Lithuanian grand duke (1392–1430) and cousin of Jogaila; defeated the Teutonic Knights in the Battle of Tannenberg (Grünwald). His reign represents the political height and greatest geographical extent of the Grand Duchy of Lithuania.

Bibliographic Essay

Since the Baltic states did not come into existence until the end of World War I, scholarship on this region focuses overwhelmingly on the twentieth century, and especially on the late twentieth century. A superb introduction to the subject is Anatol Lieven's *The Baltic Revolution: Estonia, Latvia, Lithuania and the Path to Independence* (New Haven and London: Yale University Press, 1993), which is a lively account of the struggle for independence. It also contains several interesting and enlightening chapters on the early history of the Baltic peoples. *The History of the Baltic Countries*, 3rd. Ed. (Tallinn, Estonia: AS BIT, 2002) compiled by Zigmantas Kiaupa, Ain Mäesalu, Ago Pajur, and Gvido Straube, is an excellent textbook for the general reader, with many helpful maps and illustrations.

Some of the best general histories of the Baltic countries focus on the individual experiences of Estonia, Latvia, and Lithuania. The standard work on Estonia has long been Toivo U. Raun's *Estonia and the Estonians* (Stanford, Cal.: Hoover Institution Press, 1987), which focuses primarily on the twentieth century. However, a recent textbook, *History of Estonia*, 2nd ed. (Tallinn, Estonia: AS BIT, 2002) compiled by a group of Estonian historians, devotes considerable space to the earlier history of the country. Like *The History of the Baltic Countries*, produced by the same publishing house, it is very detailed and contains ample photographs and illustrations. For Latvia the standard work is Andrejs Plakans's *The Latvians: A Short History* (Stanford, Cal: Hoover Institution Press, 1995). Also, the hefty volume by Latvian statesman and scholar Alfred Bilmanis, *A History of Latvia* (Westport, Conn.: Greenwood Press, 1951), is engaging and still useful, but it makes no pretensions to objectivity.

Unfortunately, no outstanding general history of Lithuania has been published in English in recent years. However, Alfred Erich Senn's classic *The Emergence of Modern Lithuania* (New York: Columbia University Press, 1959) still holds up well, and the lengthier *Lithuania: 700 Years* (New York: Manyland Books, 1969), edited by Albertas Gerutis, is useful though thoroughly anti-Soviet. Works by the late V. Stanley Vardys also make significant contributions, including *Lithuania: The Rebel Nation* (Boulder, Colo.: Westview Press, 1997), coauthored by Judith B. Sedaitis.

For the earliest periods of Baltic history and prehistory, see Endre Bojtár's informative study, *Foreword to the Past: A Cultural History of the Baltic People* (Budapest: Central European Press, 1999). Although somewhat dated, Marija Gimbutas's classic, *The Balts* (New York: Frederick A. Praeger, 1963), is still valuable. For the German conquest of the Baltic region, William Urban's *The Baltic Crusade* (DeKalb, Ill.: Northern Illinois University Press, 1975) is indispensable. Also see Eric Christiansen's *The Northern Crusades: The Baltic and Catholic Frontier, 1100–1525* (Minneapolis: University of Minnesota Press, 1980). An excellent study of the Baltic region in the Russian Empire is Edward C. Thaden's *Russia's Western Borderlands, 1710–1870* (Princeton, N.J.: Princeton University Press, 1984). Ed. Thaden *Russification in the Baltic Provinces and Finland, 1855–1914* (Princeton, N.J.: Princeton University Press, 1981) features chapters by several top historians on the Baltic region. For more on Russian policy in the region, also see Theodore Weeks' *Nation and State in Imperial Russia: Nationalism and Russification on the Western Frontier, 1863–1914* (DeKalb, Ill.: Northern Illinois University Press, 1996).

The literature on the Jewish experience in Lithuania is abundant. Among the best recent works are Masha Greenbaum's thorough *The Jews of Lithuania: A History of a Remarkable Community 1316–1945* (Jerusalem: Gefen Books, 1995) and Dov Levin's nicely illustrated volume, *The Litvaks: A Short History of the Jews in Lithuania* (Jerusalem: Yad Vashem, 2000).

For the establishment of the first Baltic states, the standard work remains Stanley Page's *The Formation of the Baltic States* (Cambridge, Mass.: Harvard University Press, 1959). The literature on the Baltic states during their first period of independence is surprisingly limited. The volume by Georg von Rauch, a Baltic German, titled *The Baltic States: The Years of*

Independence. Estonia, Latvia, Lithuania, 1917–1940 (Berkeley and Los Angeles: University of California Press, 1974), is still a leading account. Also see the edited collection by V. Stanley Vardys and Romuald J. Misiunas, *The Baltic States in Peace and War, 1917–1945* (University Park and London: The Pennsylvania State University Press, 1978). John Hiden's and Patrick Salmon's *The Baltic Nations and Europe: Estonia, Latvia and Lithuania in the Twentieth Century* (London and New York: Longman, 1991) is a good guide to the Baltic region's position in European diplomacy, especially during the interwar period. For interwar Lithuania see the collection edited by Alfonsas Eidintas, Vytautas Žalys, and Alfred Erich Senn, *Lithuania in European Politics: The Years of the First Republic, 1918–1940* (New York: St. Martin's Press, 1988). An important recent addition to the literature on interwar Estonia is Andreas Kasekamp's *The Radical Right in Interwar Estonia* (New York: St. Martin's Press, 2000). For the German occupation of the Baltic region, see the still unsurpassed study by Alexander Dallin, *German Rule in Russia, 1941–1945: A Study in Occupation Policies* (New York: St. Martin's Press, 1957).

For the Soviet period, *The Baltic States: Years of Dependence 1940–1990* (Berkeley and Los Angeles: University of California Press, 1993), by Romuald Misiunas and Rein Taagepera, is outstanding and is likely to remain the standard work for many years. Useful companion volumes are Tonu Pärming's and Elmar Järvesoo's edited collection, *A Case Study of a Soviet Republic: The Estonian SSR* (Boulder, Colo.: Westview Press, 1978) and V. Stanley Vardys's *Lithuania Under the Soviets: Portrait of a Nation, 1940–65* (New York: Frederick A. Praeger, 1965). Astoundingly, the latter manages to devote only a single sentence to the Jewish Holocaust in Lithuania. Joseph I. Vizulis's *Nations Under Duress: The Baltic States* (Port Washington, N.Y.: Associated Faculty Press, 1985) is surpassed by several other works but is still useful for the official documents it cites. For the nationalist and dissident movements in the Baltic republics, see Ludmilla Alexeyeva's *Soviet Dissent: Contemporary Movements for National, Religious, and Human Rights* (Middletown, Conn.: Wesleyan University Press, 1985) and Alexander Alexiev's *Dissent and Nationalism in the Soviet Baltic* (Santa Monica, Cal.: Rand Publishing, 1983); the latter contains an especially good bibliography.

There is no shortage of literature on the Baltic republics' struggle for independence from Soviet rule. Among the best are Anatol Lieven's *The Baltic Revolution* (cited above) and the essays in Jan Arved Trapans's edited collection, *Toward Independence: The Baltic Popular Movements* (Boulder, Colo.: Westview Press, 1991). To understand the Balts' struggle within the context of the Soviet collapse, see *Autopsy on an Empire* (New York: Random House, 1995) by Jack F. Matlock, the former U.S. ambassador to the USSR.

For individual country studies of the independence movements, see Rein Taagepera's *Estonia: Return to Independence* (Boulder, Colo.: Westview Press, 1993) and Richard J. Krickus's highly readable *Showdown: The Lithuanian Rebellion and the Breakup of the Soviet Empire* (Washington and London: Brassey's, 1997). Vytautas Landbergis's memoir, *Lithuania: Independent Again* (Seattle: University of Washington Press, 2000) is also of interest.

An authoritative analysis of Latvia's first post-communist decade is *Latvia: The Challenges of Change* (London and New York: Routledge, 2001) by Artis Pabriks and Aldis Purs. Also see Julia Dreifelds's *Latvia in Transition* (New York: Cambridge University Press, 1996). The story of Lithuania's struggles during the early post-communist period is told in Alexandra Ashborne's *Lithuania: The Rebirth of a Nation, 1991–1994* (Lanham, Md.: Lexington Books, 1999), a useful but repetitive and often poorly written volume. Thomas Lane's *Lithuania: Stepping Westward* (London and New York: Routledge, 2001) is a much better read and is more thorough. For Estonia, see David J. Smith's concise *Estonia: Independence and European Integration* (London and New York: Routledge, 2001), which, like the above mentioned volumes by Lane and Pabriks/Purs, is part of Routledge's impressive "Postcommunist States and Nations" series. Of comparative interest is Anton Steen's *Between Past and Future: Elites, Democracy and the State in Post-Communist Countries: A Comparison of Estonia, Latvia and Lithuania* (Brookfield, Vt.: Ashgate Publishing Co., 1997).

One of the most popular topics in post-Soviet and contemporary Baltic studies concerns ethnic tensions in the former Soviet republics. David S. Laitin's engaging study, *Identity in Formation: The Russian-Speaking Populations in the Near Abroad* (Ithaca, N.Y.: Cornell University Press, 1998), is obligatory for anyone interested in this issue. Also see Vesna Popovski's *National Minorities and Citizenship Rights in Lithuania, 1988–93* (New York: Palgrave, 1993) and Gershon Shafir's interesting comparative study, *Immigrants and Nationalists: Ethnic Conflict and Accommodation in Catalonia, the Basque Country, Latvia, and Estonia* (Albany: State University of New York Press, 1995).

For other topics of historical and contemporary interest, see the quarterly *Journal of Baltic Studies*.

Index

Abrene, 123, 188

Adamkus, Valdas, 173, 184

Agrarian Union (Latvia), 75, 91, 94, 96, 169

Agriculture, 1, 22–23, 24, 40, 41, 53, 87, 97–98, 112 n.15; since 1991, 172, 179, 181–82, 199; under Soviet rule, 117, 125–26, 128, 135, 136. *See also* Collectivization

Alcohol, production of, 42, 59, 67, 138

Alcoholism, 138, 182

Aleksandr I, 38, 41, 57, 58

Aleksandr II, 36, 50, 53, 54, 61, 69

Aleksandr III, 36, 37, 51, 53, 54, 61

Allies (World War I), 79–83, 85, 86, 87, 106. *See also under names of specific countries*

Andropov, Iurii, 142, 146

Anvelt, Jaan, 79, 111 n.9

Art, 60, 112; under Soviet regime, 131–33

Aušra (*Dawn*), 140

Awakening: in Estonia, 44–46, 50–52, 62 n.11; in Latvia, 44–50; in Lithuania, 59–60, 63 n.14

Baltic Assembly, 194

Baltic Battalion, 194

Baltic Defense College, 194–95

Baltic Entente, 105, 107, 108

Baltic Germans, 3, 14, 21–23, 24, 25, 27, 28, 29, 30, 36, 103; as ethnic minority, 66, 68, 81, 86, 99, 100, 102, 108; and land reform, 87–89; repatriation to Germany, 102, 110, 122; under Russian rule, 33, 35–39, 44–52, 54, 56, 67, 68–72, 83 n.2; during World War I, 72, 78, 80

Baltic Naval Squadron, 194
Baltische. See Baltic Germans
Banking, 20, 100, 101, 116, 170, 172, 178, 182
Barons, Krišjānis, 49, 201
Basanávičius, Jonas, 59, 60, 70, 77, 201
Belarus, 10, 17, 19, 37, 164, 196
Belarussian Soviet Socialist Republic, 81, 118, 121, 127, 155
Belarussians, 5, 39, 106, 142, 177
Bels, Alberts, 133
Berklāvs, Eduards, 130, 144 n.14
Bermondt-Avalov, Pavel, 82
Bible, 43, 133; translations of, 19, 25, 28
Birkavs, Valdis, 169–70
Birthrate, 2, 137–38, 142, 182, 199 n.12
Bolsheviks, 69, 74, 76–82, 83 n.5, 84 n.11, 96, 117
Bolshevism, 85, 86, 88, 105
Bonaparte, Napoleon, 47, 57
Book publishing, 19, 26, 28, 44–45, 46, 52
Borders: changes during 1944, 122–23; disputes, 105–6, 188; establishment of, 82, 86
"bourgeois nationalism," 123, 131, 202
Brazauskas, Algirdas, 152, 154, 156–157, 159, 160, 161, 171–72, 198 n.4, 201
Brest-Litovsk, treaty of, 77, 78, 79
Brezhnev, Leonid, 131, 138–39, 141, 146, 204
Britain: 36, 60; interwar relations with 107, 108, 109; trade with, 97–98; and World War I, 79, 87; and World War II, 109, 117
Brothers of the Sword, 13–14
Burokevicius, Mykolas, 161

Catherine II (the Great), 19, 37, 41, 53
Catholic Church, 12, 17, 20, 25, 58, 59; and education, 104; and politics in Lithuania, 91–92, 104
Catholicism, 4, 19, 24, 25, 27, 49, 58, 104, 186; conversion to, 13–14, 17, 24, 25, 26, 31 n.9, 35; under Soviet regime, 118, 134, 137, 139–41
Center Party (Estonia), 173, 174
Charles XI, 27
Charles XII, 19, 29
Chernobyl, 147
Citizenship, 7, 153, 168, 169, 170, 173, 175–78, 187, 190, 192, 198 nn.6,8. *See also under names of specific countries*
Collectivization, 118, 125–26, 127, 129, 148, 181; decollectivization, 181–82, 198–99 n.11
Commerce: and Baltic Germans, 35; in Estonia, 179; and Jews, 40, 61, 100; in Latvia, 180; in Lithuania, 180, 191–92; in the seventeenth century, 28; and sovietization, 117
Communist Party of the Soviet Union (CPSU), 117, 130, 131, 139, 145, 146, 149, 154, 181, 186; and Baltic independence movements, 151, 153, 154–64. *See also* Estonian Communist Party; Latvian Communist Party; Lithuanian Communist Party
Congress of People's Deputies (USSR), 154, 160, 165 n.11
Constitution, 89, 99, 194; of Estonia, 90, 95, 173, 174, 198 n.6; of Latvia, 91, 93, 168; of Lithuania, 91, 95, 170–71; of

Poland, 58; of USSR, 140, 150, 158
Constitutional monarchy, 23, 69
Cordon sanitaire, 83, 86
Corruption, 91, 93, 146, 170, 175, 180
Council of Baltic Sea States, 195
Courland, 21, 30 n.7; Bishopric of, 14; Duchy of Courland and Zemgale, 19, 21, 25, 26, 27; German occupation of, 72, 73, 75, 78–80; under Russian rule, 33, 37, 38, 39, 41, 43, 45, 46, 48, 49, 54, 67, 70, 83 n.2; under Swedish rule, 27–28
Couronians, 10, 11, 39
Crime, 137, 182, 190
Crusades, 12–13, 35, 204

Daugavpils, 134, 183
Defense, 79, 105, 108, 157, 168, 169, 193, 194, 195, 199 n.16
Democratic Center (Latvia), 91
Deportations: under German occupation, 74, 121, 122, 123; under Soviet occupation, 118, 120, 123, 125, 126, 127, 128, 133, 134, 143 n.3, 144 n.11, 148, 184
Dienas Lapa (*Daily Paper*), 68
Dissent, 139–41, 165 n.2. *See also under names of specific countries*
Divorce, 137, 138
Dorpat. *See* Tartu
Dorpat, University of. *See* University of Tartu
Duma, Russian State, 71, 73, 74

Ecology. *See* Environmental concerns
Economy: during interwar period, 96–98; during Middle Ages, 22; of Moldova, 196; since 1991, 169, 178–82, 191, 192; under Russian rule, 40–41, 89; in seventeenth century, 28; under Soviet regime, 136–37; of USSR, 129, 135, 136, 147, 178. *See also* Agriculture; Industry; *under names of specific countries*
Edinstvo (Unity), 153, 162
Education: under German rule, 28–29; during interwar era; 92, 99, 100, 101, 102–4; under Russian rule, 38, 43, 46, 52, 55, 61; during post-Soviet era, 183, 185, 194; under Soviet regime, 118, 129, 135, 144 n.18. *See also under names of specific countries*
Elections: in Estonia, 90–91, 93, 94, 95, 158, 173–74, 175, 198 n.6; in Latvia, 168, 169, 170, 176, 187, 192, 197; in Lithuania, 93, 95, 102, 157, 158, 171–72, 197, 198 n.4; in Russia, 71, 158; in USSR, 116, 154, 156, 165 nn.11,12, 169; in Vilnius, 106
Emigration, 2; of Baltic Germans to Germany, 71, 83 n.2, 99; of Estonians to Russia, 66, 124; of Jews, 63, 101–2, 178; of Lithuanians to Russia, 60; of Lithuanians to America, 60, 63 n.15; of Russian-speaking peoples, 177, 198 n.7
Environmental concerns, 145, 147–48, 149, 183
Estland: acquisition by Russia, 29–30, 33; and Baltic Germans, 36, 37, 79, 83; commerce in, 67; Duchy of, 27; and education, 46, 52, 54; and emancipation of serfs, 41–42; and Estonian independence movement, 77, 79; and Estonian national awakening, 50–53; and

Orthodoxy, 43–44; peasants of, 39–43, 46; population of, 38, 39, 66; religion in, 43–44; and Russian Revolution of 1905, 70–71; and Russification, 53–56; and serfdom, 37, 40, 41, 42; under Swedish rule, 27–28
Estonia, Republic of, 78, 81, 82, 86, 158; agriculture in, 88; authoritarian government in, 93–96; citizenship laws in, 7; economy of, 5, 96–98, 178–79; education in, 102–4, establishment of, 76–78; ethnic minorities in, 5, 99–100, 175, 197, 198 n.9; government of, 89–96, 173–75; land reform in, 87–89; politics in, 89–91, 173–75; population of, 86, 99–100, 199 n.12; privatization in, 180–81; relations with Finland, 6, 191; relations with Russia, 179, 187–89; relations with Western countries, 191–93; religion in, 104
Estonian Communist Party, 91, 111 nn.7,9, 117; of CPSU, 124, 130–31, 149–50, 157, 202, 204
Estonian National Independence Party, 150, 152, 174
Estonian Social Democratic Party, 90, 91
Estonian Soviet Socialist Republic, 123; cultural life of, 131–33; dissent in, 139–41; population of, 128–29, 138; religion in, 117, 134, 140; Russian-speaking population in, 152–53
Estonian Workers' Commune, 79
Ethnic minorities. *See specific nationalities and countries*
European Union (EU), 172, 173,

178, 182, 189, 190, 191, 192, 193, 194, 195, 197

Faehlmann, Robert, 50, 51, 62 n.9, 201
Farmers' Party (Estonia), 90
Fatherland Front (Latvia), 170
Fatherland League (Estonia), 95
Fatherland Party (Estonia), 174
Feminism, 185–87. *See also* Women
Finland, 4, 27, 52, 87, 94, 97, 105, 109, 110, 120, 136, 191, 195; and war with USSR, 113, 115
Foreign investment, 97, 178, 179, 191
Forest Brothers, 122, 125, 144 n.10
France, 18, 46, 57, 79, 87, 109, 114, 140, 170, 195, 197
Freikorps (German Free Corps), 80–81

Gediminas, 15, 17, 19, 201
Germany, 3, 38, 39, 43, 47, 54, 55, 56, 66, 71, 89, 133, 171, 195, 197; and Baltic Germans, 99, 102, 112 n.17; interwar relations with, 99, 105–10; trade with, 97–98, 180, 192; and World War I, 72–83; and World War II, 116, 119–22, 126
glasnost', 140, 143, 147, 148, 151
Glück, Ernst, 28
Gorbachev, Mikhail, 140, 143, 145, 165 n.17; and Baltic republics, 146–52, 154–64, 165 n.12; coup against, 164
Gorbunovs, Anatolijs, 152, 158, 169
Great Britain. *See* Britain
Great Northern War, 29–30, 31 n.9, 33, 39, 40

Great Russian chauvinism, 141, 153
Grinius, Kazys, 93
Griškevičius, Petras, 131, 146, 150

Hansa merchants, 22, 35
Hanseatic League, 22, 23, 28
Herder, Johann Gottfried, 45
Hitler, Adolph, 102, 108, 109, 112
    n.18, 115, 117, 118, 119
Homeland Union/Lithuanian
    Conservatives, 172
Hurt, Jakob, 51–52, 201

Ignalina Atomic Energy Station,
    147
Immigration, 197; Jewish, 100;
    Russian, 3, 27, 127–29, 130,
    135, 136, 138, 142, 147, 149,
    168. *See also* Russian-speaking
    population
Independence, declarations of,
    77–78, 83 n.7, 148, 150, 158–61,
    164, 168
Independent Socialists (Estonia),
    90
Industrialization, 66, 68, 69, 127,
    128, 129, 130, 136
Industry, 179, 183; destruction of,
    96, 123; evacuation of, 72;
    under German occupation,
    120–21; in interwar republics,
    97–98; nationalization of, 117;
    under Russian rule 66–68, 69;
    under Soviet regime, 117,
    125–27, 130, 134, 135, 136
Interfront (Estonia), 153, 163
Intermovement (Latvia), 153
International Monetary Fund
    (IMF), 178, 179, 180, 182
Iron Wolf Association, 95, 203
Ivan IV, 23–24

Jakobson, Carl Robert, 51
Jannsen, Johannes, 51, 62 n.11, 202

Jatvings, 10
Jews, 3, 4, 15, 66, 100, 104; in
    Lithuania, 19–20, 30 n.6, 39,
    61–63, 67, 87, 91, 98, 100–102,
    112 n.17, 143 n.2, 178, 199 n.14;
    and World War I, 72, 73; and
    World War II, 120, 123, 178,
    199 n.14
Jogaila, 15–16, 17–18, 30 n.5,
    202
Judaism, 4, 104. *See also* Jews

Käbin, Johannes (Ivan), 124, 131,
    202
Kalanta, Romas, 140
Kalevipoeg (Son of Kalev), 50, 202
Kaliningrad (*Ger.* Königsberg), 10,
    19, 22, 122, 189–90, 193
Kalnbērziņš, Jānis, 124, 130, 202
Karotamm, Nikolai, 124
Kaunas: city of, 66, 82, 104, 108,
    116, 119, 140, 150; Russian
    province, 37, 61, 66
Kettler, Gerhard, 27
KGB, 147, 153, 162, 164; and
    crackdown on dissent, 140,
    141, 142; local collaboration
    with, 183–84
Khrushchev, Nikita, 129–30, 131,
    134, 138
Klaipėda (*Ger.* Memel), 87, 105–6,
    108, 123
Koidula, Lydia, 52, 202
Köler, Johann, 51
Königsberg, 19, 22, 189. *See also*
    Kaliningrad
Kreutzwald, Friedrich Reinhold,
    50, 202
Kross, Jaan, 133, 202
Kviesis, Alberts, 94

Laar, Mart, 174, 198 n.5
Lāčplēsis (The Bear-Slayer), 49
Land Oberost, 73

Land reform, 53, 58, 84, 87–89, 90, 91, 92, 125, 181

Landsbergis, Vytautas, 157–62, 171, 184, 188, 202

Landtage, 27, 30, 41, 54, 75

Language law: in Estonia 153, 175, 192; in Latvia, 153, 170, 177, 192; in Lithuania, 102, 153, 176, 198 n.8

Larka, Andres, 93–94

Latgale, 4, 19, 26, 50, 100, 103, 104; and Latvian independence, 75, 77; under Russian rule, 33, 39, 43, 48, 49, 68

Latgalians, 10, 11, 13, 39, 41, 49

Latvia, Republic of, 1, 3, 4, 5, 6, 7, 158; authoritarian government in, 93–96; economy of, 96–98, 169, 178, 180; education in, 102–4; establishment of, 77–78, 86; ethnic minorities in, 86, 87, 88, 89, 99–100, 176, 177, 184; politics in, 91, 169–70; government of, 91–96, 168–70; land reform in, 87–89, 181; population of, 87, 199 n.12; privatization in, 180–81; relations with Russia, 187–89; relations with Western countries, 191–93; religion in, 104

Latvian Communist Party, 117; of the CPSU, 124, 129–31, 163, 168, 184

Latvian National Independence Movement (LNIM), 149, 152, 154, 170

Latvian Popular Front (LPF), 149, 158, 169

Latvian Social Democratic Party, 68, 91, 198 n.3

Latvian Social Democratic Union, 68

Latvian Social Democratic Workers' Party, 198 n.3

Latvian Soviet Socialist Republic, 123, 128; cultural life of, 131–33; dissent in, 141; language policies in, 149; population of, 127; religion in, 117, 133, 134, 140

Latvian State University, 103

Latvian Supreme Council, 158, 168

Latvian Writers' Union. *See* Union of Writers.

Latvia's Way, 169, 170

League of Independence War Veterans (Estonia), 93, 94, 96, 121

League of Lithuanian Christian Democrats, 68

Lenin, Vladimir, 4, 77, 85

"Letter of the Seventeen Communists," 141

Libau, 68

Lieven, Anatol, 147, 159

Literacy. *See* Education

Literature, 26, 45, 60, 132, 133

Lithuania, Grand Duchy of, 17–20, 74

Lithuania Minor (East Prussia), 19, 59, 105, 122, 189

Lithuania, Republic of, 158; authoritarian government in, 92–96; economy, 96–98, 172, 178–80, 191, 195; education in, 102–4; establishment of, 77–78, 86; ethnic minorities in, 86, 87, 98–99, 100–102, 176, 177; government of, 91–96, 170–73; land reform in, 88–89; politics in, 91–93, 171–73; population of, 87, 199 n.12; privatization in, 180–81; relations with Russia, 180, 187–89; relations

with Western countries,
191–93; religion in, 104
Lithuanian Christian Democratic
Party (LKDP), 92, 93
Lithuanian Communist Party, 92,
117; of CPSU, 124, 129–31,
150–52, 154, 160; and secession
from CPSU, 156–57, 161, 162
Lithuanian Democratic Labor
Party (LDLP), 171–72, 173,
177, 179, 184, 188
Lithuanian Democratic Party, 67
Lithuanian Freedom League, 151,
152, 165 n.2
Lithuanian National Council. *See*
Taryba
Lithuanian Nationalist Union, 92,
93, 95, 101, 203
Lithuanian Peasant Populist
Union (LVLS), 92
Lithuanian Social Democratic
Party (LSDP), 67, 68
Lithuanian Soviet Socialist
Republic, 123; cultural life of,
131–33; dissent in, 139–41, 165;
population of, 127, 199 n.12;
religion in, 133, 134
Lithuanian Statute, 18
Livland: acquisition by Russia,
29–30, 33; and Baltic Germans,
36, 37; commerce in, 67; and
education, 52; and Latvian
independence movement, 75,
77; and Latvian language, 45;
and Latvian national
awakening, 48–49; and
Orthodoxy, 43–44; peasants of,
39–43, 46; population of, 38,
39, 66; religion in, 43–44; and
Russian Revolution of 1905,
70–71; and Russification,
53–56; and serfdom, 37, 40–42;
under Swedish rule, 27–29

Livonia, 13, 14, 21, 30 n.7
Livonian Confederation, 21, 23,
24, 25
Livonian Order, 14, 21, 25
Livonian Wars, 24, 26
Livonians (or Livs), 3–4, 10, 13,
35
Lohse, Hinrich, 119
Lozoraitis, Stasys, Jr., 172, 173,
202
Ludendorff, General Erich, 73, 79
Luther, Martin, 24–25, 35
Lutheran Church, 30, 43, 44, 54,
55, 104, 141
Lutheranism, 4, 27, 28, 30, 35, 104;
conversion to, 24–26; under
Russian rule, 43–44, 45, 54, 55;
under Soviet regime, 117, 141

Maapäev (Estonian assembly), 76,
78
Mäe, Hjalmar, 121
Mancelius, Georg, 28
Manufacturing. *See* Industry
Marcinkevičius, Justinas, 133, 202
Marxism, 68, 69, 83 n.5, 91, 140
Marxism-Leninism, 117
Media, 6, 102, 151
Memel. *See* Klaipėda
Meri, Lennart, 5, 174, 198 n.5,
202
Mindaugas, 14–15, 132, 202
Minorities, ethnic. *See specific*
nationalities and countries
Moldavian Soviet Socialist
Republic, 155, 164
Moldova, 113, 155, 164, 196
Molotov, Viacheslav, 109, 115, 116
Molotov-Ribbentrop Pact, 109–10,
113, 148, 150–51, 154–55, 165
n.6, 196
Moravianism, 43
Munich agreement, 108, 109

Muscovy, 12, 15, 17, 18, 23, 25, 29
mutual assistance treaties, 110,
    113

Napoleon. *See* Bonaparte
Napoleonic wars, 47, 57, 63 n.1
Narva, 12, 26, 66, 70, 79, 93, 123,
    128, 183
NATO, 143 n.23; expansion of,
    172, 173, 178, 189, 191, 192–93,
    194, 195, 196, 197
National Progress Party
    (Lithuania), 92
Nationalism, 5, 35, 46–47, 71–74,
    138, 155, 156, 183, 186, 187;
    and dissent, 138–40; Estonian,
    69, 93, 138, 149, 184; Latvian,
    47–48, 103, 170, 174; Lithu-
    anian, 60, 67, 92, 95, 101, 102,
    107, 129, 150–53, 158, 169, 172;
    Russian, 53, 138, 147, 189, 198
    n.9
Nationalities policies, Soviet, 135,
    138–39, 156
Nazis, occupation policy, 119–22
Nazi-Soviet Nonaggression Pact.
    See Molotov-Ribbentrop Pact
Newspapers, 45–47, 48, 51, 59, 60,
    68, 69, 71, 95, 102, 139
Nicholas I, 44, 50, 58
Nicholas II, 36, 70, 72, 73
Niedra, Andrievs, 80
NKVD, 118
Nonaggression treaties: with
    Germany, 109; with USSR, 107.
    See also Molotov-Ribbentrop
    Pact
North Atlantic Treaty
    Organization. *See* NATO
Novgorod, 12, 22, 23
Nystad, Treaty of, 29, 33

Oil shale, 97, 108, 127, 136, 183
Old Believers, 27, 104

Olympics, 134
Order of Teutonic Knights. *See*
    Teutonic Knights
Orthodoxy, 4, 12, 13, 15, 17, 23,
    27, 63 n.12, 104, 117; conver-
    sion of Baltic peasants to, 35,
    43–44, 53–55

Paganism, 11, 13, 24, 25
Paksas, Rolandas, 173
Pale of Settlement, 20, 61
Pärnu, 66, 70
Pärt, Arvo, 133, 137
Partnership for Peace (PfP), 192,
    195
Partisans. *See* Forest Brothers
Päts, Konstantin, 69, 79, 90, 93, 94,
    95–96, 117, 202
Pelše, Arvīds, 130, 131
perestroika, 147, 149, 151, 152, 154,
    156, 157, 186, 197
Peter I (the Great), 19, 29, 36
Piłsudski, Jozef, 92, 107, 111 n.11
Poland, 3, 6, 10, 12, 23, 60, 74, 122,
    123, 156; after 1989, 172, 179,
    189, 191, 192, 195, 196;
    eighteenth century partitions
    of, 19, 33, 37, 56; during the
    interwar era, 92, 94, 101, 105,
    108, 109; Lithuania's relations
    with, 102, 105–7, 108; Nazi-
    Soviet partition of, 109–10,
    113; Polish-Lithuanian
    Commonwealth, 14–20, 24, 25,
    26, 57; under Russian rule, 53,
    58; wars with Sweden, 18; and
    Vilnius, 82
Poles, as ethnic minority in
    Lithuania, 15, 39, 61, 66, 67,
    87, 101, 102, 106, 177–78
Polish corridor, 108
Polish revolt: of 1830, 35, 53, 58,
    88; of 1863, 53, 58, 64 n.14, 88,
    159

Political parties and movements.
*See names of specific parties and
movements*
Pollution. *See* Environmental
concerns
Popular Front of Estonia (PFE),
149, 150, 152, 165 n.13
Popular Fronts. *See* Popular Front
of Estonia; Latvian Popular
Front
Population, 2, 123, 199 n.12;
according to 1897 census,
65–66; of Baltic Germans, 38,
66, 83 n.2, 99, 110, 123; of
Estonian-speaking regions, 26,
29, 31 n.13, 39, 66; Jews, 12, 20,
61, 66, 100, 119, 178; of
Latvian-speaking regions, 39,
65, 87; of Lithuanian provinces
of the Russian Empire, 57, 66;
losses in Great Northern War,
29, 39; losses in Napoleonic
wars; 57; losses in Polish-
Swedish wars, 19, 26; losses in
World War I, 86–87; losses in
World War II, 120, 123, 178; of
Moldova, 196; of Poles in
Lithuania, 177; of Republic of
Estonia, 86, 175, 199 n.1; of
Republic of Latvia, 87, 176,
199 n.12; of Republic of
Lithuania, 5, 87, 177, 199 n.12;
of Rīga, 4, 28, 65–66, 87; of
Russian-speaking peoples, 66,
128–29, 99–100, 104, 127–28,
175–77; of Soviet republics,
128–29, 136, 138, 142; of
Tallinn, 4, 66; of Tartu, 66; of
Vilnius, 4, 66
Postimees (*The Courier*), 51, 68, 95,
202
Privatization, 5, 172, 177–78,
180–81
Protestant Reformation, 24–26

Protestantism. *See* Lutheranism
Provisional Government (Russia,
1917), 74–78
Prunskienė, Kazimiera, 160–61,
162, 184, 187
Prussia, 14, 15, 19, 25, 33, 46, 56,
59, 61, 63 n.1. *See also*
Lithuania Minor (East Prussia)
Prussians, ancient, 3, 4, 7, 10, 11,
13, 35
Publishing. *See* Books;
Newspapers
Pugo, Boris, 147, 152
Pumpurs, Andrejs, 49, 202
Purges: of CPSU, 111, 116, 117,
119, 146; of Estonian
Communist Party, 124; of
Latvian Communist Party,
130–31, 133, 202
Putin, Vladimir, 193

Red Army (USSR), 3, 114; and
Bolshevik advance, 79–80, 82,
85; and Soviet-Finnish war,
110; and Soviet occupation of
Baltic republics, 115–16, 117,
119, 121, 122; and Tblisi
demonstration, 155, 162
Reform Party (Estonia), 174
Reichskommisasariat Ostland
(RKO), 118–20
Religion. *See under names of specific
countries and specific religions*
Resistance: anti-German, 121–22;
anti-Soviet, 121, 125, 126, 144
n.10
Revolution of 1905. *See* Russian
Revolution
Rīga, 5, 6, 26, 44, 45, 49;
Archbishopric of, 14, 15, 21;
economic development of, 22,
68; founding of, 13; German
occupation of, 119; and
Latvian independence

movement, 146, 148, 155, 162,
163; population of, 4, 28,
65–66, 87; under Russian rule,
53, 68, 70; under Soviet rule,
116, 127, 130; and World
War I, 72, 75, 76, 79–80, 87
Rīga Association of Women,
48–49
Rīga Latvian Association, 48, 53
Riigikogu (Estonian parliament), 5,
90, 95, 99, 173, 174, 175
Riigivanem, 90
Ritterschaften, 30, 54, 99
Rosenberg, Alfrēd, 119–20
RSFSR (Russian Socialist Federal
Soviet Republic), 117, 123, 127,
128, 135, 138, 160, 161, 163,
164, 187, 188, 189
Rubiks, Alfreds, 157, 163, 199 n.13
Russian Federation, 19, 188, 190;
relations with Baltic countries,
187–89, 192–93
Russian Orthodoxy. *See*
Orthodoxy
Russian republic (of USSR). *See*
RSFSR
Russian Revolution: of 1905, 60,
63, 68, 69–71, 73, 131; of
February 1917, 73–77; of
October 1917, 76–78, 84 n.9
Russian Social Democratic
Workers' Party (RSDWP), 69,
77, 90
Russian-speaking populations, 5,
6, 7, 55, 99–100, 173, 189, 196,
197, 198 n.9; emigration from
Baltic countries, 198 n.7; in
Estonia, 175; in Latvia 176,
177; in Lithuania, 176–78;
immigration to Baltic
republics, 127–29; under
Soviet rule 135–36, 152–53
Russification: under Soviet
regime, 127–29, 135, 137, 145,

176; under tsarist rule, 35, 37,
49, 50, 51, 53–56, 58–60, 61, 69,
71, 83 n.2
Rüütel, Arnold, 158, 159, 174

Saeima (Latvian parliament), 88,
91, 94, 99, 168, 169, 176, 198
n.2
Sąjūdis, 150–52, 154, 157, 159–61,
171, 177, 188
samizdat', 140, 141
Savisaar, Edgar, 149, 165 n.13,
173, 174, 203
sblizhenie, 135, 138
Seimas (Lithuanian parliament),
91, 95, 102, 111 n.10, 171, 182
Selonians, 10, 13, 39
Serfdom: abolition of serfdom, 37,
40–43, 49, 50, 66, 69; under
German barons, 14, 18, 22–23,
28, 30, 35, 40
Settlers' Party (Estonia), 90
Sigismund II Augustus, 18, 25
Singing Revolution, 7, 52, 146,
150
Sirge, Rudolf, 133
Sirk, Andres, 93, 94, 203
Skrunda, 188
Šleževičius, Adolfas, 172, 182
Sluckis, Mykolas, 133
Smetona, Antanas, 75, 77, 92, 93,
95, 96, 110, 115, 117, 203
Sniečkus, Antanas, 124, 127, 131,
138, 203
Socialist Revolutionaries (SRs), 69
Socialist Workers' Party (Estonia),
90–91, 93
Song festivals, 52, 133–34, 146,
150, 155
Songaila, Ringaudas, 150, 152
Soviet Union, 2, 72, 81, 108, 109;
Baltic states' interwar relations
with, 98, 106–7; collapse of, 3,
4, 162–64; and occupation of

Baltic states, 3, 89, 94, 96, 110–11, 113, 115–18, 121–64, 167

Sovietization, 117–18, 123–29

sovnarkhozy, 136

St. George's Day Uprising, 14, 30 n.4

Stalin, Josef, 131, 132, 146, 167, 174; death of, 127, 128, 129, 132; occupation of Baltic states, 115, 119, 123, 139, 146, 149; and pact with Hitler, 102, 109, 110, 113, 117, 119; and purges, 116, 124, 130

Stalinism, 131, 150, 165 n.6

Stender, Gotthard, 45

Stulginskis, Aleksandras, 92, 203

Supreme Council: of the Republic of Estonia, 158; of the Republic of Latvia, 158, 168, 169; of the Republic of Lithuania, 157, 159, 161, 171

Supreme Soviet: of Estonian SSR 150, 158; of Latvian SSR, 152, 158; of Lithuanian SSR, 152, 157; of RSFSR, 161; of USSR, 147, 186

Suvałki, 62 n.1, 66

Sweden, 3, 12, 18, 23, 105, 191, 194, 195; as rulers of Baltic area, 20, 24, 26–29, 30 n.7, 33, 40

Swordbrothers. *See* Brothers of the Sword

Tallinn, 4, 26, 66, 69, 70, 78, 79, 93, 100, 111 n.9, 191; as Hanseatic city, 15, 22; under Soviet rule, 116, 129, 137; and struggle for Estonian independence, 146, 150, 155, 163; and World War I, 79; and World War II, 123

Tartu, 22, 52, 66, 70, 93, 123, 138; Bishopric of, 14; Treaty of, 81; University of, 28, 38, 54, 62 n.9, 101, 103

Taryba, 75, 77–78, 83 nn.7,8

Tautininkai. *See* Lithuanian Nationalist Union

Teataja (*The Herald*), 69, 71

Teemant, Jaan, 90, 203

Television, 6, 136, 162, 177

Teutonic Order (or Teutonic Knights), 13–15, 17, 24, 26, 35, 49, 204

Thaw, The, 130, 132–34

Tõnisson, Jaan, 68–69, 76, 90, 93, 95, 203

Trade: in ancient times, 11–12, 15; with Britain, 98, 107; with Finland, 191; with Germany, 98, 108, 180; and Hansa merchants, 22, 35; and Jews, 20, 40, 61, 100, 101; with the Russian Federation, 179, 191; under Russian rule, 67; under Swedish rule, 26; with USSR, 97, 98, 107; with Western countries, 96, 97, 178, 179, 180, 191–92

Ukraine, 6, 17, 19, 37, 55, 60, 118, 164; Ukrainian SSR, 122, 128, 155

Ukrainians, as ethnic minority, 5, 142, 177

Ulmanis, Guntis, 169, 203

Ulmanis, Kārlis, 75, 80, 81, 94, 96, 97, 101, 117, 169, 203

Undeutsche, 14, 22, 36, 38, 40

Union of Lublin, 18

Union of Writers: of Latvian SSR, 148–49; of USSR, 132

Union Treaty (USSR), 164

United Agrarian Party (Estonia), 90, 93, 111 n.8

United Nations, 5, 140, 164

United States of America, 79, 87, 97, 138, 142, 159, 180, 186, 187, 191, 192, 195, 199 n.16; emigration to, 60, 64 n.15; and Soviet annexation of Baltic republics, 117, 167, 168

University of Lithuania, 104

University of Tartu (Dorpat), 28, 38, 54, 62 n.9, 101, 103

University of Vilnius, 57, 58, 104

Urbanization: under Russian rule, 52, 65–66, 98; under Soviet regime, 127–29, 134, 137

USSR. *See* Soviet Union

Uudised (*The News*), 69, 71

Vagris, Jānis, 152, 154

Vaino, Karl, 131, 146, 149–50

Valančius, Motiejus, 59, 203

Valdemārs, Krišjānis, 48, 203

Väljas, Vaino, 150

Valters, Miķelis, 75

Vīķe-Freiberga, Vaira, 170, 187, 203

Vilnius: Bishop of, 26; Diet, 70–71; city of 3, 57, 60, 66, 67, 77, 105, 109, 119, 173, 190, 199; and Jewish community, 15, 20; and Lithuanian independence movement, 147, 150, 151, 155, 156, 157, 159, 161, 162, 163; Lithuanian-Polish dispute over, 82, 105, 106–7, 108, 109; under Polish control, 87, 101,

177; population of, 4, 66; Russian province, 37, 66; transfer to Lithuania, 110, 112 n.17, 122, 188; University of, 57, 58, 104; during World War I, 81–82

Vitebsk, 39, 48, 49, 68

Voldemaras, Augustinas, 92, 95, 97, 111–12 n.14, 203

Von Buxhoevden, Albert, 13, 204

Von der Goltz, Rüdiger, 80–81

Voss, Augusts, 131, 147, 204

Vyshinskii, Andrei, 116

Vytautas, Magnus, 17, 19, 104, 204

War crimes, 184, 199 n.14

Wars of Independence, 78–83, 86–87

Warsaw, Grand Duchy of, 57

Wilhelm II, 72, 78, 79, 80

Women, 48–49, 89, 185–87

World War I, 65, 72–80, 85–87, 100, 101, 107, 108, 113, 120

World War II, 3, 110–11, 113, 115–23, 124, 131, 195, 196

Yakovlev, Aleksandr, 151, 165 n.6

Yazov, Dmitri, 162

Yeltsin, Boris, 160, 161, 163, 164, 189, 193

Zamut, 12

Zemgale, 25. *See also* Courland

Zemgalians, 10, 11, 14, 39

About the Author

KEVIN O'CONNOR is Assistant Professor of History at Southern
Illinois University, Carbondale.

Other Titles in the Greenwood Histories of the Modern Nations
Frank W. Thackeray and John E. Findling, Series Editors

The History of Argentina
Daniel K. Lewis

The History of Australia
Frank G. Clarke

The History of Brazil
Robert M. Levine

The History of Canada
Scott W. See

The History of China
David C. Wright

The History of Congo
Didier Gondola

The History of Cuba
Clifford L. Staten

The History of France
W. Scott Haine

The History of Germany
Eleanor L. Turk

The History of Holland
Mark T. Hooker

The History of India
John McLeod

The History of Iran
Elton L. Daniel

The History of Ireland
Daniel Webster Hollis III

The History of Israel
Arnold Blumberg

The History of Italy
Charles L. Killinger

The History of Japan
Louis G. Perez

The History of Mexico
Burton Kirkwood

The History of Nigeria
Toyin Falola

The History of Poland
M. B. Biskupski

The History of Portugal
James M. Anderson

The History of Russia
Charles E. Zieger

The History of Serbia
John K. Cox

The History of South Africa
Roger B. Beck

The History of Spain
Peter Pierson

The History of Sweden
Byron J. Nordstrom

The History of Turkey
Douglas A. Howard